FAMOUS REGIMENTS
OF THE
BRITISH ARMY

'Pride of regiment and love for the regiment's history and tradition is the sacred Ark of the Covenant on which the British soldier depends in battle and on which Britain, through him, has again and again survived and won through to victory.'
Sir Arthur Bryant

'If Socrates and Charles XII of Sweden were present in any company and Socrates said "Follow me, and hear a lecture on philosophy"; and Charles, laying his hand on his sword, to say, "Follow me, and dethrone the Czar" a man would be ashamed to follow Socrates. Sir, the impression is universal; yet it is strange.'
Doctor Johnson

FAMOUS REGIMENTS
OF THE
BRITISH ARMY

A PICTORIAL GUIDE AND CELEBRATION
VOLUME ONE

DORIAN BOND

The History Press

For Deborah, Anna and Nicholas.

First published 2009

The History Press
The Mill, Brimscombe Port
Stroud, Gloucestershire, GL5 2QG
www.thehistorypress.co.uk

British Library Cataloguing in Publication Data.
A catalogue record for this book is available from the British Library.

ISBN 978 1 86227 473 0

Typesetting and origination by The History Press
Printed in Malta

Page 2: Drummer of His Majesty's 1st Life Guards by Sir Alfred
Munnings, 1922. Reproduced by kind permission of the Household
Cavalry Museum, © The Life Guards.

CONTENTS

'The Art of War is of vital importance to the State. It is a matter of life and death, a road either to safety or to ruin. Hence it is a subject of enquiry which can on no account be neglected.'

Sun Tzu, *The Art of War*

There is a place where voices
Of great guns do not come,
Where rifle, mine, and mortar
For evermore are dumb:
Where there is only silence,
And Peace eternal and rest,
Set somewhere in the quiet isles
Beyond Death's starry West.
O God, the God of battles,
To us who intercede,
Give only strength to follow
Until there's no more need
And grant us at that ending
Of the unkindly quest
To come unto the quiet isles
Beyond Death's starry West.

G. B. Smith, Lancashire Fusiliers, killed in action 3 December 1916, aged 22 years.

INTRODUCTION

In writing this book I have of course been unable to include many regiments in a single work with this kind of approach. I have started with just 35, so inevitably questions will be asked as to why certain regiments have been omitted, at least in this volume.

One incident illustrates my dilemma. I was reading about the West Yorkshire Regiment, the 14th, and came across this story. On the morning of July 1st 1916, the 10th Battalion, the West Yorkshire Regiment, led by their officers, Lieutenant Colonel Dickson and Major Knott, went into action at 7.30 a.m. at a place called Fricourt near a river called the Somme. On that summer day they faced a terrible trial of murderous machine gun fire and in the ensuing hours lost 700 men including those two officers. This was the highest battalion loss in a single day in the whole of the British Army during the whole war. But the West Yorkshires are not in this volume. It is unforgivable.

'*The civilian who attempts to write a military history is of necessity guilty of an act of presumption.*' Sir John Fortescue's words in the introduction to his monumental work on the history of the British Army were accurate. His own presumption was well-justified and like only a handful of master historians he had the courage to voice opinions and draw conclusions rather than just enunciate facts and figures. My book is of course much more limited in its ambitions. It is an attempt to inform readers a little about the famous regiments from these islands that have played such a shining part in our history.

I have chosen them from stories in my childhood and school years where names such as Blenheim, Dettingen, Quebec, Salamanca, Waterloo, Inkerman, Balaclava, Rorke's Drift, Ypres, Gallipoli, the Somme, Dunkirk, El Alamein, Monte Cassino, D-Day and Arnhem were a matter of national pride and admiration, many of them linked to particular regiments. There has been no selection process according to merit or geography, they are just names I am familiar with, names I have grown up with. Others would make a different list.

Further volumes will set out to remedy the unavoidable omissions. And what do you do with a Corps such as the Royal Engineers or the Royal Army Medical Corps, whose histories are long, fascinating and just as full of heroic deeds as the fighting regiments? The saying 'First in, last out' perfectly describes the Sappers and when you think about their work in terms of combat, it heightens one's admiration of these men. I should mention a personal link here; my grandfather was a 24-year-old Captain in the Royal Canadian Engineers. A career officer, he was killed before dawn, leading a party into No Man's Land, cutting the wire to prepare openings for the first day of the Allied attack on Hill 60 on August 15th, 1917. He was just another soldier doing his duty in the face of the enemy. No hero he, no individual medals for gallantry.

The idea of the book is to inform, to interest, to intrigue and, hopefully, to move the reader with tales of these extraordinary bodies of men and the individuals who served in them. If forgotten heroes can be brought back into our consciousness, it would not be a bad thing. Duty, discipline, patriotism, kindness and imagination are fine human qualities and these often tribal and traditional regiments displayed them in abundance, and still do. It was these qualities and the adherence to them that created the greatest Empire the world had seen since Imperial Rome's legions watched over its furthest frontiers. These regiments were the true successors of the legions of Rome.

But we should always be mindful that the true face of battle is terrible to behold. And courage is not a quality exclusive to the British, as attested by a French officer at the Schellenburg during Marlborough's dazzling Blenheim campaign: '*The English infantry led this attack with the greatest intrepidity, right up to our parapet, but there they were opposed with a courage at least equal to their own. Rage, fury and desperation were manifested by both sides, with the more obstinacy as the assailants and assailed were perhaps the bravest soldiers in the world. The little parapet which separated the two forces became the scene of the bloodiest struggle that could be conceived. It would be impossible to describe in words strong enough the details of the carnage that took place during this first attack, which lasted a good hour or more. We were all fighting hand to hand, hurling them back as they clutched at the parapet; men were slaying, or tearing at the muzzles of guns and the bayonets which pierced their entrails; crushing under their feet their own wounded comrades, and even gouging out their opponents' eyes with their nails, when the grip was so close that neither could make use of their weapons.*'

Another dilemma for any student of British military history is one of scale. Is Bushey Run as important as Waterloo in regimental terms or was Busbecque as significant as Salamanca? The effectiveness of officers in battle in leadership terms, the discipline and courage of the men, has equal strength in whatever situation they may find themselves. They can only deal with their corner of the battlefield. So in regimental terms combat situations have equal merit while obviously in strategic and historical terms one battle can far outweigh another and a regiment's presence there can only enhance its reputation. A number of battle-hardened Peninsula regiments missed out on Waterloo, which must have irked them.

In this sense the First World War far outweighs anything that comes before and most of what came after. During my research one fact illustrated this to me better than anything I had encountered before. A census was taken over a 24-hour period on one road leading up to the front line during the battle of the Somme in July 1916. Every individual soldier, officer, horse, and vehicle was accounted for. The totals counted came to more than the size of the British forces in the whole of the Crimean War. This puts things into perspective. Although this is significant, it does not take away from the courage of the infantry at Inkerman or the cavalry at Balaclava. A military unit can only respond to what is put in front of it.

I have endeavoured to give as much information as possible about each regiment within the space available and have made mention of their museums, which are dotted about the country. Unlike many other of our great institutions, the regiments rarely had one home, were often on the move in foreign climes, so few great libraries of information accompany them. Their members were men of action and, with a few exceptions, men of few words. Their deeds and accomplishments were often not recorded and if they were, they are embroidered in single words on Colours now consigned to traditional places of worship or those small but proud museums.

The regiments of which I write watched over our frontiers knowing that what they did, and are still doing, was putting themselves in positions of danger, when called to do so, for the sake of their fellow countrymen. I salute them.

Dorian Bond
Winchester, England

ACKNOWLEDGEMENTS

The list of people who have helped me is long. Here are some without whom I could not have completed the task: Brigadier Colin Sibun at the Ogilby Trust, Ken Gray and Christine Pullen at the Royal Green Jackets Museum, Johnny Kaye, John Nettleton, Robert Macgregor-Ockforde, Steve Shannon, Ian Chatfield, Lisa Heighway at the Royal Archives, Windsor Castle, David Read at the Soldiers of Gloucestershire Museum, Grenville Bint, Special Air Service Association, Major David Innes-Lumsden and Major Patrick Timmons of the Queen's Royal Hussars, Gavin Edgerley-Harris at the Gurkha Museum, Michael Stevens and Rachel Holmes of the Hampshire Regiment Museum, Ian Carter and Yvonne Oliver of the Imperial War Museum, Tony Strason of the Lancashire Fusiliers, Sarah Taylor and Susan Langridge at the Green Howards, Jonathan Ferguson and Margaret Wilson of the National War Museum of Scotland, John Cornish, King's Royal Hussars, Ian Martin at the Kings Own Scottish Borderers, Major Proctor and Tommy Smyth at Balhousie Castle, Malcom Ross at the Gordon Highlanders Museum, Mike Galer, Curator at Derby Museum, Colonel Steele and David McMasters at the Royal Highland Fusiliers, Clive Morris, Curator, Queen's Dragoon Guards, Major Edward Crofton, Sergeant Gorman, Colonel Tom Bonas, Lieutenant Colonel O'Gorman, Lieutenant Colonel Conway Seymour, Colonel Henry Hanning, Stan Evans and Warren Williams of the Welsh Guards, Lieutenant Colonel Roger Binks, Robin Mclean, Curator, Royal Scots Dragoon Guards Museum, Edinburgh, Karen O'Rourke, Assistant Curator, Liverpool Museums, Major Martin Everett, Curator, Royal Regiment of Wales, Juliet McConnell at the National Army Museum, Lieutenant Colonel R.P.Mason of the Royal Scots Regimental Museum, John Lange, Curator, Household Cavalry Museum, Maurice Gibson, Regimental Secretary, the Highlanders, Dr. Alix Powers-Jones of the Highlanders Museum, Captain Mick Holtby of the Queen's Royal Lancers, Valerie Bedford, Stuart Wheeler and Janice Tate at the Tank Museum, and of course the team at the History Press, Shaun Barrington, Max Hubbard and Miranda Jewess. All illustrations and photographs are provided by the regimental museums unless otherwise indicated. Regimental cap badges have been kindly provided by G. L. D. Alderton, from his book *Cap Badges of the British Army 1939–45*, published by the History Press.

I would also like to thank Tim Reese and Jerome Lantz for their illustrations.

Bayonet attack by the Guards at Inkerman. From Dickinson's *The Officer's Portfolio*.

one

THE GUARDS REGIMENTS

'Up, Guards and at 'em!'

Duke of Wellington at Waterloo, June 18th 1815

'We were lying next to the Guards and you couldn't help admiring them. They were in exactly the same conditions as we were. It had rained on them just the same as it had on us. We were all in the open air, but we were all scruffy and dirty and they were clean and tidy. We didn't know how they did it! Their Quarter Guard was spick and span. Their sentry was on his beat, marching up and down, saluting officers and presenting arms as if they were all still at home in barracks. What discipline! It was marvellous!'

A description of the Guards on the Somme, July 1916

'There are three bodies no sensible man directly challenges: the Roman Catholic Church, the Brigade of Guards and the National Union of Mineworkers.'

Harold Macmillan, Prime Minister

LIFE GUARDS

'Piccadilly Butchers'; 'Tins'

Dates	1658 to present
Motto	*Honi soit qui mal y pense*, Shame on him who thinks evil of it.
Alumni	Ronald Ferguson, father of the Duchess of York, 7th Marquess of Bath, eccentric novelist and politician, James Blunt, pop singer, Philip Dunne, commando, Tommy Cooper, comedian.
Anniversaries	18 June, Waterloo Day
Battle Honours	Dettingen, Vitoria, Peninsula, Waterloo, Tel-el-Kebir, Ladysmith, Mons, Ypres, Somme, Passchendaele, Arras, Cambrai, El Alamein, Arezzo, North West Europe, Gulf, Basra.

The number one regiment in the British Army and the senior cavalry regiment. The Life Guards, together with the Blues and Royals, form the Household Cavalry Regiment.

The ceremonial image of the regiment in their splendid red tunics, white breeches, high black boots, shining breast plates and white plumed helmets is known throughout the world. But though the Household Cavalry Mounted Regiment escorts the Sovereign to the State Opening of Parliament or foreign dignitaries on State Visits to Britain, it is also an armoured reconnaissance unit within the British Army. Make no mistake, the Life Guards are a serious fighting regiment with a list of battle honours to prove it. Take for example two Commanding Officers: Lieutenant Colonel Edwin Cook, Commanding Officer of the 1st Life Guards, died of wounds during the First Battle of Ypres on 4 November 1914 during the valiant defensive fighting of the British Expeditionary Force against a German Army five times its strength. Major, the Honourable Hugh Dawnay, Commanding Officer of the 2nd Life Guards was also killed two days later in this desperate battle. His was a heroic death of which any regiment would be proud. When the Prussian Guard broke through a French sector of the line, Major Dawnay personally led his men into battle, he with sword and revolver, they with bayonets fixed like infantrymen, and, inflicting severe casualties, stemmed the enemy advance. He was killed in the exchange. John Buchan, lamenting the loss of such an excellent officer, quoted the words of William Napier describing the heroism of Colonel Ridge of the 5th at Badajoz, *'No man died that night with more glory. Yet many died, and there was much glory.'*

The ranks in the Life Guards, other than officers, are unique in the British Army. There are no Sergeants. In the past no cavalry regiments had the rank of sergeant, originally only an infantry rank, and the Household Cavalry has kept this tradition alive. A Sergeant is known as a Corporal of Horse and a Corporal as a Lance Corporal of Horse. This may come from the regiment's foundation when all members of the regiment were gentlemen and members of the aristocracy pledged to protect the king. This tradition continued on into the 18th century and was not a tradition in the Blues, who were a Regiment of Horse by origin and were thus more like Line cavalry regiments in structure.

The regiment was first raised in 1658 as a Troop to protect the exiled King Charles II in Bruges, though mounted guards who looked after the life of the King went back as far as 1651. They were known as *His Majesty's Own Troop of Horse Guards* from 1661. Another Troop, to look after his younger brother, the future King James II, was known as *The Duke of York's Troop of Horse Guards* from 1660.

British Off.^r of Heavy Cavalry.
2.nd Reg.^t of Life Guards.

An officer of the 2nd Life Guards, 1815.

In 1659 another Troop, the Duke of Albermarle's Troop, was raised to protect General Monck on his return to London to re-establish the Monarchy, and a further Troop a year after the Restoration in 1661. These Troops were made up exclusively of Royalist gentlemen and even the corporals were commissioned as lieutenants. This anomaly persisted for a hundred years; a regiment made up of officers only.

They first saw action at the Battle of Sedgemoor in 1685 during the rebellion of the Duke of Monmouth against King James II. The officer commanding the army on that day went by the name of John Churchill, later the great commander the Duke of Marlborough.

During the next hundred years these Troops of Royal bodyguards, a sort of Praetorian Guard, evolved into the 1st and 2nd Life Guards. Their first battle honour was at the Battle of Dettingen, 1743, under the overall command of King George II, where they famously made a successful charge. Handel composed a Te Deum and an anthem in honour of the battle. The Horse Grenadier Guards also were at Fontenoy where they covered the Allied retreat. They were recalled to England on the outbreak of the second Jacobite rebellion in 1745. In 1788 the 1st and 2nd Life Guards were formed from the original Troops of Horse Grenadiers and Troops of Royal Horse

Life Guards at Trooping the Colour.

Guards and much of their ceremonial uniform dates from this period.

In 1812 the regiment was sent to Spain to serve under the future Duke of Wellington. In the summer of 1813 they were part of the Peninsula Army and took part in the victory at the Battle of Vitoria; for this and other actions, as the army drove the French over the Pyrenees into France, they received the 'Peninsula' battle honour.

In May 1815, following the escape of Napoleon from Elba, the regiment was sent to the Low Countries as part of the Household Cavalry Brigade under Major General Lord Somerset. At Genappe on 17 June they made an important charge that stopped the advance of the French Lancers, who had just inflicted heavy losses on the 7th Hussars and the 23rd Light Dragoons, and were looking to attack the withdrawing British infantry.

Early in the afternoon of the following day at the Battle of Waterloo, the 1st and 2nd Life Guards, alongside the Royal Horse Guards and the Royal Dragoon Guards, formed the front line of the charge which began to turn the day in the Duke of Wellington's favour and put paid to the main French attack under Marshal Ney. In this decisive attack they soundly defeated the French Cuirassiers.

The regiment did not serve abroad again until the Egyptian campaign of 1882 where they took part in a moonlight charge led by Colonel Ewart on 28 August at Kassassin, which routed the enemy infantry and destroyed their guns. A few days later the regiment took part in the swift victory in the Battle of Tel-el-Kebir.

Shortly after this time, with Sudan in turmoil due to lack of control from Egypt, elements of the Life Guards, alongside officers and men from other cavalry regiments, volunteered for service in the Heavy Camel Regiment which was part of the column sent to rescue General Gordon in Khartoum. They fought against the Mahdists at the Battle of Abu Klea on 17 January 1885, but the ultimate purpose of the expedition failed to achieve its objective.

The regiment, as part of the Household Cavalry Regiment, was much involved in the Boer War in South Africa. On 15 February 1900, after a spectacular high speed advance across the veldt, losing many horses on the route through sheer exhaustion, the Cavalry Division relieved Ladysmith under Lieutenant General John French. A few days later at the battle of Paaderberg they located the retreating Boer units which led to their encirclement and surrender on 27 February 1900.

During the First World War a squadron of the regiment was briefly part of the Household Cavalry Composite Regiment during the Retreat from Mons and Ypres. They then were part of the 7th Cavalry Brigade until 1917. At Zandvoorde two squadrons were completely wiped out. They converted to become the 1st and 2nd Guards Machine Gun Battalions in 1917 and fought at Bethune, the Somme and on the Hindenburg Line in 1918. In 1922 the 1st Life Guards and 2nd Life Guards were amalgamated to become the Life Guards (1st and 2nd) and in 1928 the Life Guards.

In the Second World War, as part of the 1st Household Cavalry Regiment, the Life Guards saw action against Vichy France in Syria, then were on operations in Iraq and Persia before taking part in the Battle of Alamein and the Italian campaign.

The 2nd Household Cavalry Regiment was an armoured car unit, operating as reconnaissance, in the Guards Armoured Division that landed in Normandy and fought its way across North West Europe, liberating Brussels and taking the bridge at Nijmegen alongside US forces, before reaching the Polish Parachute Brigade near Arnhem in 1944. They then advanced through the winter of 1944-5 to the German border and beyond by the time of the German surrender. Its Corps commander, Lieutenant General Sir Brian Horrocks described it as *'the finest armoured car regiment I have ever seen.'*

To Horse, to Horse

How do you actually end up on a horse if you join? Having enlisted in the Household Cavalry to serve with either The Life Guards or The Blues and Royals, you will join the Guards Company in the Army Training Regiment at Pirbright for basic military training – something that all recruits joining the Army experience. At the end of this 12-week period, those not becoming mounted dutymen move to Bovington for Royal Armoured Corps training either as an AFV (Armoured Fighting Vehicles) Driver or a Gunner. After this six-week course you join either The Life Guards or The Blues and Royals squadrons of the Household Cavalry Regiment. Those selected for mounted duty remain at Windsor for another 16 weeks in Riding School. This is when you get your horse. When you can ride to an acceptable standard you begin sword drill and cavalry foot drill. A final four weeks are spent riding in ceremonial uniform before the Passing Out Parade in front of the Commanding Officer. Your new home is now Hyde Park Barracks.

In 1992, with Army reductions, the Life Guards and the Blues and Royals united to form the Household Cavalry Regiment, but, uniquely, keeping their own uniforms and colonels. The Life Guards have mounted guard, with the Blues and Royals, outside the building called Horse Guards on Whitehall since the Restoration of the monarchy in 1660. They are the personal body guards of the reigning monarch. Horse

Kettledrum overall.

Guards was originally the only entrance to the Royal Palaces and was so right up until 1841. To this day nobody can ride or drive through without Royal permission. When the monarch is in London the Household Cavalry form what is known as a Long Guard. This consists of one officer, one Corporal Major who carries the Standard, two non-commissioned officers, one trumpeter and ten troopers. When the monarch is not in London, this is reduced to a Short Guard which is two non-commissioned officers and ten troopers. There is a sentry on duty all night at Horse Guards and only people who know the password can have access. So, the Life Guards, as part of the unique Household Cavalry Regiment, continue to be both the personal bodyguard of the Sovereign and, at the same time, a fully participating unit of the British Army on active duty.

MUSEUM: Household Cavalry Museum, Horse Guards, Whitehall, London SW1A 2AX Tel 0207 9303070

ROYAL HORSE GUARDS

'The Blues'

Dates	1650-1969
Motto	*Honi soit qui mal y pense*, Shame on him who thinks evil of it.
Alumni	Prince William, Prince Harry, Evelyn Waugh, writer, Auberon Waugh, journalist, General Sir William Napier, Peninsular war veteran and military historian, Jack Charlton, footballer, Andrew Parker-Bowles, first husband of the Duchess of Cornwall.
Anniversaries	18 June, Waterloo Day
Battle Honours	Dettingen, Minden, Warburg, Waterloo, Balaclava, Tel-el-Kebir, Relief of Kimberley, Paardeberg, Marne, Ypres, Arras, Cambrai, Iraq, Syria 1941, El Alamein 1942, Arezzo, Florence, Amiens, Nijmegen, Brussels 1944, Falklands 1982, Iraq 2003.

This is the only regiment in the British Army in which the 2nd lieutenants are known as Cornets, the original name used in all cavalry regiments for junior officers. This swank unit forms one half of the Household Cavalry Regiment, along with the Life Guards. Ironically, it was originally raised as a Parliamentary republican regiment, since it can trace its origins back to 1650 when Oliver Cromwell formed it as a Regiment of Cuirassiers. It is one of only two regiments, along with the Coldstream Guards, which was part of the New Model Army and survived the return of the monarchy in 1660. Royalist officers took over and it became, in 1661, the Earl of Oxford's Royal Regiment of Horse, the 1st Regiment of Horse with a blue uniform, hence the 'Oxford Blues' and later the 'Blues.' They became part of the Royal Household in 1687 and the Royal Regiment of Horse Guards in 1689.

They fought in Ireland at the Battle of the Boyne in 1690. In the War of the Austrian Succession along with the Life Guards, their first battle honour is at the Battle of Dettingen in 1743. In 1745 they also fought at the Battle of Fontenoy and the following year they ceased to be a line cavalry regiment and were given special status as the Royal Regiment of Horse. In 1750 they were named the Royal Horse Guards (Blue).

The Blues on parade at
Horse Guards, 1830.

Blues and Royals at
the wheel during
the Trooping of the
Colour.

In the Seven Years War they fought at the Battle of Minden in 1759, the Battle of Warburg in 1760, Vellinghausen in 1761 and Willemstahl in 1762, when the Marquis of Granby was their colonel. It was on July 31st 1760 at Warburg that the Marquis, a balding man, lost his hat and wig during the charge but still managed to salute his generals as he passed them. This gave rise to the expression 'going at it bald-headed'. The Blues to this day can salute when not wearing headwear. After the Seven Years War the Marquis set up many unemployed non-commissioned officers in the regiment as publicans, hence the large number of pubs in England bearing the name 'The Marquis of Granby'.

The Blues fought with success in the Peninsula campaign gaining the battle honour of Vitoria in 1813 and at the Battle of Waterloo where they were part of the Heavy Cavalry Brigade under the command of Major General Somerset. They were in the charge that drove the attacking French infantry off the

The Blues making their way to the Trooping of the Colour.

Allied ridge and signalled the beginning of the end for Napoleon's Grande Armée. A detachment of the Blues formed the Duke of Wellington staff during the battle, since, from 1813, he had been their Colonel.

They were incorporated as part of the Household Cavalry by King George IV in 1820 and in 1875 were renamed the Royal Horse Guards (The Blues). They were part of the British force sent to Egypt in 1882 to support the Khedive during the uprising led by Colonel Arabi Pasha, which culminated in the overwhelming British victory at the Battle of Tel el Kebir, in which the regiment took part in mopping up operations. The Royal Horse Guards were sent to South Africa as part of the Household Cavalry Regiment during the Boer War. They took part in the heroic and costly gallop across the veldt to relieve the town of Kimberley. Under the command of Lieutenant General John French the men drove their horses so hard that many foundered and had to be destroyed. A few days later they were part of French's cavalry that identified the retreating Boers and took part in the definitive Battle of Paardeburg, which effectively ended the Boer resistance.

The Travel Writer

Lieutenant Colonel Frederick Burnaby was a well-known member of the Royal Horse Guards. He was a Victorian soldier, journalist and traveller. He had crossed the Channel in a balloon and ridden by horse across Turkey and Southern Russia, writing books on the subject. He unofficially joined the Suakin Campaign in 1883 where he was wounded at the Battle of El Teb in 1884 while operating as an intelligence officer under General Valentine Baker. A year later he was killed at the Battle of Abu Klea fighting valiantly against the dervishes during General Wolseley's advance to relieve General Gordon in Khartoum.

When the First World War broke out in 1914 the Blues briefly formed part of the Household Cavalry Composite Regiment and were sent to the Front taking part in fighting at Mons and Ypres. By the end of the year they were reassigned to the 7th Cavalry Brigade, part of the 3rd Cavalry Division, until the end of 1917. In March 1918 they were converted to form 3rd Battalion, Guards Machine Gun Regiment, which fought successfully at Cambrai and on the Hindenburg Line.

At the First Battle of Ypres, Lieutenant Colonel Gordon Wilson, Commanding Officer of the Blues, was killed in action at Zillebeke on 6 November 1914 leading his regiment in the heroic defensive action of the British Expeditionary Force.

In the Second World War the Blues, as part of the 1st Household Cavalry Regiment, saw action against Vichy France in Syria, Iraq and Persia before taking part in the Battle of Alamein and in the Italian campaign. The 2nd Household Cavalry Regiment was an armoured car unit (operating as reconnaissance) in the Guards Armoured Division which landed in Normandy and fought its way across North West Europe. Their World War II experience is of course the same as that of the Life Guards (see above).

Firefight

Trooper Chris Finney G.C. On 28 March 2003 while driving a Scimitar armoured vehicle north of Basra, Finney came under fire. He managed to get out of the burning vehicle but immediately returned to rescue his gunner. Still under fire he dragged his comrade clear and tended to his wounds. Though wounded himself, he then attempted to rescue the crew of the accompanying vehicle but was beaten back by the flames. For his gallantry he was awarded the George Cross with his citation reading, 'Finney displayed clear-headed courage and devotion to his comrades acting courageously and with complete disregard for his own safety throughout the entire episode.'

In the post-war period the Blues served in a number of trouble spots around the world including Germany, Cyprus and Malaya. One of their most interesting challenges was to form the ceremonial personal bodyguard to the young Queen Elizabeth II on her Coronation Day in 1953. This was no mean feat for a regiment which had been mechanised more than a decade before and therefore suffered from a distinct shortage of equestrians.

In 1969 the Blues amalgamated with the Royal (1st) Dragoons to become the Blues and Royals, the Royals now being incorporated into the Household Cavalry. In 1992 the Household Cavalry Regiment was formed, which is unique in the British Army. The Blues and Royals and the Life Guards each provide two squadrons for operational purposes but each regiment keeps its own regimental headquarters, traditions, uniforms and colonels. This regiment is an armoured reconnaissance regiment as it was during the Second World War. It has four squadrons, one of which is permanently attached to the 16th Air Assault Brigade, an elite rapid reaction force deployed throughout the world to trouble spots. Both the Blues and Royals and the Life Guards combine to form the Household Cavalry Mounted Regiment.

MUSEUM: Household Cavalry Museum, Horse Guards, Whitehall, London SW1A 2AX Tel 0207 9303070

The Blues fighting at the battle of Abu Klea, January, 1885. In barely a quarter of an hour of combat, nine officers and 65 other ranks were killed and over a hundred wounded. More than 1,100 Mahdists died in those few short minutes.

ROYAL (1ST) DRAGOONS

'The Royals'; 'Tangier Horse'

Dates	1661–1969 VCs 1
Motto	*Spectemur agendo*, We are Judged by our Deeds.
Alumni	Edward Hyde, Earl of Clarendon, governor of New York, Julian Grenfell, poet, Frank Rhodes, soldier and war correspondent, brother of Cecil, Prince Francis of Teck, brother of Queen Mary, John Churchill, Duke of Marlborough, general.
Anniversaries	18 June, Waterloo
Battle Honours	Tangier, Dettingen, Fontenoy, Fuentes de Onoro, Waterloo, Balaclava, Inkerman, Ladysmith, Ypres, Loos, Arras, Hindenburg Line, El Alamein, NW Europe 1944–5

The 'Royals' were first raised from the remnants of Cromwell's New Model Army and Monmouth's Horse in 1661 to garrison Tangier, which formed part of Catherine of Braganza's dowry. Their four original Troops became known as the Tangier Horse and have Tangier on their battle honours, which is the oldest battle honour in the British Army.

An officer of the Royals walking with a Hussar officer, 1810.

The Dragon

The name *dragoon* comes from *dragon*, the French word for the shortened muskets suitable for use by mounted troops. Its cocking piece had the curvature of a dragon and the flash of gunpowder released as it fired was perhaps another reason for the name. Dragoons originated as mounted infantry armed with these muskets. Their horses were more a means of moving swiftly to trouble spots than for use in charges.

Captain Clark-Kennedy and Corporal Stiles of the 1st Royal Dragoons, capturing the eagle of the 105th Regiment at Waterloo.

In 1674 they were named the 1st Dragoons, immediately becoming the senior cavalry regiment of the Line which they remained until being incorporated into the Guards in 1969. On their return to England in 1683 they were re-titled the King's Own Royal Regiment of Dragoons serving King Charles II. The brilliant young commander, John Churchill, later the Duke of Marlborough, was appointed their colonel and raised further troops for the regiment in St. Albans. When King James II came to the throne, the regiment fought at the Battle of Sedgemoor in 1685 where Churchill commanded the Royalist army in defeating the Duke of Monmouth's uprising. In 1690 they were re-named The Royal Regiment of Dragoons.

Not Forgotten

On 26 June 1917 Second Lieutenant John Dunville was leading a patrol in front of the trenches. In spite of enemy fire he continued calmly to direct his men in their operations and, though severely wounded, stayed with a Royal Engineer who was cutting the wire. The work completed, Dunville was carried back to the lines but died the next day from his wounds. The inscription on his memorial stone reads, *'To commemorate John Spencer Dunville, VC, 2nd Lieut. Royal Dragoons, second son of John and Violet Dunville; he gave his life for his country in the Great War and died of his wounds in France on 27 June 1917 aged 21 years, buried at Villiers Faucon, was awarded the Victoria Cross for conspicuous bravery. Let those who come after see to it that his memory is not forgotten.'*

Above, from left
Private, 1st Royal
Dragoons, 1815.

Trooper, 1st Royal
Dragoons, 1810, in
Peninsular campaign
dress.

A Royals Sergeant,
1815. (Tim Reese)

In 1743, during the War of the Austrian Succession the Royals charged famously against the French Black Musketeers at the Battle of Dettingen, thereby winning the right to their black plumes and black backing to their badges. Two years later the regiment fought during the Second Jacobite uprising of 1745 and took part in the Battle of Culloden. In 1751 they were named as the 1st (Royal) Regiment of Dragoons.

They served in the Peninsular War and then the Waterloo campaign, where they captured the colours of the French 105th Infantry, incorporating the eagle and the numerals 105 into their regimental crest. The eagle insignia is still worn by the Blues and Royals to this day.

In the Crimean War, on 25 October 1854, the Royals were part of the Heavy Brigade at the Battle of Balaclava. Under the command of Major General James Scarlett they took part in an epic charge against the Russian cavalry, which was a complete success, driving the enemy from the battlefield. Unfortunately, this success was overshadowed later in the day by the disastrous but valiant charge of the Light Brigade.

During the Boer War the Royals were initially part of Lord Dundonald's Mounted Brigade and were present at a number of actions against the enemy – including the Battle of Colenso – all of which were efforts to relieve Ladysmith. A year later the regiment was in Colonel Pulteney's column alongside the 6th Inniskilling Dragoons operating with no little success against an elusive and dangerous enemy.

In the First World War the regiment was sent from South Africa where it was stationed and arrived in France in September 1914. They formed part of the 3rd Cavalry

Division in the separate fighting to hold the German advance during the next few weeks. Between mid October and the end of November the division sustained casualties of more than 8,000 men and three hundred officers. Though the cavalry regiments such as the Royals were not given many opportunities, if any, to operate as they were trained, one thing is sure. Their participation in the First Battle of Ypres ensured that the Allies were not defeated in the first weeks of the war, which is what happened in 1940. The regiment then won battle honours at Ypres, Loos and the Hindenburg Line.

When the Second World War broke out, the regiment was stationed in Lydda, Palestine. Within a year it was mechanised with armoured cars and saw action against Vichy French Forces in Syria and the Italians as part of the 8th Army in the Western Desert. They led the advance across hundreds of miles to Benghazi, where they were the first troops to enter, on Christmas Day 1941. During Rommel's advances early in 1942 units of the Royals formed the rearguard during the retreat to Tobruk and to the defensive line at El Alamein.

The Duke of Wellington, the second great commander with whom the regiment is forever associated, through the incorporation of the French eagle into the regimental crest following Waterloo. The first is John Churchill, the future Duke of Malborough. (Though both leaders would be Colonels of the following regiment.)

Behind the Lines

During the Battle of Alamein A and C troop managed to slip through the German front lines. On the night of 1 November 1942 C Squadron, under the command of Major Roderick Heathcoat-Amory, negotiated their way through the German defensive minefields. It took until daybreak before they broke out, proceeding to wreak havoc behind enemy lines, destroying more than a hundred transport vehicles, a tank and several artillery pieces, as well as taking a large number of prisoners. Heathcoat-Amory's citation for his Military Cross records his *'conspicuous ability and devotion to duty throughout this hazardous operation covering four days behind enemy lines.'*

The regiment led the southern wing of the Eighth Army's rapid advance across North Africa, which ended with the expulsion of Axis forces from North Africa in May 1943. 'A' Squadron took part in the invasion of Sicily and the early part of the Italian

Above, from left
A caricature of the Royals in Full Dress, 1830s.

Trooper of the Royals (1st) Dragoons.

campaign, then, in late 1943, the regiment was recalled to England for preparation for the invasion of Normandy. They were equipped with waterproof vehicles and artillery before embarking for Normandy in July and advancing with Montgomery's army through France and Holland into Germany. They ended up near Lübeck in Northern Germany, capturing 10,000 German prisoners and liberating 16,000 Allied Prisoners of War before sweeping north into Denmark, liberating Copenhagen, to the delight of the Danish people. As had been the case during the North African campaign in Libya and a year later at El Alamein, the Royals were always in the forefront of operations and, in the final exchanges of the war inside Germany, General Montgomery utilised them as forward reconnaissance units alongside the 51st Highland Division and the 5th Scottish Division.

After the war they were on active service in Egypt during the Suez crisis, Malaya and Northern Ireland. The Royals amalgamated with the Royal Horse Guards in 1969 to become the Blues and Royals, the only regiment of the line ever to have been elevated to Guards status in modern times.

MUSEUM: Household Cavalry Museum, Horse Guards, Whitehall, London SW1A 2AX Tel 0207 9303070

GRENADIER GUARDS

'The Bill Browns'

Dates	1656 to present VCs 13
Motto	*Honi soit qui mal y pense,* Shame on him who thinks evil of it.
Alumni	Lord Carrington, politician, Winston Churchill, statesman and soldier, Terry Waite, hostage, Harold Macmillan, Prime Minister, Brian Johnson, cricket commentator, John Churchill, 1st Duke of Marlborough, military genius, Peter Fleming, writer brother of Ian, Osbert Sitwell, aesthete, Field Marshal Lord Gort VC.
Anniversaries	18 June, Waterloo, 5 November, Inkerman, second Sunday in May, Regimental Remembrance Day.
Battle Honours	Tangier 1680, Blenheim 1704, Ramillies 1706, Oudenarde 1708, Malplaquet 1709, Waterloo 1815, Alma, Inkerman 1854, Peking 1876, Ypres 1914, Somme 1915, Cambrai 1917, El Alamein 1942, Mareth 1943, Salerno, Anzio, Monte Camino, Nijmegen 1944, Gulf 1991.

'The First or Grenadier Regiment of Foot Guards', the Grenadier Guards, are, without question, the most famous Regiment in the British Army, if not the whole world. They are the senior infantry regiment in the British Army and their colonels have included Britain's two finest commanders, John Churchill, Duke of Marlborough and Arthur Wellesley, Duke of Wellington. Though well known for their ceremonial duties at the Trooping of the Colour and guarding the Sovereign, they have had more than their share of battle honours, numbering seventy eight, from the great victories of the first Duke of Marlborough through to the Second World War and beyond.

They were originally known as Lord Wentworth's Regiment, and formed as bodyguard to the exiled King Charles II in Bruges in the Low Countries during the rule of Oliver Cromwell. They returned to England with the King in 1660 and in 1665, following Lord Wentworth's death, combined with John Russell's Regiment of Guards to form the First Regiment of Foot.

Captain in Frock Coat Order and Guardsman in Full Dress. Watercolour by Douglas N. Anderson.

There is much rivalry with the Coldstream Guards who were, in fact, formed before them, but are the Second Regiment of Foot by virtue of the fact that the Grenadiers were formed for the King and the Coldstream for Cromwell's New Model Army; a small bone of contention.

The Grenadiers are the only regiment of Foot Guards to have fought in all four of the Duke of Marlborough's legendary victories over the armies of Louis XIV during the War of the Spanish Succession. In fact they were the only Foot Guard Regiment present at both the Battles of Blenheim and Ramillies. They were part of Marlborough's Army that daringly marched four hundred miles deep into Bavaria and fearlessly led the attack during the storming of the Schellenburg Fortress on 2 July 1704, which opened the way for the great victory at Blenheim exactly a month later.

In the War of the Austrian Succession the regiment fought at the Battle of Dettingen in 1743 and famously at the Battle of Fontenoy two years later where they advanced holding their line with magnificent discipline against murderous enemy fire. It was there that Lord Charles Hay, a Captain in the regiment, on seeing the Gardes Francaises in front of him, Guards against Gardes, rode forward and challenged their commander, the Comte d'Auterroche, politely, *'We are the English Guards. We remember you from Dettingen and intend to make you swim the Scheldt as you swam the Main. Please, fire first!'* The battle was not a British victory. It is said that the hard-earned victory of the French was driven home by the final attacks of Irish foot regiments in the French Army. Charles Hay was wounded.

A Field Marshal's Baton in his Knapsack

John Vereker, 6th Viscount Gort, was commissioned into the Grenadier Guards in 1905. As a young officer he commanded the party carrying the coffin of King Edward VII. During the First World War he was mentioned in despatches eight times, winning the MC and the DSO and two bars. On 27 September 1918 during the Battle of Canal du Nord in France, Lieutenant-Colonel Gort led his battalion into the attack under very heavy fire. When the battalion was held up, though wounded, he ran across open ground and led a supporting tank into an attacking position. Though wounded again, he continued to direct the attack to success, capturing over 200 of the enemy, two batteries of field-guns and numerous machine-guns. He only left the field of battle for medical treatment when his battalion had achieved their objectives. For his gallantry he was awarded the Victoria Cross. In 1940 he commanded the ill-fated British Expeditionary Force in France and was later commander in Gibraltar and Malta rising to the rank of Field Marshal. Here he presents the George Cross to the people of Malta in 1942.

During the Seven Years Wars the regiment fought at two major engagements in Europe against the French armies: the Battle of Vellinghausen on 15 July 1761, when the Guards Brigade was commanded by a Major General Julius Caesar, and the Battle

The Grenadier Guards attacking at Waterloo.

of Wilhelmstahl on 24 June 1762. In both battles the 1st Guards fought with their customary discipline and courage.

In the American War of Independence the 1st Guards fought in a composite Guards battalion from the early success of the Battle of Long Island in 1776 to the humiliation of Yorktown five years later. In 1793 and 1799 the regiment was deployed in inconclusive campaigns in the Low Countries against the marauding French revolutionary armies.

VCs in the Crimea

Brevet Major Sir Charles Russell was awarded the VC for his bravery in the face of the enemy at the Battle of Inkerman on November 5th 1854. He personally led a volunteer group of Grenadiers in vicious hand-to-hand fighting, driving the Russian infantry off the Sandbag Battery high ground position with their bayonets.

Captain Lord Henry Percy was an experienced officer aged 37 when, though wounded, he personally led more than fifty men, from his own regiment and other infantry regiments, after they had charged too far against the Russian defences and had been surrounded, back to the British lines in safety. He then located fresh ammunition and led the men back into action. For his outstanding bravery he was awarded the Victoria Cross.

OBITUARY.

SIR CHARLES RUSSELL, V. C.

The death of Lieut.-Col. Sir Charles Russell, V. C., is announced in a London dispatch. He was born at Southern Hill, Reading, on June 22, 1826, and received his education at Eton. He succeeded his father as third Baronet on April 19, 1852. Having been appointed to the Thirty-fifth Regiment at the age of 17, he served with it in Mauritius, and in 1847 was transferred to the Grenadier Guards. He accompanied the expeditionary force to Malta, in February, 1854, and saw active service through the Crimean war. Sir Charles was present at the landing at Old Fort and at the battles of Balaklava, Alma, Inkermann, and the siege of Sebastopol. His valiant service in the field earned for him the rank of Brevet Major, and after the battle of Inkermann he was honored with the Victoria Cross, the Crimean medal, and four clasps, the Turkish medal and order of the Medjidie, and the order of the Legion of Honor. He was a Conservative representative for Berkshire in the Parliament of 1865-8, vacating his seat for that county under the operation of the minority vote, and was returned for Westminster in 1874. Sir Charles was Honorary Colonel of the Forty-sixth Middlesex Volunteers, a Deputy Lieutenant, and a Justice of the Peace for Berkshire.

The New York Times
Published: April 15, 1883

The next significant action for the 1st Guards was the harsh campaign in the Spanish Peninsula under Sir John Moore in the autumn of 1808, which ended with the desperate defence of Corunna and the evacuation of the British Army. During the difficult retreat across the harsh terrain of Northern Spain, the 1st Guards lost less men to desertion, sickness or indiscipline than any other regiment in Moore's army. When Sir John Moore was mortally wounded it was a party of the 1st Guards who carried him from the battlefield.

It was at the Battle of Waterloo on 18 June 1815 that the regiment gained undying fame and their name. Late in the afternoon they famously repulsed the last desperate attacks of the French Grenadiers of the Imperial Guard, Napoleon's elite regiment, breaking them and forcing them into retreat. In honour of this great victory they were renamed the First or Grenadier Regiment of Foot Guards and became the only regiment in the army to be called after their opponents in battle. They also took the grenade with seventeen flames as their badge and took to wearing the famous bearskin.

Just over forty years later, on 5 November 1854, the Grenadier Guards fought at the Battle of Inkerman during the Crimean War. The Grenadiers consider this engagement particularly significant since the action was fought largely at close quarters in hand to hand combat. Every man had to play his part. The Grenadiers fought unflinchingly throughout the day, particularly at Sandbag Battery, ending exhausted with losses of nine officers and two hundred and twenty five men, virtually half their number. Not an inch of ground was conceded to the enemy and not one man was taken prisoner. The regiment was the only one to carry their Colours into battle and

Below, from left
Private 1st Guards, 1751.

The 1st Guards at Waterloo.

defended them valiantly. Not for nothing is Inkerman known as the 'Soldiers' Battle'. Inkerman Company within the regiment proudly bears the name, as Nijmegen Company remembers the bravery of the Grenadiers in 1944.

The Grenadiers fought for the last time in their red coats at the Battle of Tel-el-Kebir in Egypt in 1882. Then in the winter of 1899 in the Boer War they fought in khaki at the engagements of Belmont and Graspan, the Modder River and Magersfontein in the north west of the Cape Colony.

For the killing fields of the First World War the Grenadier Guards raised five battalions and sustained 12,000 casualties. In the desperate combat during the first Battle of Ypres, where the British Army was making a fighting retreat, the 1st and 2nd battalions took appalling casualties. By the middle of November 1914 only eight officers and three hundred and forty men were left standing. Harold Macmillan, later to become Prime Minister, served in the regiment during much of the war and was noted for his bravery. An expression was coined by his men, *'Nearly as brave as Mr Macmillan.'*

During the Second World War three battalions of the Grenadiers fought with the British Expeditionary Force in France in 1940, again against enormous odds and, by defending the perimeter of Dunkirk, enabled the army to embark from the beaches and escape back to England. In the course of the next year a further three battalions were raised.

Three battalions of the Grenadier Guards fought in North Africa and Italy and three landed in Normandy in 1944, forming part of the Guards Armoured Division and the 6th Guards Tank Brigade involved in heavy fighting at Nijmegen in Holland alongside the U.S. 82nd Airborne. Since the Second World War the regiment has continued to play its central role in the traditional pageantry of the United Kingdom alongside its military role as a peacekeeping or fighting unit wherever it has served in trouble spots throughout the world from Palestine, Malaya, Cyprus, Northern Ireland, to the Gulf, and in more recent times, Iraq and Afghanistan.

Scipio

The regimental slow march is *'Scipio'* written by George Frederick Handel. It is about the legendary Roman general Scipio Africanus, victor of the Carthaginian Wars. Many think it was taken from the opera and used by the regiment. This is not the case. In fact Handel wrote the tune specifically for the 1st Regiment of Foot Guards and only later put it into the opera which was first performed in 1726.

MUSEUM: Guards Museum, Wellington Barracks, Birdcage Walk, London SW1E 6HQ Tel 0207 4143430

COLDSTREAM GUARDS

'The Lilywhites'

Dates   1650 to present   VCs 13
Motto   *Nulli Secundus*, Second to None.
Alumni Edward Fox, actor, Alistair Horne, historian, Michael Howard, military historian, Laurie McNenemie, football manager, Stephen Potter, writer, Lord Brabourne, film producer.
Anniversaries   23 April, St. George's Day, first Sunday in May, Black Sunday
Battle Honours   Tangier, Namur, Oudenarde, Malplaquet, Egypt, Talavera, Salamanca, Waterloo, Alma, Inkerman, South Africa, Mons, Ypres, Loos, Somme, Arras, Dunkirk, Tobruk, Salerno, NW Europe, Gulf.

A member of the regiment should be referred to as a Coldstreamer and the regiment as the Coldstream, never the Coldstreams. Their cap badge should only be referred to as their cap star with its design based on the Garter star. Her Majesty's Coldstream Regiment of Foot Guards holds 117 battle honours and has won 13 VCs. A proud record, second to none.

On 13 August 1650 the regiment was first raised by one of Cromwell's officers, Colonel George Monck. This regiment was known as Monck's Regiment of Foot, as was the custom with regiments and their colonels for the next one hundred years, and fought on the side of Parliament against the future King Charles II two weeks later at the Battle of Dunbar. A medal of thanks was raised for the officers and men of the New Model Army who had participated in this victory, a forerunner of campaign medals awarded in later times. This action makes the Coldstream Guards the oldest regiment in the British Army to have been in continuous service. They are the only surviving regiment of the first professional English army, Cromwell's New Model Army.

A decade later, on 1 January 1660, with Cromwell's regime at an end and England once again in political turmoil, Monck assembled his regiment at a village called Coldstream on the Anglo-Scottish borders and began his long march to London. He arrived there in February in time to influence Parliament to call for the return of the monarchy. He personally met King Charles II at Dover a few weeks later, and though the New Model Army was disbanded by order of Parliament, Monck's Regiment was reprieved at the last minute to control unrest in London. As a result of this, on 14 February 1661, the regiment assembled on Tower Hill and, having put down their arms as old members of the Republican army, immediately took them up again as Royalist soldiers in the New Standing Army. They at once became Household troops and were placed second in the Army list. The regiment has never accepted this, hence their motto. On Monck's death in 1670, they were renamed the Coldstream Regiment of Foot Guards.

In the next years the regiment saw action as part of the Tangier garrison for King Charles II and his Consort, Catherine of Braganca, who had brought the Moorish city as part of her dowry, at the Battle of Sedgmoor in support of King James II, and the Siege of Namur in support of King William III in 1695.

During the next century the regiment was involved in many actions including the Duke of Marlborough's last two great victories at Oudenarde and Malplaquet, and in the War of the Austrian Succession at the Battle of Dettingen and the Battle of Fontenoy in 1745 where, as part of the Guards Brigade, they took part in an historic advance, taking withering fire, then calmly taking aim and decimating the enemy ranks and breaking them. If ever there was an example of courage under fire, this was it.

Three Guards companies fought in the American War of Independence under Colonel Matthew of the Coldstream Guards with the Coldstream contributing more than 300 men. Their first encounter with the enemy was at the Battle of Long Island on 27 August 1776 when the British under General Howe drove Washington and the Americans from Brooklyn and New York. At a further engagement at Fort Washington three months later they were part of the force that drove the rebels from Manhattan Island. They also fought successfully at the Battles of Brandywine Creek and Germantown the following year. However they suffered considerable losses at the Battle of Guilford Courthouse in South Carolina on 15 March 1781 where the two battalions of Foot Guards lost 11 officers out of 19 and 200 men out of 450. The Coldstream only returned to Britain after the surrender of General Cornwallis at the Battle of Yorktown in Virginia on 19 October of that year.

Lieutenant Colonel James Macdonnell, one of the defenders of Hougoumont. Wellington called him 'the bravest man at Waterloo'.

Instruments of Great Things

'The town of Coldstream, because the General did it the honour to make it the piece of his residence for some time, hath given title to a small company of men whom God hath made instruments of Great Things; and though poor yet honest, as ever corrupt Nature produced into the world, by the no inconsiderable name of Coldstreamers.'

Thomas Gumble, 1671

When war broke out with revolutionary France, the Coldstream, alongside the other Foot Guards, saw action in the Low Countries in 1799 as part of the 2nd Brigade under the command of Major General Burrard in Sir Ralph Abercrombie's Division. A

Above, from left
Grenadier sergeant,
2nd (Coldstream)
Guards, 1792. Print
after Edward Dayes.

Lieutenant Colonel Sir
Henry Sullivan, killed
during the sortie from
Bayonne, 14 April 1814.

Sergeant of the
Coldstream Regiment
of Foot Guards, 1815.

year later in Egypt they fought in the closely contested Battle of Alexandria in March
1801, which was won largely by the accurate firing and discipline of the infantry. In
1809 the 1st battalion embarked for Portugal to form part of Sir Arthur Wellesley's
Peninsula Army, while the 2nd battalion had the misfortune of being part of the larger
40,000-strong army sent on the Walcheren Expedition to the Low Countries, which
was withdrawn a few months later having seen no major actions and having lost 10 per
cent of their number to malaria. The 1st battalion fought in many famous victories of
the Peninsular War including the battles of Talavera, Fuentes d'Onor, Ciudad Rodrigo,
Salamanca, Vitoria and over the Pyrenees into France to Nivelle, Nive and Bayonne.

In June 1815, the 2nd battalion Coldstream formed part of the 2nd Guards Brigade
in the Duke of Wellington's Anglo-Dutch Army which was facing Napoleon's Grande
Armée close to the village of Waterloo in Belgium. Wellington ordered them to take
up position in the strategically important farm buildings of Hougoumont, on the
right of his line. Realising that to carry the day this strongpoint would have to be
taken, the French decided to attack.

Jacob the Goose

In 1838-42 the 2nd Battalion were in Canada dealing with a rebellion of settlers.
The story goes that one night rebels approached in a surprise attack and the men
were woken by the noise that Jacob the Goose made, thus saving their lives. Jacob
was brought back to London and looked after by the regiment in recognition of his
bravery. He was later run down in the street by a hansom cab but he is preserved in
the regimental museum, the closest thing to a mascot the regiment has ever had.

They made their first assault at 11 o'clock in the morning and for the next eight hours continued the onslaught almost continually against the Guards Brigade commanded initially by Lieutentant Colonel Lord Saltoun and later by Lieutenant Colonel Macdonnell, of the Coldstream. At one point the struggle was so precarious that Macdonnell, helped by Sergeant Graham, actually managed to close the courtyard gates against hand to hand French attacks. In all the French lost about 8,000 men in their relentless attacks and a British force of little more than 3,000 held 15,000 French troops at bay.

The Duke of Wellington was later asked to select the *'bravest man in England'* for the £500 award given by a benefactor and chose Lieutenant Colonel Macdonnell who at once shared his prize with Sergeant Graham. Every year this heroic action is celebrated in the Sergeant's Mess of the Coldstream Guards in the *'Hanging the Brick'* ceremony.

In 1831 King William IV granted the regiment the right to wear the bearskin headdress with a red plume on the right side to distinguish them from the other Foot Guard regiments.

In the Crimean War four members of the Coldstream were awarded the newly instituted Victoria Cross and the regiment won battle honours at Alma, Inkerman and Sevastopol. At the Alma River, the Coldstream, alongside the Grenadiers and the Scots Guards, advanced on a broad front and took the Heights above the river, forcing the Russian defenders into retreat.

In 1882 the regiment took part in the Egyptian campaign against the Arabi Pasha rebellion culminating in the Battle of Tel-el-Kebir, where the Guards fought in their full red jackets for the last time. In 1885 the regiment also fought in the Suakin campaign in the Sudan.

World War I recruitment poster for the Coldstream Guards.

Campbell, Father and Son

Lieutenant Colonel John Campbell won the Victoria Cross on September 15th 1916 at Ginchy in France during the maelstrom that was the Battle of the Somme. He was commanding the 3rd battalion Coldstream Guards when the first two waves of attackers had been mown down by machine gun fire and the advance was faltering. He personally stood in No Man's Land blowing his hunting horn amidst the thunder of the artillery and, rallying his men, led them on into the German defences, capturing their guns and taking important strategic positions. For his leadership and heroism, in what must have been the most desperate of situations, he was rightfully awarded the supreme award for gallantry. Campbell's father, Captain Ronald Campbell, also of the Coldstream Guards, was killed leading a heroic action during the Zulu Wars on 28th March 1879 and should probably have been recommended for a VC. His commanding officer wrote, *'I never saw a man play a more heroic part than he did yesterday.'*

An officer of the Coldstream Guards, 1815. (Tim Reese)

They played a major role in the Boer War, fighting at the Battle of Modder River where they were the first infantry to advance against the enemy fire and at the catastrophic Battle of Magersfontein where they attempted to draw fire away from the pinned down Highland brigade.

During the First World War the regiment's three battalions were in the line almost continually from 1914 to the Armistice in 1918. In one week at the end of October and early November in the autumn of 1914 the 1st battalion was twice virtually wiped out, on both occasions losing all their officers and being reduced to about 100 men. During the ensuing four years the regiment suffered casualties of more than 500 officers and 13,000 men. After the War, King George V bestowed the honour of calling soldiers in the Brigade of Foot Guards (by now numbering five regiments) Guardsmen rather than Privates as in other regiments.

In the Second World War the Coldstream raised five battalions, losing more than 300 officers and 4,500 men. Starting the war, as they had in 1914, the 1st and 2nd battalions were part of the British Expeditionary Force sent to France in 1940 taking the brunt of the German onslaught. Through a fighting retreat they reached the French coast where they were cut off by German Army Group A, and formed part of the outer defences as the army was evacuated from Dunkirk. Throughout these difficult days ending on 4 June 1940 their discipline and fighting qualities held firm in the most testing of circumstances.

They then saw action in North Africa and Italy. The 1st and 3rd battalions formed part of the Guards Armoured Division which landed in Normandy towards the end of June 1944, fighting its way across France into Belgium and Holland, through to the Rhine and the borders of Germany in the spring of 1945.

Both Ends of the Bridge

Captain Ian Liddell won the VC on 3 April 1945 when his units were held up on the River Ems by a bridge that had been set with explosives. He ran forward alone in the face of enemy fire, scaled a wall and defused the explosives at each end of the bridge before signalling his unit to move forward. He was killed in action two weeks later by German sniper fire just a few days before the end of the war.

Though the Coldstream Guards are now only one battalion, their proud traditions live on. Since 1945, despite numerous military cutbacks, they have served in Malaya, Aden, Northern Ireland the Gulf, Bosnia, Iraq and Afghanistan in addition to carrying out their ceremonial duties for which they are famous.

MUSEUMS: Guards Museum, Wellington Barracks, Birdcage Walk, London SW1E 6HQ Tel 0207 4143428

Coldstream Museum, 12 Market Square, Coldstream, Berwickshire TD12 4BD Tel 01890 882630

SCOTS GUARDS

'Jock Guards'

Dates	1642 to present VCs 11
Motto	*Nemo me impune lacessit*, No one assails me with impunity.
Alumni	David Stirling, founder of the SAS, Willy Whitelaw, politician, Robert Runcie, Archbishop of Canterbury, Derek Oldham, opera singer, George Mann, England cricket captain.
Anniversaries	30 November, St. Andrew's Day.
Battle Honours	Namur, Dettingen, Talavera, Fuentes de Onoro, Salamanca, Waterloo, Alma, Inkerman, Sevastopol, Modder River, Mons, Ypres, Somme, Hindenburg Line, Norway, Tobruk, North Africa, Salerno, Anzio, Monte Camino, North West Europe 1944-5, Falklands, Gulf War.

Interestingly, no plume is worn in the bearskin of the Scots Guards since traditionally they formed the centre of the line, being the 3rd Foot Guards, with the Grenadiers (1st) on their right and the Coldstream (2nd) on their left. Plumes for recognition would only be necessary for flanking troops.

They should not be confused with the Garde Ecossaise raised by King Charles VII of France in the 15th century as a personal bodyguard for the French monarch, who were only disbanded in 1830 with the demise of the last Bourbon, King Charles X.

The Scots Guards were originally raised by the 1st Marquis of Argyll during the Civil War in 1642, so theoretically are an older formation than the two foot guard regiments ranked above them. They fought for the King in Ireland and then for the future Charles II at the defeats of Dunbar and Worcester being called the *'Lyfe Guard of Foot'*. At the former they fought against Monck's regiment, later to become the Coldstream Guards. Soon after the accession of King Charles II they became known as the Scottish Regiment of Foot Guards.

At the Battle of Bothwell Brig in 1679 under their colonel, the Earl of Linlithgow, their charge against the rebels won the battle but due to their humane treatment of

Uniform of 3rd
Guards, *c.*1750.

Uniforms from
1899–1901.

the enemy in defeat they were described by a chronicler of the events as *'the gentlemen of Linlithgow's regiment'.*

In 1686 they were officially incorporated into the British Army, fighting under the Duke of Marlborough in the campaign in the Low Countries of 1691-2 where they distinguished themselves. Three years later they were given precedence behind the Grenadier Guards and the Coldstream Guards and in the same year they won their first battle honour at the Siege of Namur.

Unrest in Scotland during the first few years of the 18th century prevented them from partaking, like their brother Foot Guard regiments, in the great victories of the Duke of Marlborough. But in 1709 they finally did take part in the War of the Spanish Succession when they captured Saragossa taking 72 Spanish colours, only to be surrounded and forced to surrender in their next engagement.

As part of the Guards Brigade the regiment fought with distinction at the Battle of Dettingen in 1743 and at the Battle of Fontenoy two years later. During the latter part of the 18th century they were used in the London area for the suppression of civil unrest, resulting in the King thanking them for *'so disagreeable a service'* which, as Scotsmen keeping order in an English town, resulted in some degree of unpopularity.

With the outbreak of the Napoleonic Wars the three battalions of the regiment continued to play a central role in our nation's history. In the Egyptian campaign of 1801 they took part in the Battle of Alexandria and now have the sphinx encrypted with 'Egypt' on the colours. In 1809 the 1st battalion arrived in Portugal to serve

A.E. HASWELL MILLER 1958

1899 — SOUTH AFRICAN WAR — 1901.

1890 — — — — — — 1899			1890 — — — — — 1901	
OFFICER PRIVATE	OFFICER	PRIVATE	OFFICER	DRILL SERGEANT LANCE-SERGEANT
Undress – in Camp. Marching Order (serge).	*Marching Order,*	*Marching Order.*	*Service Dress,*	*Drill Order. Guard Order.*
	(Embarkation).		*(1901)*	

QUARTERMASTER BANDMASTER	PRIVATE	PRIVATE	PRIVATE	1902			1902
Full Dress. (Playing out).	*Full Dress,*	*Marching Order,*	*Marching Order,*	OFFICER		MEDICAL OFFICER	PRIVATE
	Marching Order.	*(1899).*	*(1907).*	*Mounted Infantry,*		*Full Dress.*	*Mounted Infantry,*
				(in England).			*(in England).*

in Wellington's army continuously for the next five years, fighting their way across Spain, the Pyrenees and into France and winning five major battle honours in the process. In 1810-11 they took part in the Battles of Talavera, Busaco, the Torres Vedras Line and Fuentes d'Honor. This was followed by the stunning victory at Salamanca and the driving of the French armies out of Spain. The 2nd battalion won a further battle honour at Barrosa defeating a French force of more than twice their number. Once in France the 1st battalion took a major part in both the Battle of Nive and the siege of Bayonne, which were the last major actions of the Peninsular War and gained them the battle honour 'Peninsula'.

The 2nd battalion achieved perhaps the greatest of the regiment's battle honours at the Battle of Waterloo when they, alongside the Coldstream, were the mainstay in the valiant defence of Hougoumont farm, the key position on the right of the Allied positions, against continuous and formidable French onslaughts. Sergeant Fraser of the Scots Guards won a special medal for his gallantry that day.

Dog Soldier

Bob was a butcher's dog in Windsor who became entranced with the 1st battalion, Scots Fusilier Guards when they were based there in 1853. Maybe it was their disciplined marching that attracted him after a lifetime of trying to control unruly sheep and cattle. Anyway, whenever they were on parade he was there too, trotting along at the front. He was popular with all the men. To describe him is difficult. In sum he was a bit of a mixture, certainly there was terrier blood and maybe a drop of English bull-dog. In 1854 on the outbreak of the Crimean War the regiment was posted to the Crimea and it was Bob who was the first ashore. Within days he was at the Battle of Alma rushing at the enemy with the men of his battalion. But after the Russian counter attack which drove the regiment back from the Greater Redoubt he could not be found and only turned up some weeks later at the Battle of Balaclava. Two weeks after that he witnessed his third battle at Inkerman where he saw the many casualties the regiment suffered.

Bob endured the terrible winter of 1855 and after two years, and the award of a medal for good conduct which he proudly wore around his neck, he returned with the regiment (now depleted by half) to London where he accompanied them on their homecoming parade. Sadly, Bob was run over in February 1860 and was given a proper send off by the men of the regiment. He was later stuffed and still resides as a museum piece in the Naval and Military Club in London, a club for senior military men. This was no ordinary dog's life.

In 1831 the name of the Regiment was changed by King William IV to the Scots Fusilier Guards. In 1877 this was changed to the Scots Guards on the orders of Queen Victoria. Forty years were to pass before the regiment was again able to excel in battle. It was in 1854 in the Crimean War, that the 1st battalion won four VCs at the Battle

Robert Lloyd-Lindsey, later Lord Wantage, won the VC at the age of 22 for two separate acts of heroism at the battle of Alma on 20 September and Inkerman on 5 November 1854. He later became an MP and philanthopist.

of Alma and fought valiantly at the Battle of Inkerman and at the Siege of Sevastopol where they, along with the rest of the British Army, survived an appalling Russian winter.

In 1882 in Egypt the regiment wore their scarlet uniforms and carried their colours into battle for the last time at the Battle of Tel el Kebir. The regiment fought throughout the Boer War in a number of actions including the Modder River and Magersfontein, this time in camouflage.

During the First World War the two fighting battalions of the regiment served the full four years in the trenches gaining 33 battle honours, winning five VCs and losing nearly 3,000 officers and men in the process. At the First Battle of Ypres, one of the most heroic and effective battles ever fought by the British Army, overshadowed by the events and carnage of the ensuing four years, the Scots Guards lost three-quarters of their number fighting an army five times their size.

First Scots Guards VC

Private James Mackenzie was 25 years old on December 19th 1914 when he displayed extraordinary gallantry in rescuing a severely wounded colleague right in front of the German trenches. A stretcher party had already tried and failed to bring the wounded man back owing to the heavy enemy fire. Later in the day Mackenzie again went to the aid of another wounded soldier but this time he was killed as he ran out into the withering fire. He was awarded the VC posthumously. This was the first VC won by the Scots Guards during the First World War and the first to be won under their new name, changed from the Scots Fusilier Guards.

In the Second World War five battalions were raised fighting in Norway, North Africa, Italy and NW Europe, winning 41 more battle honours and losing more than a thousand men. The 1st battalion was deployed in Norway in April 1940 fighting in defensive actions until withdrawn in June. Then they fought in North Africa and Italy, taking part in the Salerno and Anzio landings, and finally in North West Europe through to the end of the war.

After the war the regiment distinguished itself in Malaya during the Communist insurgency, in Suez, Borneo, Northern Ireland. The regiment once again fought with distinction in the Falklands War. On 1 June 1982 the 2nd battalion landed at the San Carlos bridgehead. On the night of 13 June they attacked the Argentine defenders at the Battle of Tumbledown Mountain and after fierce fighting captured it as the last major obstacle on the way to liberating the capital, Stanley.

North African VC

During the North African campaign against the Afrika Korps in Tunisia, Captain Charles Lyell, 2nd Baron Lyell was leading his company of the 1st battalion, Scots Guards against German defensive positions on 27 April 1943. Holding up the advance the enemy had an 88mm gun and a heavy machine gun in separate dug-in positions. Captain Lyell decided to attack with a small party of men. Leading the assault he took out the machine gun with a grenade then, covered by the only man left unwounded, he attacked the larger gun position with pistol and bayonet. Though the enemy position was put out of action, Lyell was killed. But his actions had cleared the enemy defensive positions thus allowing the battalion's advance to continue. For his heroism he was awarded the VC posthumously.

MUSEUM: Guards Museum, Wellington Barracks, Birdcage Walk, London SW1E 6HQ Tel 0207 4143428

Clockwise from top left
1st Battalion Scots Guards march past their Colonel-in-Chief during the ceremony of Trooping the Colour, 1995.

The Scots Guards wear no plume in their bearskin.

Modern uniforms; the button cluster of three denotes the Scots Guards.

IRISH GUARDS

'The Fighting Micks'

Piper and musician
in Home Service
dress. Watercolour by
Douglas N. Anderson.

Dates	1900 to present	VCs 6
Motto	*Quis Separabit*, Who shall separate us.	
Alumni	Francis Brown, priest and photographer, Jean, Grand Duke of Luxembourg, former ruler of Luxembourg, Liam O'Flaherty, Irish writer, Josef Locke, singer, Jack Kipling, only son of Rudyard Kipling.	
Anniversaries	17 March, St. Patrick's Day.	
Battle Honours	Mons, Ypres, Loos, Somme, Passchendaele, Cambrai, Arras, Hindenburg Line, Norway 1940, Boulogne 1940, Mont Pincon, Nijmegen, Rhine, North Africa 1943, Anzio, Italy 1943-4, Basra 2003.	

In a speech at the end of the Second World War, Winston Churchill said, *'When I think of these days … I do not forget… Irish heroes that I could easily recite, and all bitterness by Britain for the Irish race dies in my heart. I can only pray that in years, which I shall not see, the shame will be forgotten and the glories will endure.'*

At the end of February 1900 Ladysmith in South Africa was relieved after a four-month siege. A number of Irish regiments such as the Dublin Fusiliers and the Connacht Rangers had been instrumental in the battles to relieve the town. On the eve of her visit to Ireland, Queen Victoria gave orders that a regiment of Foot Guards should be raised in honour of these brave fighting Irishmen in the British Army. Three days before her arrival in Dublin the Irish Guards were formed on 1 April 1900. James O'Brien of Limerick was the first recruit on 21 April 1900 and many other Irishmen followed him on transfers from all over the British Army. Officers often came from prominent Roman Catholic families, though not exclusively. The men of the regiment were originally recruited from all over Ireland, including the Republic, but sadly this system ceased during the Troubles, for security reasons.

Lord Roberts VC.

From Mafeking to Ypres

Brigadier General Charles FitzClarence VC, a direct descendant of King William IV, joined the Irish Guards on their formation in October 1900. He had already won his VC a year before in series of heroic actions against the enemy during the siege of Mafeking when he was serving with the Royal Fusiliers. By 1909 he had become the commanding officer of the 1st battalion. He was later promoted to the rank of Brigadier General and commanded the 1st Guards Brigade with the British Expeditionary Force sent to France in August 1914. During the First Battle of Ypres he was killed on November 11th whilst organising a counter attack against overwhelming odds. This was after he had miraculously stalled the German advance ten days earlier when he chanced across the 2nd battalion, Worcestershire Regiment and placed them into the line where they bravely held up the German advance.

Every year on St. Patrick's Day a shamrock is presented to each member of the regiment to wear in their cap badge by a member of the Royal family. Vivid blue plumes of St. Patrick are worn on the right of their bearskins. The regimental mascot is always an Irish wolfhound named after one of the ancient Kings or High Chieftains of Ireland. He is looked after by a drummer in the regimental band.

A Novel Recruitment Approach

At a place called Cuinchy in France on 1 February 1915, Lance Corporal Michael O'Leary won the first VC for the Irish Guards. As part of a storming party he attacked and captured a German barricade killing five of the enemy. He then attacked a second barricade killing three more of the enemy and taking two prisoner. The story goes that his father was then approached by the War Office to make recruiting speeches in Ireland. At the first speech which he made in Gaelic, he said that the boys should join up, otherwise the Germans would invade Ireland and do to them what the British had been doing for 700 years! His services were not called upon again. A further footnote to this story is that in 1981 the regiment purchased Michael O'Leary's VC and is the only regiment in the British Army to hold all its own VCs.

The new regiment was inspected by their first colonel, Field Marshal Lord Roberts VC, a week after the outbreak of the First World War on 4 August 1914 and placed in the line near Mons. From 23 August, when the Germans first attacked until 5 September when the line held, the regiment was involved in an epic 200-mile fighting retreat known to veterans as the Retirement. On 1 September, in their first serious contact as a regiment they sustained casualties of more than a hundred men, including in the following days their commanding officer and

Lieutenant Colonel
George Morris.

second-in-command, killed. Lieutenant Colonel George Morris was the first man to lead the Irish Guards into battle. On 12 August 1914 he led his men to France to form part of the 4th (Guards) Brigade. Fighting against a numerically far stronger enemy he was killed leading his men in the rearguard of the 2nd Division of the British Expeditionary Force. Major Herbert-Stepney took command of the battalion during the next few desperate days as the withdrawal continued until the line held firm on 5 September. He too was killed, on 6 November. The Irish Guards crossed the Aisne river by pontoon later in September and then fought in the First Battle of Ypres, losing another 700 men.

For the next four years the Irish Guards took part in many of the grim battles of the conflict, Loos, the Somme, Arras, Ypres, and Cambrai, with more than 2000 officers and men killed. During this time they were awarded four VCs and 67 MCs. They ended the war in the trenches at Maubeuge just a few miles from Mons where they had started. The death of his only son at Loos prompted Rudyard Kipling to write the greatest regimental history ever produced, *The Irish Guards in the Great War*, (published by the History Press) of which the author said, 'This will be my great work – it is done with agony and bloody sweat.'

Mystery Man

In the last days of April 1943 the 1st battalion, Irish Guards were holding rising ground to the West of Allied positions in their encirclement of Tunis. This area was subject to desperate German counter attacks and it was critical that it was held when it came under further attack from Panzer Grenadiers. The citation for the award of the Victoria Cross to Lance Corporal John Patrick Kennealy that day describes the scene. *'Single handed he charged down the bare slope straight at the enemy firing his Bren gun from the hip. He repeated this remarkable action two days later and it was only when he was noticed hopping from one position to another that it was discovered he had been wounded. The magnificent gallantry of this Non-Commissioned Officer under heavy fire, his unfailing vigilance, and his remarkable accuracy were responsible for saving many valuable lives during days and nights in the forward positions and influenced the whole course of the battle. His courage in fighting all day when wounded was an inspiration to all ranks.'* John Patrick Kennealy was apparently not his real name. He was born illegitimately, Leslie Jackson, to an 18-year-old Birmingham girl and a wealthy businessman. His mother raised him and gave him a good education. Joining the Honourable Artillery Company early in the war, he went absent without leave, was arrested and for a while languished in Wellington Barracks. It was there he determined to join the Irish Guards and after taking another man's identity, did just that.

In 1940 the 1st battalion Irish Guards were sent into action in Norway maintaining a successful rearguard action at Narvik, despite having lost a number of their senior officers in an enemy air attack before they had even landed. During the spring of 1943, the 3rd battalion arrived in North Africa and in heavy fighting won their first VC of the war. Later they were involved in the Anzio landings in Italy where they took such heavy casualties (only 20 officers and about 250 men returned to England) that they were later withdrawn from the line and incorporated into the other two battalions.

The Last Victoria Cross in Europe

'On the morning of 21st April 1945, Guardsman Edward Charlton was co-driver in one tank of a Troop, which, with a Platoon of infantry, seized the village of Wistedt. Shortly afterwards, the enemy attacked this position under cover of an artillery concentration and in great strength, comprising as it later transpired, a Battalion of 15th Panzer Grenadiers, supported by six self-propelled guns. All the tanks, including Guardsman Charlton's, were hit; the infantry were hard pressed and in danger of being over-run.

Thereupon, entirely on his own initiative, Guardsman Charlton decided to counter-attack the enemy. Quickly recovering the Browning from his damaged tank, he advanced up the road in full view of the enemy, firing the Browning from his hip. Such was the boldness of his attack and the intensity of his fire that he halted the leading enemy company, inflicting heavy casualties on them.

This effort at the same time brought needed relief to the infantry. For ten minutes, Guardsman Charlton fired in this manner, until wounded in his left arm. Immediately, despite intense enemy fire, he mounted his machine gun on a nearby fence, which he used to support his wounded left arm. He stood firing thus for another ten minutes until he was again hit in the left arm, which fell away shattered and useless.

Although twice wounded and suffering from loss of blood, Guardsman Charlton again lifted his machine-gun onto the fence, now having only one arm with which to fire and reload. Nevertheless, he still continued to inflict casualties on the enemy, until finally he was hit for a third time and collapsed.

He died later of his wounds, in enemy hands.

The heroism and determination of this Guardsman in his self-imposed task were beyond all praise. Even his German captors were amazed at his valour.

Guardsman Charlton's courageous and self-sacrificing action not only inflicted extremely heavy casualties on the enemy and retrieved his comrades from a desperate situation, but also enabled the position to be speedily recaptured.'

The 2nd and 3rd battalions landed in Normandy with the Guards Armoured Division in June 1944, fighting their way across France and the Low Countries where Lieutenant Colonel Joe Vandeleur led the Irish Guards contingent over the bridges of Holland in fierce fighting in the attempt to relieve the paratroopers who were holding the bridge at Arnhem, *'a bridge too far'*, as General 'Boy' Browning

Clockwise from above
A warrant officer in dress uniform.

2nd and 3rd battalions on the move to Valkenswaard, the Netherlands, September 1944, during Operation *Market Garden*.

The Irish Guards in Iraq.

had so wisely cautioned. The Irish Guards fought on to the borders of Germany and had the honour of winning the last VC awarded in Europe during the Second World War.

Since 1945 the Irish Guards have served around the world from Aden to Northern Ireland to Belize and Hong Kong. In 2003 they were part of British forces that moved into Iraq to occupy Basra and the south of the country alongside U.S. forces.

The Irish in the British Army

Lance Corporal Ian Malone was killed by a sniper's bullet serving with the Irish Guards in Basra in 2003. He was an Irish citizen but a British soldier, and proud of both. At his funeral service in Ireland his coffin was carried by fellow Guardsmen from the Irish Guards. This apparent anomaly of Irishmen fighting with courage and loyalty in the British Army is a fortunate legacy from the days when Britain and Ireland were one country. Perhaps it was best put by the Irish patriot and poet Francis Ledwidge, himself killed near Ypres in 1917 fighting with the Inniskilling Fusiliers: *'I joined the British Army because she stood between Ireland and an enemy common to our civilization.'* No doubt Malone had similar feelings.

MUSEUM: Guards Museum, Wellington Barracks, Birdcage Walk, London SW1E 6HQ Tel 0207 4143430

WELSH GUARDS

'The Taffs'

Dates	1915 to present	VCs 2
Motto	*Cymru am Byth*, Wales Forever.	
Alumni	Michael Heseltine, politician, General the Lord Charles Guthrie, Chief of the Defence Staff, Rex Whistler, artist, Jock Lewes, original SAS member and inventor of the Lewes bomb, Maurice Turnbull, Welsh rugby international and English Test cricketer.	
Anniversaries	1 March, St. David's Day.	
Battle Honours	Loos, Somme, Bapaume, Arras, Passchendaele, Hindenburg Line, Boulogne, Tunis, Perugia, Arezzo, North West Europe 1944-5, Italy 1944-5, Falklands 1982.	

Over the years the regiment has had so many recruits with names like Williams, Evans, Davis and Jones that Guardsmen use their regimental number by way of referring to each other. So they might be called *'twenty two'* or *'ninety eight'* or *'forty two'*. This custom is known as *'the Last Two'*.

The Welsh Guards, the last of the Foot Guard regiments to be formed, are easily identified by their badge of the Welsh leek, the white, green and white plume on the left side of their bearskins and their buttons arranged in groups of five to indicate that they are the fifth Foot Guard regiment. (No other regiment has a vegetable as one of its insignia.) Few regiments in the space of less than one hundred years have played so large a part at the heart of the nation's history.

The Welsh Guards were formed at the request of King George V on 26 February 1915 to create a Welsh presence in the Guards regiments. After all, England, Scotland and Ireland were already represented in the Foot Guards, so why not Wales, particularly with its fine combative traditions? The officer in command of the Household Division in London, Lieutenant General Sir Francis Lloyd, himself a Welshman, promised the King that he would muster a regiment the following day and on the day after that they would form the Palace Guard. Welshmen from other Guards regiments were

Clockwise from above
Sergeant Robert Bye
VC receiving his
Victoria Cross from
His Majesty King
George V.

1 Company, 3rd Welsh
Guards at Arezzo.

Welsh Guards
marching during the
Somme.

2 Company, 3rd Welsh
Guards at Arce.

encouraged to join and the Grenadiers supplied three hundred men including NCOs, plus the regiment's first commanding officer, Lieutenant Colonel Murray-Thriepland. Regimental Sergeant Major Stevenson came from the Scots Guards. Three days later, on St. David's Day, the regiment, still dressed in their old uniforms, duly mounted the King's Guard on duty at Buckingham Palace. In August the regiment travelled to France and joined the Guards Division in the trenches of Flanders; a baptism of fire indeed, from ceremonial duties to full combat in a matter of weeks. But this is one of the qualities that the Guards Division prides itself in – the ability to perform ceremonial duties as well as fighting as 'real' soldiers. And the Welsh Guards adapted very quickly.

An Honourable Soldier

On 24 May 1940, Lieutenant the Honourable Christopher Furness was officer in charge of transport near Arras when the order was given to move all vehicles to Douai. As the battalion got on the road, units of German armour were encountered. Furness decided to attack and most of the battalion's light tanks and transports were knocked out by the numerically superior enemy. Despite this Furness continued to attack until he himself was killed. His selfless actions drove the enemy temporarily back, enabling most of the battalion vehicles to get away. For his gallantry beyond the call of duty in the face of the enemy he was honoured with the Victoria Cross.

The regiment won their first battle honour, the first of twenty-one, at the Battle of Loos the following September. Here they advanced successfully on Hill 70 but took severe casualties. In August 1916 they were on the Somme near Beaumont-Hamel and attacked the enemy defences near Lesboeufs on 16 September. The attack started behind a creeping artillery barrage in bad weather conditions over muddy ground and within a few hours they had taken one hundred and forty-four casualties and made little progress against a well dug-in enemy. The attack was suspended and the next day the regiment was replaced by fresh troops.

They won their first VC in July 1917 at the start of the Third Battle of Ypres, or Passchendaele as it is more widely known. On 31 July 1917 the Welsh Guards went into the attack at Pilkem on the Yser Canal just inside Belgium. As the men advanced in heavy rain 27-year-old Sergeant Robert Bye, realising that a German block-house defensive position was causing casualties to his men, rushed the German position and put it out of action. Having reached one of their targets Bye then turned back and cleared the other German defensive strong-points before the battalion moved forward to achieve its final objectives. His heroic actions, during which he took more than seventy prisoners, ensured that his men advanced with minimum losses. His was the first VC awarded to the Welsh Guards.

Six months later, and again on the Somme, the Welsh Guards took part in the pursuit of the German army to the Hindenburg Line. On the evening of 4 March, the

Above, from left
Falklands 1982.

The Welsh Guards on
patrol in Iraq.

village of Sailly-Saillisel was reached, the Guardsmen taking up their positions under heavy shell fire which continued throughout the night and next day. These days have been described as *'one of the hardest tours of duty the battalion ever had'*. The shelling was so intense that their trenches were utterly destroyed and the enemy snipers *'waited to catch men moving from one foxhole to another.'* At the end of the First World War, the Welsh Guards along with the other Foot Guards Regiments, were allowed by King George V to call their private soldiers Guardsmen, in honour of the brave service they had given to their country. A total of 849 men of the regiment had sacrificed their lives for their country.

The Welsh Guards raised three battalions during the Second World War. In 1940 the 1st battalion were part of the British Expeditionary Force to France where, at the Battle of Arras, ground upon which they had fought a little more than twenty years before, the regiment won their second VC with the heroic actions of Lieutenant the Honourable Christopher Furness who was killed in the execution of his duties. The regiment then retreated to Dunkirk where they were one of the units that escaped back to England. The 2nd battalion also took part in this campaign in the defence of Boulogne.

During 1943 and 1944 the 3rd battalion fought in the North African and Italian campaigns while the 1st and 2nd battalion were prepared as part of the Guards Armoured Division for the forthcoming invasion of Europe. The 1st battalion remained as infantry while the 2nd battalion were converted to an armoured role but they combined in operations as a unit. Having been landed in Normandy in late June 1944 they were at the spearhead of the Allied advances which liberated Brussels on 13 September 1944 after a spectacular 100-mile advance in a single day, later described as, *'an armoured dash unequalled for speed in this or any other war'*.

After the war, the regiment, now reduced to one battalion, served in Palestine during the creation of modern Israel, in West Germany, Aden, Cyprus and Northern Ireland. During the 1970s the regiment lost a number of men in the Northern Ireland 'Troubles'.

In 1982 after the invasion of the Falkland Islands by the military junta in the Argentine, the regiment formed part of the Task Force sent to liberate the Falkland

Islands. As part of the 5th Infantry Brigade, under the command of Lieutenant Colonel Johnny Rickett, part of the regiment was put aboard the landing ship *Sir Galahad*. They were then transported to Fitzroy on East Falkland for a landing designed to put infantry into a more forward position in the attack on Stanley, the capital.

On 8 June *Sir Galahad* and her sister ship *Sir Tristram*, which was putting supplies ashore, both came under air attack from the Argentine Air Force. A bomb went straight down into the hold of *Sir Galahad* where ammunition was being prepared and a flash fire started. The regiment suffered the loss of 32 NCOs and Guardsmen in a total casualty figure of 48 dead, along with many serious casualties, particularly from burns. Badly wounded was Guardsman Simon Weston, amongst others, who suffered nearly fifty per cent burns but bravely recovered and was awarded the OBE in 1992 for his charitable works.

For their conduct during the Falklands campaign the regiment gained one Military Cross and three Military Medals as well as one further battle honour. *Sir Galahad* was later towed out into the South Atlantic, scuttled and officially designated as a War Grave.

On 6 September 1997 twelve Guardsmen from the regiment under the command of Captain Richard Williams formed the Honour Guard for Diana, Princess of Wales's coffin as it was carried from Kensington Palace to Westminster Abbey by a troop of the Royal Horse Artillery. In more recent years they have been operational in Bosnia, Kosovo, Iraq and Afghanistan.

Though the Welsh Guards may not be as old as the other Foot Guards regiments or indeed as old as many other regiments in the British Army, in their comparatively brief history they have stepped forward to take up the sword of duty with the patriotism and courage that true Welshmen pride themselves in.

MUSEUMS: The Guards Museum, Wellington Barracks, Birdcage Walk, London SW1E 6HQ Tel 0207 4143430
The Welsh Guards Collection, Park Hall, Oswestry, Shropshire SY11 4AS
Tel 01691 671123

The 71st Highland Light Infantry at Sevastopol, 1854.

two

THE LINE INFANTRY REGIMENTS

'The infantry is the best portion of the British army.'

General Maximilien Foy

'The result of a hundred battles and the united testimony of impartial writers of different nations have given the first place amongst the European infantry to the British.'

Sir William Napier

'I don't know what effect these men will have upon the enemy, but, by God, they terrify me.'

Arthur Wellesley, Duke of Wellington

ROYAL SCOTS REGIMENT (1ST)

'Pontius Pilate's Bodyguard'

Dates   1633 – 2006   VCs 6

Motto   *Nemo me impune lacessit,* No one assails me with impunity.

Alumni   Sir Thomas Burke, Irish sportsman, Sir Gordon Drummond, Canadian soldier and Governor General, Walter Lyon, First War poet, Lewis Nott, Australian doctor and politician, Ian Robertson, Scottish advocate, Marquess of Linlithgow, Viceroy of India.

Anniversaries   2 August, Blenheim, 18 June, Waterloo.

Battle Honours   Tangier, Sedgemoor, Steinkirk, Blenheim, Ramillies, Oudenarde, Malplaquet, Fontenoy, Cullodden, Quatre Bras, Waterloo, Alma, Sevastopol, South Africa 1900-2, Dunkirk, Kohima, Gulf.

Sometimes known as the Royal Regiment, the Royal Scots was the oldest regiment in the British Army and thus the senior infantry Regiment of the Line, *'First of Foot, right of the Line and the pride of the British Army.'*

Some say it was also the oldest regiment in the world, tracing its origins right back into the Dark Ages. A group of Scotsmen formed a bodyguard for King Charles III of France in 882 A.D. which became the Garde Ecossaises of the French monarchy. The only competitor for the title of the oldest regiment in the world is the French Regiment de Picardie. The story goes that there was once an dispute between the two ancient regiments as to which was the senior. Finally a French officer scornfully remarked *'Well, if you really want to win this argument, why don't you claim to have been part of Pontius Pilate's bodyguard?'* A Scot replied *'If we had mounted the guard over the Holy Sepulchre, then we would not have slept on duty!'*

They were first raised in 1633 under a Royal Warrant from King Charles I by Sir John Hepburn, that formidable Scottish warrior. Within two years Hepburn's Regiment had grown to over 8,000 men including many veterans of the Green Brigade who had fought for King Gustaphus Adolphus of Sweden, 'the Lion of the North, the bulwark of the Protestant faith', in the Thirty Years War. It is said that Hepburn only left the service of the Swedish king because Gustaphus had made one joke too many about Hepburn's Catholicism. Shortly after signing up with the English monarch Hepburn took his men to France where they remained, campaigning until the Restoration of the monarchy in England.

In 1661, under their new colonel, Lord George Douglas, the regiment marched south to support the newly restored King Charles II. Their structure was copied for the setting up of a new army to replace the disgraced New Model Army of Cromwell and his republicans. Since there was no campaigning to be done in Restoration England, they once more returned to France where they remained for most of the next twenty years. But they returned to the fold finally in 1680 when they were posted to Tangier as part of the garrison there. They never strayed again and at Tangier won the first of one hundred and forty-nine battle honours taking part in virtually every major British military campaign right up to the Gulf War in 1991.

On their return to England in 1684, King Charles II gave them the title of the Royal Regiment of Foot. A year later shortly after the accession of King James II, they were on the right of the line at the Battle of Sedgemoor, defeating the Duke of Monmouth's rebel army. When Monmouth saw they were his opponents he observed, *'I know these men, they will fight. If I had but them, all would go well.'* In 1686 they were increased in size to two battalions, a structure they would retain for the next two hundred and sixty-three years. In 1692 they again proved themselves under a new monarch, King William III, at the Battle of Steenkirk in the Low Countries, where he witnessed their valour against the French and was suitably impressed.

It was in the early years of Queen Anne's reign that they fought in the Duke of Marlborough's series of great victories over the French in Germany and the Low Countries during the War of the Spanish Succession, Blenheim, Ramillies, Oudenarde and Malplaquet.

At the Battle of Fontenoy in 1743, during the War of the Austrian Succession, the regiment lost 277 men in the valiant but futile attacks on the French defences. When the regiments of the British Army were numbered in 1751, the Royal

Sir Robert Douglas, Colonel of the Royal Scots, killed at the Battle of Steenkirk, 24 July 1692.

The Royal Regiment of Foot, later the Royal Scots, during the siege of Namur in 1695. Watercolour by R. Simkin.

Regiment was given the honour of the number one, so becoming the First or Royal Regiment of Foot.

During the Seven Years War the regiment took part in the capture of Montreal in 1760 and the capture of Havana in 1762 but during another posting to the West Indies starting in 1793 they lost nearly 400 men and five officers to disease, which was half their battalion strength.

Death in the Final Days

Just three weeks before the Armistice, on 22 October 22 1918, Lieutenant David McGregor of the Royal Scots was attached to the 29th Machine Gun Corps supporting an infantry advance that was stalled by winnowing cross-fire from the enemy. Realising he would not be able to bring his guns forward in support quickly enough, he ordered the driver to gallop over open ground to get into a firing position. As they moved forward he lay prone on the limber completely exposed to the enemy fire. Once in his forward position, he was able to give covering fire to the advancing units until he was killed. For his heroism in the face of the enemy he was awarded the Victoria Cross. The last part of his citation reads, *'His great gallantry and supreme devotion to duty were the admiration all ranks, and especially of the officers and men of the 1st Border regiment, who witnessed this extraordinary action.'*

During the ensuing years of the wars against revolutionary and Napoleonic France, the regiment was increased in size to four battalions. The 1st was continually in North America and the West Indies. The 2nd battalion took part in the capture of Egypt in 1801. The 3rd were at Corunna in 1808 and fought Busaco in 1810, Fuentes de Onoro in 1811,

Private Prosser and family.

Salamanca in 1812 and Vitoria in 1813. On Napoleon's escape from Elba they joined Wellington's army in the Low Countries and fought at both Quatre Bras and Waterloo. During those few days in June 1815 they suffered casualties of 363 out of a total complement of 624. But they had added another proud chapter to their regimental history.

In the Crimean War they fought at the Battle of Alma and the Siege of Sevastopol. Private Joseph Prosser won the regiment's first VC at Sevastopol for two individual acts of heroism in No Man's Land, one of them unusual. On 16 June 1855 he apprehended a deserter and in the second, on 11 August, he saved the life of a wounded soldier of the 95th Derbyshire Regiment, carrying him back to safety. On both occasions he was under constant enemy fire but continued to carry out his missions successfully. The presence of a soldier of the 95th at the Siege is interesting. This gallant regiment had taken severe casualties at both Alma and Inkerman and were left with only about a hundred fighting men. At Inkerman they had become the last British regiment to carry their Colours into battle. Due to the savage hand-to-hand fighting expected, regiments were ordered to leave their Colours in safe keeping, but the 95th had been in the front when the Russians attacked and had no time to carry out the order. They did not surrender their Colour that day.

Hong Kong GC

Douglas Ford was a 23-year-old Captain in the 2nd battalion Royal Scots in Hong Kong when they were defeated by the Japanese in December 1941. He, along with other members of the regiment, was imprisoned in Sham Shui Po POW camp. He was planning a major breakout which was discovered by the Japanese authorities. Ford was brutally interrogated and sentenced to death. But he never betrayed his co-conspirators. Having been forced to dig his own grave, he was executed on December 18th 1943. For his outstanding bravery he was awarded the George Cross. He lies buried in the graveyard of Stanley Prison on Hong Kong Island.

The First World War brought combat on quite a different scale, with the regiment increased in size from two battalions to thirty-five, with fifteen of those being front line troops in Flanders and France, the Dardanelles and Russia, losing more than 11,000 killed and 40,000 wounded, winning seventy-one battle honours and six VCs.

In the Second World War the 1st battalion was sent to France with the ill-fated British Expeditionary Force. Fighting a heroic defensive battle near Bethune on 25-27 May 1940 against the onslaught of the German Panzers, many Royal Scots were killed, wounded or captured with only a few even reaching Dunkirk to escape. The regiment alongside them was the Royal Norfolk Regiment (9th) which was also decimated. One hundred Norfolks taken prisoner, and probably a number of Royal Scots, were summarily shot at Le Paradis by the advancing German Waffen SS units. The German commander was tried and executed after the war for these crimes. About 18 months later the 2nd battalion suffered a similar fate when they had to face

Below, from left
Soldiers of the 1st Royal Scots prepare for the battalion attack on Ywathitgyi on the Mandalay railway, 31 January 1945.

Ken Howard's watercolour depicts soldiers of the 1st Royal Scots on crowd-control duties in Belfast in the early 1970s.

Clockwise from top left
An officer of the Royal
Scots, 1704. (Tim Reese)

A recreation of the
Royal Scots in action
in Canada, 1812.

Lieutenant, Battalion
Company, Royal Scots,
1815.

the invading Japanese in Hong Kong. Though fighting heroically in the true tradition
of Scottish regiments, they too were crushed by overwhelming odds. The 1st battalion
was later reformed and took part in the Arakan campaign in Burma and the savage
Battle of Kohima in 1944. The 2nd battalion was also reconstituted and fought in Italy
from July 1944, while the 7th, 8th and 9th battalions fought across North West Europe
after D-Day ending up in Germany at the close of the war.

In 1949 the two battalions of the regiment were amalgamated. This was the first
time since 1686 that the regiment had had only one battalion. In the following years
the Royal Scots were deployed in Korea, Aden, Cyprus, Northern Ireland and the
Gulf. In 1983 the regiment celebrated its 350th anniversary.

On 28 March 2006 the six Scottish regiments were brought together in six bat-
talions to form the new Royal Regiment of Scotland. It should be remembered that
this date was exactly three hundred and seventy three years to the day from when the
Royal Scots had first lined up as soldiers on duty for their King. The first battalion
would be the Royal Scots. On 1 August 2006 the Royal Scots merged with the King's
Own Scottish Borderers to form the battalion which was named the Royal Scots
Borderers, 1st battalion The Royal Regiment of Scotland. The reason why the Royal
Scots, the most senior line regiment in the British Army, was chosen to merge was
that all the other battalions were already made up of merged regiments. Old Sir John
Hepburn would have given a wry smile and been rightly proud of the regiment he
had founded and which had carved its name in glory on many of the battlefields that
crowd the history of these islands, Blenheim, Waterloo, Alma, Ypres, to name a few.

MUSEUM: The Royal Scots Regimental Museum, The Castle, Edinburgh EH1 2YT
Tel 0131 3105016

QUEEN'S ROYAL (WEST SURREY) REGIMENT (2ND)

'The Lambs'

Dates	1661–1966 VCs 9
Motto	*Pristinae Virtutis Memor*, Mindful of their former Glory; *Vel Exuviae Triumphans*, Victorious even in Adversity.
Alumni	General Hubert Hamilton, Dirk Bogarde, movie star, David Napley, lawyer, John Richardson, novelist, John Hamilton MC, artist, Vivian Galbraith, scholar and historian, Kenneth Lockwood, Colditz survivor, Norman Cohn, historian, Sir Reginald Dorman-Smith, diplomat, Richard Holmes, military historian.
Anniversaries	1 June, Glorious 1st of June, 9 September, Salerno.
Battle Honours	Tangier, Namur, Vimeiro, Corunna, Salamanca, Vitoria, Nivelle, Toulouse, Ghuznee, Afghanistan 1839, Peking 1860, Burma, Tirah, Relief of Ladysmith, South Africa 1899-1902, Mons, Somme, Messines, Gallipoli, Mesopotamia, North West Europe 1940,44-5, Tobruk 1941, El Alamein, Tunis, Salerno, Anzio, North Arakan, Kohima.

The Princess of Wales's Royal Regiment, within which the former Queen's Regiment forms the 1st battalion, provided the British Army with the first Victoria Cross of the new century when Private Johnson Beharry won the highest award for heroism under fire in Iraq in 2006.

The Queen's Regiment was the second regiment of the Line and the most senior English regiment of the Line. They were known originally as Kirke's Lambs, an ironic choice perhaps because their Colonel, Piercy Kirke, who had fought under the Comte d'Artagnan in the Low Countries, had a brutal reputation. Another explanation is that King Charles II's consort, Queen Catherine of Braganca, had strong links with

We'd never have kom if we'd known
der QUEEN'S were here

Above, from left
World War I postcard
from an illustration by
Lawrence Colborne.

Shooting Team,
The Queen's Royal
Regiment (West
Surrey), 1937.

the Lamb image at her family palace in Portugal. This seems the most likely answer, coupled with the fact that the regiment used her symbol of interlinked Cs when they were named after her. The Paschal Lamb was also a Christian symbol adopted in Tangiers during the long struggle against the Muslim Moors.

The regiment has had associations with many Queens in British history, starting with Catherine of Braganca and more recently with Diana, Princess of Wales, who would have become queen if history had taken a different turn.

The regiment was first raised to form part of the garrison that would hold Tangier against the Infidel, the city having been part of Queen Catherine's dowry. They first paraded on Putney Heath under the command of their first colonel, the Earl of Peterborough, in October 1661. Early in 1662 they embarked for Tangier where they remained for the next twenty-two years. Their primary function was to secure the city which guarded the gates of the Mediterranean from the threat of the Moors. They finally returned to England in 1684 and it was then they were given the sobriquet of the Queen's regiment for the first time. Their oldest battle honour, 'Tangier', is the oldest one in the British Army and is only held only by one other regiment, the Blues and Royals.

In 1685 they fought on the side of King James II at Sedgemoor against the Duke of Monmouth and his rebel army, the last battle fought on English soil. Four years later, in 1689, following the Glorious Revolution, the regiment was fighting for King William III against their former King James II at the battle of the Boyne in Ireland. There they fought well and their reputation began to grow. After service in Ireland the Queen's were transferred to the Low Countries where they fought at the battle of Landen and at the Siege of Namur in 1695.

Soon afterwards, on the outbreak of the War of Spanish Succession, the regiment distinguished itself at the battle of Tongres, near Liège. Fighting under the command of a Dutch general, Marshal Overkirk, they, alongside a Dutch regiment, managed to resist a French army of over 40,000 for over a day and in the process gained their two mottoes and were given the title 'Royal'. They were taken prisoner after the action but were released three months later. They were then deployed to Spain fighting in the defeat at Almanza in 1707. In 1730 they were posted to Gibraltar and they remained overseas for the next 45 years, mainly on garrison duty. During this time Lieutenant General Kirke died, on 1 January 1741 after thirty years as commanding officer. The regiment returned to Gibraltar in 1789 for a further nine years, and, while there, were commanded for six months by the Duke of Kent, Queen Victoria's father.

In 1794 a detachments of the 2nd were placed on five ships of the Royal Navy including Admiral Howe's flagship and fought on June 1st in his famous victory, losing one officer and six men killed in the action. In recognition of this the regiment were given the honour of the naval crown superscribed with '1 June 1794' on the Colour. A year later they were posted to the West Indies where disease thinned the ranks. A second battalion was raised and also sent out. The losses of both battalions was so bad that in July 1797 they returned home with only seventy fit men from the original total of more than a thousand who had left England.

They were then part of the force General Abercrombie sent to Egypt campaigning successfully against the French army there. In July 1808 the Regiment joined the Army of Sir Arthur Wellesley in Portugal. They remained in the Peninsula until the final victory at Toulouse in 1814, taking part in the battles of Vimeiro, Corunna, Talavera, Salamanca, Vitoria and the Nivelle. The crossing of the Pyrenees involved ten major actions in nine days of engagement. Wellington wrote of the Queen's, *'It is impossible for troops to behave better.'*

In 1825 they embarked for India and in 1838 they fought in the 1st Afghan War. On 23 July 1839 they took part in the battle of Ghuznee when, in a pre-dawn attack, they stormed the fort, which opened the road to Kabul from Kandahar, losing 37 officers and men in the process. It was the first battle honour awarded in the reign of Queen Victoria.

The 2nd had sixteen survivors from a total of 51 men in the tragedy of SS *Birkenhead*, wrecked off the South African coast in February 1852. Captain Wright of the 91st, later the Argyll and Sutherland Highlanders, a witness to the events, wrote, *'The order and regularity that prevailed on board, from the time the ship struck until she totally disappeared, far exceeded anything that I thought could be effected by the best discipline; and it is*

Below, from left
Woven badge of the Glorious 1st of June.

Officer's uniform, 1830.

Queen's Regimental battle honours of World War I.

The 2nd Queen's Royal Regiment in its previous incarnation as the First Tangier Regiment.

The Glorious First of June.

the more to be wondered at, seeing that most of the soldiers were but a short time in the Service. Everyone did as he was directed and there was not a murmur or cry amongst them until the ship made her final plunge. I could not name any individual officer who did more than another. All received their orders and had them carried out as if the men were embarking, not going to the bottom; there was only this difference, that I never saw any embarkation conducted with so little noise or confusion.' It was this account of the disaster that the King of Prussia had read out to his troops to show them the meaning of true discipline. (See also Highland Light Infantry.)

In 1857 the 2nd battalion was re-raised, serving in the Mediterranean and the West Indies before arriving in India in 1878. In 1886 they campaigned successfully in the Burma War. The 1st battalion fought in 1860, alongside the 31st Regiment, as part of the victorious Anglo-French force at the Taku Forts and Peking in China.

In 1881 the regiment became the Queen's Royal (West Surrey) Regiment. In the Boer War the 2nd battalion, alongside the 2nd East Surreys fought at Colenso, Tugela River, Spion Kop and the Relief of Ladysmith.

During the First World War the regiment formed 31 battalions, lost 7,399 officers and men killed and won five VCs and 73 battle honours. The losses were appalling and started right from the off. During the First Battle of Ypres the 1st battalion had only 32 survivors by 1 November. By 7 November, the 2nd battalion had suffered 676 casualties. By November 1918 when the 1st battalion finally came out of the line, there were just seventeen men standing who had travelled to France in the late summer of 1914. Loos, the Somme, Arras and Cambrai had added to the tally. Other battalions of the regiment played their full parts on the Western Front as well as Gallipoli, Palestine, Mesopotamia and even Vittorio Veneto, fighting alongside the Italians against the Austro-Hungarians.

The 1st battalion spent the whole of the Second World War on operations in the Far East, fighting in Burma in the Arakan, at Kohima and in the Irawaddy region. The 2nd battalion was in the Western desert, then transfered to India from where in 1943 they became part of General Orde Wingate's Chindits, fighting the Japanese behind the lines.

The six territorial battalions, brigaded as 131 and 169, fought in France in 1940 and in 1942 were posted to North Africa where they became part of the Eighth Army. The three battalions of the Queen's Regiment that made up 169 Brigade were ordered at the end of March 1943 to join the Eighth Army in Tunisia. They journeyed from Iraq 3,300 miles in 31 days going straight into battle at Enfidaville in Tunisia on 28 April. Some days later they took part in the capture of Tunis. This advance averaged more than 100 miles a day and is probably the longest in military history by any unit. The two brigades took part in the capture of Tunis in 1943, the Salerno landings (where the replacement of one brigade by another, all consisting of the one regiment was a rare, almost unheard of, event) and Anzio, as well as numerous other actions all the way up the Italian peninsula. The 5th battalion fought into Germany in 1945 ending up in Hamburg and took part in the victory parade in Berlin in front of Winston Churchill. The Queen's battalions had won 39 battle honours in the preceding five years fighting on every front, save Norway, and fulfilling the proud fighting traditions of the regiment.

The Earthquake

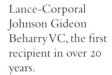

On 31 May 1935 the regiment was stationed in Quetta in the North West Provinces of India. There was a devastating earthquake that virtually destroyed the town and thousands of people were killed or trapped in the rubble. Lance Corporal George Henshaw and Private Arthur Brooks (right) were both awarded the Empire Gallantry Medal for their courage in rescuing individuals while putting themselves in great danger. These medals were converted to the George Cross by King George VI shortly after his accession to the throne.

Following the War the regiment served in Korea and Malaya during the Emergency, 1954-57. On 14 October 1959 the Queen's Royal Regiment (West Surrey) amalgamated with the East Surrey Regiment to form The Queen's Royal Surrey Regiment bringing to an end just short of 300 years of service for King, Queen and Country. The 2nd Regiment of Foot had been a fine regiment, certainly second to none, and certainly mindful of its former glory.

In 1966 this regiment was once again transformed into the Queen's Regiment, made up of the Queen's Royal Surrey Regiment (the 2nd, 31st and 70th), the Queen's Own Buffs, the Royal Kent Regiment (3rd, 50th and 97th), the Royal Sussex Regiment (35th and 107th), the Middlesex Regiment, Duke of Cambridge's Own (57th and 77th) into four battalions bearing the names of their former regiments. Further cut-backs in 1973 resulted in the 4th Battalion (the Middlesex) being disbanded. In 1992 the remaining three battalions were amalgamated with the Royal Hampshire Regiment to form the two battalions of the Princess of Wales's Royal Regiment (Queen's and Royal Hampshires).

On 1 May 2004, Lance-Corporal Johnson Beharry was driving a Warrior TAV through Al Amarah, Iraq, when it was hit by RPGs. Beharry drove through the ambush under fire and led five other Warriors to safety. On 11 June – he did it again, this time sustaining serious shrapnel injuries to the face and brain. Johnson Beharry VC displayed 'unquestioned valour' – twice.

MUSEUM: Queen's Royal Surrey Regiment Museum, Clandon Park, West Clandon, Guildford, Surrey GU4 7RQ
Tel 01483 223419

Lance-Corporal Johnson Gideon Beharry VC, the first recipient in over 20 years.

BUFFS (ROYAL EAST KENT REGIMENT) (3RD)

'Howard's Buffs'; 'The Old Buffs'

Dates	1572 –1961 VCs 5
Motto	*Veteri Frondescit Honore,* It Flourishes in Ancient Honour.
Alumni	Anthony Bridge, artist and priest, William Douglas-Home, playwright and pacifist, Wolfgang von Blumenthal, Prussian aristocrat and English barrister and historian, Archibald Douglas, Earl of Forfar, colonel of the regiment mortally wounded at the battle of Sherrifmuir in 1715.
Anniversaries	16 May, Albuhera Day.
Battle Honours	Blenheim, Ramillies, Oudenarde, Malplaquet, Dettingen, Albuhera, Vittoria, Toulouse, Sevastopol, Taku Forts, South Africa, Ypres, Loos, Somme, Arras, Passchendaele, Jerusalem, Baghdad, France 1940, El Alamein, Italy.

Contrary to myth, *'Steady, the Buffs,'* was not said at Waterloo, nor at Rorke's Drift. The Royal East Kent Regiment, the Buffs, were not present at either encounter. *'Steady the Buffs'* was not a command issued in a moment of crisis on the battlefield. The story is more mundane. The Buffs were on garrison duty in Malta in 1858. They were doing drill one day under the command of a Scotsman, Adjutant Cotter, who had previously served in the 21st, the Royal North British Fusiliers. As luck would have it, the Fusiliers were the other regiment on the base. To ensure his men performed well Cotter called out *'Steady the Buffs, the Fusiliers are watching!'* This much amused the Fusiliers, who proceeded to call out *'Steady the Buffs'* whenever they saw the Buffs on parade. The phrase became common throughout the British Army and now in the language, meaning to remain calm in a difficult situation.

Certainly, the Buffs were one of the oldest and most famous regiments in the British Army. They were originally raised in 1572, during the reign of Queen Elizabeth I, and known as Thomas Morgan's Company of Foot, part of the London Trained Bands which existed until 1648. They campaigned in the Low Countries in support of the Protestants against the Spanish for a number of years, hence, when they came to England, their name reflected this.

In 1665 they became known as the 4th (Holland Maritime) Regiment and in 1668 the 4th (The Holland) Regiment, then the 4th (the Lord High Admiral's) Regiment. Since Prince George of Denmark, consort of Queen Anne, was Lord High Admiral at this time, they became known in 1689 as Prince George of Denmark's Regiment. In 1707 the dragon was included on their colours in reward for their service and reflecting the royal connection with Queen Elizabeth I.

In 1906 the link with the Danish royal family was revived with the appointment of King Frederick VII of Denmark as their Colonel-in-Chief. This tradition continued until the amalgamation of the regiment with the West Kent Regiment in 1961.

During the War of the Spanish Succession the 3rd fought in all four of the Duke of Marlborough's historic victories, Blenheim, Ramillies, Oudenarde and Malplaquet. At Malplaquet they took many casualties in the fighting through the woods, losing fifteen officers.

The regiment then fought in the First Jacobite rebellion on 13 November 1715 at the Battle of Sherrifmuir where their colonel, the Earl of Forfar was mortally wounded. In 1782 the official connection with the county of Kent was made when the regiment was named the East Kent Regiment of Foot.

The Buffs title had originated in the 1740s, when the 3rd and the 19th Regiments of Foot, both regiments with buff-coloured facings on their uniforms, were campaigning in Holland under the command of gentlemen with the family name of Howard. Since regiments at that time tended to be called after their colonel, each regiment was called Howard's Regiment of Foot.

To sort out this confusion on a battlefield, the 3rd became known as Howard's Buffs, hence Buffs, and the 19th as the Green Howards taking their name from the facings of their uniforms. The buff colour of the 3rd was seen on their breeches, waistcoats and stockings. The name game was further confused when at the Battle of Dettingen in 1743 George II called out enthusiastically to the 31st Regiment of Foot (the Huntingdonshire Regiment of Foot, later the East Surrey Regiment), *'Bravo, the Buffs!'* When advised this was not the Buffs, he corrected himself with the cry of *'Bravo, the Young Buffs!'* Hence the regiment called themselves the *'Old Buffs.'* The main claim to fame of the Buffs at Dettingen is that they stopped King George's horse from bolting and carrying him off the battlefield.

During the Peninsular War the Buffs fought at the engagements at Douro, Talavera, Albuhera and Vitoria. At the battle of Douro, they were the first to cross the river and fought bravely taking many casualties but holding the position, which forced the French to retreat. At Talavera they again held the line against constant French attacks. The Battle of Albuhera was particularly brutal for the regiment and their casualties were appalling. From a total of just over 700 men, only 85 managed to answer roll call at the close of the battle. But the reputation of the Buffs was magnified that wet day in May in southern Spain.

A French illustration of an officer of the Buffs.

Officer of the Buffs, *c.* 1815. From a watercolour by by R. Wymer.

The Buffs encamped in the Bois de Boulogne.

An officer of the Buffs, 1854. (Tim Reese)

At the battle, fought on 15 May 1811, sixteen-year-old Ensign Thomas was guard to the Regimental Colours. The 3rd were put to the sword by a savage French cavalry attack and Ensign Thomas, when surrounded, was called upon to surrender. He refused, saying *'Only with my life,'* and was promptly cut down by the enemy, defending the Colour to the end. After the battle he was buried by a sergeant and a private soldier from his company, the only two out of sixty-three to escape from the battle unscathed. The reason the Buffs had been put at a disadvantage in the engagement was that there was a downpour of rain just before the battle began and they had difficulty firing their muskets with their powder damp.

Sergeant Gough of the Royal Fusiliers (7th) recaptured the Colour during the battle and it was returned to the 3rd.

After the crossing of the Pyrenees and the final battles of Nivelle, Nive, Orthez and Toulouse in France, the Buffs were deployed to North America to take part in the closing stages of the war in September 1814 at Lake Champlain and Plattsburgh. A number of battle-experienced regiments took this posting which resulted in them not attending at Waterloo. When Napoleon escaped from Elba, the Buffs were recalled to England, just missing the Waterloo campaign and ending up as part of the army of occupation in Paris.

During the next decades the Buffs served in Australia from 1821 to 1827, then India during the Gwalior campaign. At Punniar in 1843, they defeated a Maratha attack alongside the 50th Queen's Own West Kent Regiment.

In May 1855 the regiment arrived to serve in the Crimean War where they endured the harsh conditions of the Siege of Sevastopol, winning two of the medals newly instigated as the highest award for bravery in the face of the enemy, the Victoria Cross for valour. On 8 September 1855 Brevet Lieutenant Colonel Frederick Maude was in charge of the covering and ladder party of the 2nd Division in the assault on

The Buffs at the attack of Chuenpee, during the First Opium War.

the Redan, a Russian strongpoint in the defences of the city. Despite furious enemy counter-attacks and being seriously wounded, he continued to hold his position with just a handful of men until he was forced to withdraw. On the same day Corporal John Connors also won the VC for his extreme bravery in rescuing an officer of the 30th who was surrounded by the enemy. Frederick Maude's cousin, Captain Francis Maude, Royal Artillery, also won the VC during the Indian Mutiny at Lucknow, almost exactly two years later, on 25 September 1857, when he continued to fire on the enemy though losing many of his men to enemy attacks, thus ensuring the success of the operation.

In 1860 the regiment, as part of the Anglo-French Force, were sent to Tienstin to enforce trading agreements with China. On 12 August they took part in the capture of the Taku Forts just outside Peking and then in the occupation of the city. Private John Moyse was captured during this, the Second Opium War when British and French forces attacked the Taku Forts outside Peking. He refused to *kow-tow* before a local Chinese Mandarin and as a result was executed. For his loyalty to the Crown and the British Army he rightly became a national hero and a ballad was written about his heroism, *A Private of the Buffs* by Sir Francis Doyle, which ends with the lines

> *So let his name through Europe ring,*
> *A man of mean estate,*
> *Who died, as firm as Sparta's king,*
> *Because his soul was great.'*

The Buffs later fought in the successful conclusion to the Zulu War at the battle of Ulundi in 1879, on the North West Frontier and in the Boer War where they won further battle honours at the Relief of Kimberley and the Battle of Paarderberg.

During the First World War the regiment raised nine battalions and lost some 6,000 men. On 16 March 1916, during an attack near Hohenzollern Redoubt, Acting Corporal William Cotter had one leg blown off and was wounded in both arms. Despite this, he dragged himself across 50 yards of open ground in the face of enemy fire to a crater where his men were defending against a German counter-attack. Controlling their fire and organising the men, he held the position for a further two hours, only allowing his terrible wounds to be roughly dressed. He could not be moved back into the lines for a further fourteen hours but all the time he kept up the morale of the men by his cheerful disposition. He died of his wounds a week later. For his extraordinary gallantry without regard to his own suffering, he was awarded the VC.

Saving the King's Colour

At the Battle of Albuhera, Ensign Walsh was in charge of the King's Colour. He was surrounded and about to be taken prisoner when Lieutenant Latham grabbed the Colour to save it. He was savagely attacked and horribly wounded, losing his arm and half his face from sabre slashes. But he managed to hold on to the broken Colour and when rescued by the 4th Dragoons he handed it to them for safe-keeping, retrieving it from under his coat. Amazingly, Latham survived his terrible wounds, served with the regiment for a further nine years, achieved the rank of Captain and was awarded a special gold medal by his brother officers. A silver depiction of the scene was made for the regimental dinner service entitled the 'Latham Centrepiece' and this is in the regimental museum.

In 1935 the Buffs were finally rewarded with the title of 'Royal' which would seem somewhat overdue. During the Second World War the Buffs raised 10 battalions fighting in France in 1940, then in the North African campaign including the Battle of El Alamein, in Sicily and Italy as well as Burma.

In 1961 the Buffs amalgamated with the Queen's Own Royal West Kent Regiment (50th/97th) to form the Queen's Own Buffs, the Royal Kent Regiment. They had won 116 battle honours in three hundred years of service to the Crown. In 1966 this regiment became the 2nd battalion (Queen's Own Buffs) The Queen's Regiment, alongside battalions from Surrey, Sussex and Middlesex.

In 1992 the Queen's Regiment was amalgamated with the Royal Hampshire Regiment to form two battalions of the Princess of Wales's Royal Regiment (Queen's and Royal Hampshires). At the present time the Queen's Regiment, within which the Buffs existed for their last 26 years, soldiers on within the Territorial Army as B (Queen's Regiment) Company, The London Regiment.

MUSEUM: The Buffs, Royal East Kent Regiment Museum Collection, Royal Museum and Art Gallery, 18 High Street, Canterbury CT1 2RA Tel 01227 452747

King's Regiment (Liverpool) (8th)

'The Leather Hats'; 'the King's Hanoverian White Horse'

Dates	1685-1958 VCs 11
Motto	*Nec aspera terrent,* Difficulties be Damned.
Alumni	Major General Eric Bols, World War II commander, Arent DePeyster, native of New York, leader of Indian fighters and friend of Robert Burns, General Sir Harold Briggs, General Daniel Hogton, Peninsular War hero, Sir Charles Harington, soldier.
Anniversaries	13 August, Blenheim, 1 July, Somme, 14 September, Delhi
Battle honours	Namur, Blenheim, Ramillies, Oudenarde, Malplaquet, Dettingen, Warburg, Egypt, Niagara, Delhi, Peiwar Kotal, Burma, Siege of Ladysmith, Mons, Ypres, Loos, Somme, Passchendaele, Macedonia, Italy, Normandy, Burma.

Private soldiers of the regiment were referred to as Kingsmen. They were named after King George I, in recognition of their loyalty to the Crown fighting bravely at the battle of Sheriffmuir during the first Jacobite uprising in 1715. At the battle they lost more than a hundred men and were rewarded with the White Horse of Hanover as their badge.

The regiment was first raised in 1685 as Princess Anne of Denmark's Regiment of Foot. When she became Queen of England in 1702, the regiment was briefly known as the Queen's Regiment. They fought initially in Ireland at the Battle of the Boyne and other actions under the command of John Churchill, later to become the Duke of Marlborough. They then campaigned with their new King, William of Orange, in the Low Countries, notably at the Siege of Namur.

With the outbreak of the War of the Spanish Succession they were part of Marlborough's army in the Low Countries. They fought at the storming of the

Schellenburg fortress and the Battle of Blenheim in 1704. In the following years they continued to campaign in the Low Countries under 'Corporal John' Marlborough, fighting at his other historic victories at Ramillies, Oudenarde and Malplaquet as well as numerous other actions now long forgotten. They returned to Britain in 1715 and fought at the battle of Sheriffmuir where they sustained heavy casualties against the Jacobites.

They were at Dettingen and Fontenoy in the War of the Austrian Succession in 1743-5. Returning from the continent on the outbreak of the Jacobite rebellion they fought at Falkirk and then Culloden. In 1746 they fought at the battle of Roucoux, then the following year at Lauffeldt. In all these contacts with the enemy they displayed coolness and courage despite taking severe casualties. They were numbered as the 8th Regiment of Foot in 1751. During the Seven Years War they fought in a number of actions in Northern Germany including the battles of Warburg, Kloster Kamp and Wilhelmstahl.

The Memorial

The following words are engraved on the Memorial to the fallen of the King's Regiment in St John's Gardens, Liverpool, *'The King's Liverpool Regiment, this monument is erected by the officers, non-commissioned officers and men of the regiment and by the grateful people of Liverpool in memory of their comrades and fellow citizens who died during the campaigns in Afghanistan 1878-80, Burma 1885-87 and South Africa 1899-1902. Some fell on the field of battle, some died of wounds and some of disease, but all gave their lives for the honour of the regiment their city and their country.'*

While the Kings were on campaign in America during the 1760s, a Lieutenant John Caldwell of the regiment absconded. He had fallen in love with an Indian girl and married her. He joined her tribe of Chippewas, took the Indian name of 'The Runner', and later became the chief of the tribe. It was during their posting in America that Arent DePeyster, a New Yorker from a Dutch family, became an officer in the King's and developed the idea of working with the native American tribes in battle. They were used as scouts and raiders, often operating with the light sections of the regiment. It was this type of action that led to the foundation of the light infantry and rifle regiments.

After fighting the French across the continent of America, the regiment was soon to be up against the local population in the American War of Independence. In 1776 the regiment won the battle of Cedars, taking and holding the Cedars position near Montreal with the help of native Americans. In 1777 they fought at the unsuccessful siege of Fort Stanwix alongside the 34th, later the Border Regiment, and under the command of Lieutenant Colonel Barry St Leger. During the next five years the regiment campaigned all across the eastern seaboard of America, marching hundreds of miles in virgin territory. On one occasion Captain Henry Bird of the 8th led a foray deep into Kentucky and a return march, with more than 300 prisoners, all the way back up to Detroit. In 1785 the regiment, now under the command of Colonel DePeyster, returned to England. It was the centenary of their foundation, and the King's Regiment had spent more than 75 years abroad.

In 1793, they were part of the force sent on the relatively unsuccessful campaign against the French revolutionary army in the Low Countries under the overall command of the Duke of York. They fought at the relief of Njimegen. In 1801 having been initially posted to Minorca, they took part in the successful campaign led by Sir Ralph Abercromby against the French in Egypt.

When the American War broke out in 1812, the King's Regiment was once again stationed in America in Quebec so they were inevitably involved in numerous actions during the next few months including the defeat at Chippewa and the bloody battle of Lundy's Lane, where both sides lost more than 800 men. The regiment won the battle honour 'Niagara' as a result.

The Bishop's Son

The story of Captain Noel Chavasse is quite remarkable. He served with the King's Regiment 10th battalion, the Liverpool Scottish, during the First World War. The son of the Bishop of Liverpool, he was an outstanding athlete and scholar while at Oxford University and became a doctor. Working as a medical officer in the trenches he was awarded the VC for his actions on 9 August 1916, when he persistently tended to the wounded and dying during the course of the whole day and the following night, despite being wounded himself, saving the lives of more than twenty seriously wounded men. A year later, between 31 July and 2 August 1917, he was badly wounded while moving an injured man in for medical treatment. Despite his wound, and with no respite for food, medical attention or sleep, he continued to bring in the wounded in appalling weather conditions, saving many lives. He died of his wounds some days later and was again awarded the supreme medal for gallantry in the face of the enemy, one of only three men in history to have achieved this. If there must be one Liverpool hero, then one need look no further than Noel Chavasse.

After years of service in Ireland, the Mediterranean and the West Indies, the regiment was posted to India. At the outbreak of the Indian Mutiny the regiment fought at the taking of Delhi, the relief of Lucknow and the battle of Cawnpore. As a result of the Mutiny, a second battalion was raised in 1857, which was sent to India and served in the Second Afghan War fighting at the battle of Peiwar Kotal on 2 December 1878. In 1885 they took part in the Third Burmese War, which involved a campaign against insurgent guerrillas costing the regiment nearly 300 casualties.

In 1873 the regimental depot was moved to the City of Liverpool and in 1881, with the Army reforms, the regiment was renamed the King's (Liverpool) Regiment,

Private of the 8th
Regiment *c.*1742.

2nd Battalion, 8th
Regiment – Malta
*c.*1865.

cementing their close affiliation to the city. The 1st battalion was in South Africa training as mounted infantry when the Boer War began. The 2nd battalion were one of the units pinned down at the Siege of Ladysmith. It was during its defence that the regiment was to win its first VCs. On 21 August 1900 Sergeant Harry Hampton and Lance Corporal Henry Knight both won the supreme gallantry award at Van Wyk's Vlei while under enemy fire.

The King's regiment raised 49 battalions in the First World War, 22 of which served in the front lines with losses of nearly 14,000 men killed, an average of about 650 men per battalion. They also won a further 58 battle honours.

A bandsman. He wears the pattern of collar badge introduced in 1895.

The Earl of Derby proposed 'Pals' battalions and four were raised. He addressed the volunteers, *'This should be a battalion of Pals, a battalion in which friends from the same office will fight shoulder to shoulder for the honour of Britain and the credit of Liverpool.'* In the ensuing three years the Liverpool Pals sustained nearly 3,000 casualties, killed or wounded. By the end of the War the regiment's battalions had fought at all the major engagements such as Mons, Ypres, Loos, the Somme, Passchendaele, Arras as well as in the Balkans, Archangel in Russia and Afghanistan in 1919.

Ten battalions were raised during the Second World War, serving in Burma as part of the Chindits, in the intense fighting in Italy and in the invasion of North West Europe. Two battalions of the regiment landed on D-Day; the 5th on Sword with the 3rd Infantry Division and the Liverpool Irish on Juno with the Royal Winnipeg Rifles. When the War ended they saw service in Palestine, Germany and with the United Nations forces in Korea.

The regiment officially amalgamated with the Manchester Regiment on 1 September 1958 to form the King's Regiment (Manchester and Liverpool). There was some connection between the two regiments by virtue of the fact that the 63rd (West Suffolk) Regiment of Foot had originally been raised as the 2nd battalion of the 8th in 1756. It was this battalion of Kingsmen that had merged with the 96th to become the Manchester Regiment in 1881. In 2006 this regiment, in turn, amalgamated with the Queen's Lancashire Regiment and the King's Own Royal Border Regiment to form the Duke of Lancaster's Regiment (King's, Lancashire and Border).

MUSEUMS: The King's Regiment Museum, Museum of Liverpool Life, Pier Head, Liverpool L3 1PZ Tel 0151 4784065

The Liverpool Scottish Regimental Museum, The former TA Centre, Botanic Road, Edge Lane, Liverpool Tel 07952 169285

GREEN HOWARDS, ALEXANDRA PRINCESS OF WALES'S OWN (YORKSHIRE REGT) (19TH)

Historically, 'The Green Howards' is a nickname

Dates	1688–2006 VCs 18
Motto	Fortune Favours the Brave.
Alumni	Donald Bell VC, professional footballer, George Howard, chairman of the BBC and owner of the stately home Castle Howard, Herbert Read, poet, writer and art critic, Herbert Sutcliffe, cricketer, Hedley Verity, cricketer, Len Hutton, cricketer.
Anniversary	20 September, Alma
Battle Honours	Namur, Malplaquet, Belle Isle, Alma, Inkerman, Sevastopol, Paarderberg, Ypres, Loos, Somme, Gallipoli, Archangel, Norway, Dunkirk, El Alamein, Italy, Burma.

Crimean shako of the 19th. The word 'shako' comes from the Hungarian for peaked cap. It was part of the uniform of the Hungarian hussar in the 18th century and was adopted by many regiments and armies from 1800.

This is a proud North Yorkshire regiment, albeit with early origins in the West Country. Their name, originally their nickname, the Green Howards originated in 1744, during the war of the Austrian Succession, when there were two British Regiments of Foot commanded by gentlemen with the name of Howard, the Honourable Charles Howard who commanded the 19th and Colonel Thomas Howard who commanded the 3rd. Since they were both known as Howard's Regiment of Foot, they were given different colours for their uniform facings. Green for the 19th and buff for the 3rd, hence the Green Howards and the Buff Howards, the Buffs. The green facings are worn by the regiment to this day despite various attempts to abandon it over

the years. It is described as Brunswick green and was used by the Royal House of Hanover, whose dynasty began in 1714 with George I.

The regiment was originally formed in November 1688 at Dunster Castle, Somerset, by Colonel Francis Luttrell during the Glorious Revolution. It was raised from independent companies in Devonshire in support of William, Prince of Orange, who had landed at Torbay earlier in the month. Under their new king, they fought at the Battle of the Boyne in Ireland in 1690, then campaigned with him in the Low Countries, taking part in the siege of Namur in 1695. They fought sturdily at the victory of Malplaquet in 1709, the Duke of Marlborough's final field battle where the casualty toll was more than fifteen thousand men on each side. During the War of the Austrian Succession, though not present at Dettingen, the regiment fought at Fontenoy in 1745, Roucoux in 1746 and Laufeldt in 1747. In 1751 they became the 19th Regiment of Foot. During the Seven Years War against France, in 1761 they took part in what nowadays would be called combined operations against Belle Isle, an island off the Atlantic coast of France, when they were the first regiment ashore successfully, driving off the French defenders and enabling more units to land and capture the island.

The regiment saw a number of actions during the American War of Independence and when they returned home in 1782 they became the 19th (1st Yorkshire North Riding Regiment) of Foot '*to cultivate a connection with the County which might at all times be useful towards recruiting*'. But it was 90 years later that the regiment moved to Richmond and began its real connection to the county. During the French Revolutionary Wars and the subsequent campaigns culminating at Waterloo, the 19th only took part in the Siege of Ostend in 1794. One mystery of the regiment has only recently been cleared up. Though the Green Howards were not at the Battle of Waterloo, officers in the Mess have Marshal Ney's silver snuff-box taken from the battlefield that day and presented to the regiment in later years. It appears that during the 19th century a serving officer whose father had been at Waterloo gave it to the regiment.

In 1796 the 19th were posted to the Indian sub-continent where they spent the next twenty-five years campaigning in the Kandy wars in Ceylon and against Tipoo

Above, from left
Marshal Ney's silver snuff box, given to the regiment in the 19th century.

One of the Russian drums captured at Alma in the Crimean War, paraded on all important regimental occasions.

Above, from left
Lieutenant, 1823.

Grenadier company,
19th Regiment *c*.1751.
Illustration by R.
Caton Woodville.

Sahib in India. Disease took a terrible toll and accounted for most of their losses.

On 18 November 1852 the regiment was one of those selected to line the route at one of the great occasions of the Victorian era, the dramatic State Funeral of the Duke of Wellington in London, where they stood in the Mourn Arms position in respect for the Iron Duke near St. Paul's Cathedral.

During the Crimean War the regiment fought valiantly at Alma on 20 September 1854, the first major engagement of the war. As part of the Light Division, fighting alongside the 23rd, Welsh Fusiliers, and the 33rd, the West Riding Regiment, they took severe casualties in the first assault on the Russian Great Redoubt and its subsequent capture. They also captured six Russian drums from the Borodino, Minsk and Vladimir Regiments, these drums are paraded on all important regimental occasions. During the ensuing months the regiment fought at Inkerman and at the Siege of Sevastopol, during which they suffered more than 300 casualties out of an original total of little more than 1,000 men. On the final assault on the Redan they lost nearly half their total, many of the men dying of their wounds and suffering in the Russian winter. After the war, the famous journalist, William Russell, wrote of the Light Division, of which the Green Howards were a part, *'This gallant body behaved so well at the Alma, and maintained its reputation at Inkerman, suffered as severely as it did gaining the former great victory, and an examination on their return will, I fear, show that the winter, the trenches, and careless recruiting have done their work.'* Alma Day is particularly significant for the regiment since it was the first battle honour bestowed on them, Malplaquet and Belle Isle being awarded at a later date.

The regiment was posted to India in 1857 in the wake of the Mutiny and remained there for fourteen years, taking part in the successful Hazara Campaign of 1868 when they were the only regiment present from the British Army. They returned to England in 1871. In 1875 with the presentation of new Colours to the 1st battalion by the Princess of Wales they became the Princess of Wales's Own. The cap badge, designed by the Princess herself, became the Princess's cipher 'A' behind a Danish cross and coronet, since Princess Alexandra was from the Danish royal family.

In 1895 the Green Howards were sent to the Sudan against the Mahdi uprising and fought at the battle of Ginnis, the last time that they wore the red coat of the British infantry. In 1897 they returned to India and took part in the Tirah Campaign on the North West Frontier before being posted to South Africa in 1899 where they remained on operations during the whole of the Boer War, winning a further VC at the Battle of Paardeberg.

In 1902 the regiment eventually became Alexandra, Princess of Wales's Own (Yorkshire Regiment). The strong connection to Denmark, and subsequently Norway,

Clockwise from top left
Transport, Shanghai, 1927.

2nd Battalion, Green Howards – Larnaca, Cyprus, 1955.

Green Howards, World War II.

From left
Portrait of Stanley Hollis VC by Albert Lembert; and Company Sergeant Major Stan in more relaxed mood, after winning his VC.

continued and the King of Norway was the colonel in chief of the regiment until 2006, following his father and grandfather in the tradition which had started at the height of the Second World War in 1942 when the Norwegian Royal family were in exile in England. Though Princess Alexandra was Danish, her daughter married the second son of the King of Denmark who, in 1905, became King Haakon VII of Norway.

The Scots Adventurer

Private Samuel Evans was a Scotsman who had originally joined a Scottish regiment, the 26th, the Cameronians, and served with them in India and China. On his return home he wanted to serve overseas again so he switched to the Green Howards who were scheduled to go to South Africa. But they were diverted to the Crimea on the outbreak of war with Russia and Evans fought at Alma and Inkerman. At the Siege of Sevastopol on 13 April 1855, he volunteered to go into an embrasure to repair a breach. He and another Private leapt into the embrasure, where they carried out the necessary repairs under continuous and very heavy fire. For his gallantry in the face of the enemy and without any regard for his own safety, he was awarded the Victoria Cross. On 8 September of the same year he was seriously wounded in an assault on the Great Redan, and after time in hospital in Scutari, in all probability in the care of Florence Nightingale, he was sent back to England and discharged from the Army in 1856. He later retired and lived in Edinburgh but in old age was invited to stay with the regiment in Ireland and Yorkshire on separate occasions. After his death in 1901, the regiment built a memorial to Evans over his grave. In his will, he bequeathed his medals to the Green Howards for their kindness to him and to his wife.

In the First World War the Green Howards raised 24 battalions with 65,000 men serving in the regiment, suffering casualties of 7,500 killed and 24,000 wounded. They also fought in Russia in 1919 towards the end of the Revolutionary War. During this period they won 12 VCs.

During the Second World War they raised 12 battalions fighting in Norway, the Western Desert, Italy and North West Europe.

1st Battalion on Exercise 'Gryphon's Flight' at Catterick, North Yorkshire, 1990.

Two of the Green Howard battalions were among the first to land on D-Day and in that action they were the only British regiment to win a VC. At dawn on 6 June 1944, the 6th battalion of the Green Howards came ashore under heavy fire on the beaches of Normandy with no protection from the Patton tanks that had been promised. They battled forward and Sergeant Stanley Hollis of D Company cleared the beach exit enabling his comrades to advance to the village of Crepon, where, later in the day, he again saved the lives of a number of his men, winning the supreme award for gallantry, the Victoria Cross.

Tale of the Brothers Seagrim

Lieutenant Colonel Derek Seagrim (right) was appointed commanding officer of the 7th battalion Green Howards just prior to the Battle of El Alamein. After the victory, the battalion advanced with the Eighth Army across North Africa into Tunisia. On 20/21 March 1943 at the Mareth line, a German defensive position, Seagrim's extraordinary courage and cool leadership led directly to the capture of an important objective. When early attacks failed under heavy fire, he took his men forward, leading from the front. Placing a scaling ladder over an anti-tank ditch, he led his men across and attacked and knocked out two machine-gun posts, killing or wounding about twenty enemy soldiers. The next day he held the position, calmly rallying his men during enemy counter attacks. For his extreme bravery he was awarded the Victoria Cross. Within two weeks of this gallant action he was cut down in battle and died of his wounds on April 6th 1943.

Major Hugh Seagrim was Derek's younger brother and joined the British Indian Army where he served with the 20th Burma Rifles, becoming an expert in Burmese dialects. When Japan invaded Burma in 1941 he raised guerrilla forces largely from the indigenous Karen people, fighting behind the lines against the Japanese Army. Despite desperately difficult conditions, he continued to sabotage the enemy until massive reprisals against the local people made him decide to give himself up in March 1944. He was held prisoner in appalling conditions until September 22 when he was executed along with some of his co-fighters. For his bravery he was awarded the George Cross.

This is the only case of two brothers winning the two supreme awards for bravery, both posthumously. They both attended Norwich School, the alma mater of Horatio Nelson, England's greatest hero. Like Nelson, their father was an Anglican vicar.

From 1949 to 1952 the regiment were part of operations against the Communist threat in Malaya. Since that time the regiment has distinguished itself all over the world, from Cyprus to Northern Ireland, the Gulf War and Bosnia.

In 2006 the new Yorkshire Regiment was formed, made up of famous Yorkshire regiments: the Prince of Wales's Own Regiment of Yorkshire, formerly the West Yorkshire Regiment (14th) and the East Yorkshire Regiment (15th) which came together in 1958, became the 1st battalion; the Green Howards became the 2nd battalion and the Duke of Wellington's Regiment, 33rd and 76th who had come together in 1881, formed the 3rd battalion. At the time the Green Howards were one of only five regiments of the line that had never amalgamated in their entire history. They shared this honour with the Royal Scots, the 22nd (Cheshire) Regiment, the Royal Welch Fusiliers, and the King's Own Scottish Borderers.

MUSEUM: Green Howards Regimental Museum, Trinity Church Square, Richmond, North Yorkshire DL10 4ON Tel 01748 826561

LANCASHIRE FUSILIERS (20TH)

'The Minden Boys'; 'The Young Fusiliers'

Dates	1688–1968 VCs 18
Motto	*Omnia Audax,* Daring in All Things.
Alumni	General James Wolfe, hero, J.R.R. Tolkien, scholar and writer, Archibald Arnott, doctor to Napoleon on St. Helena, Air Chief Marshal Sir Trafford Leigh-Mallory, commander of RAF Fighter Command in the Battle of Britain, Neville Laski, QC, Richard Porritt, the first MP killed in World War II.
Anniversaries	25 April, Gallipoli, 1 August, Minden Day, 5 November, Inkerman Day.
Battle Honours	Dettingen, Minden, Corunna, Vimeiro, Albuhera, Vitoria, Alma, Inkerman, Sevastopol, Lucknow, Khartoum, Spion Kop, Ladysmith, Mons, Ypres, Suvla Bay, Somme, Passchendaele, Cambrai, Monte Cassino, Burma, Chindits.

Captain R.R. Willis leading a party through wire entanglements, Gallipoli, 25 April 1915. He was one of six members of 1st Battalion to be awarded the Victoria Cross.

'Six VCs before breakfast' was the phrase coined for the Lancashire Fusiliers at Gallipoli. To observe the battle honours of this regiment and to note the number of its VCs is to realise that it has written in blood on the pages of English history.

It was originally raised in 1688 in Devonshire by Colonel Peyton during the Glorious Revolution of 1688. It was known, as was the custom in those days, as Peyton's Regiment of Foot. The regiment first saw action at the Battle of the Boyne on the side of King William III in 1690, then captured Athlone and took part in the Siege of Limerick in 1691. They were in Gibraltar in 1728 during the siege by the Spanish, successfully holding the city. But their first official battle honour was won at the Battle of Dettingen in 1743. They also fought at the Battle of Fontenoy in 1745 and the defeat of the Jacobites at Culloden in 1746. They were officially numbered the 20th Regiment of Foot in 1751.

Above, from left
2nd Battalion, India, 1893.

Lancashire Fusiliers, 1913. Lieutenant and colour sergeant, full dress; sergeant and private service dress, marching order. The officer wears the Queen's South Africa Medal and the colour sergeant the Sudan, Queen's and King's South Africa Medal.

In 1759 during the Seven Years War, the regiment won immortal glory at the Battle of Minden, under the command of their Colonel Kingsley, winning a laurel wreath to be worn on their Colours and a rose to be worn in their head dress every year on August 1st in memory of their forbears, who picked roses to put in their hats when they returned from the battle. The regiment, alongside their comrades – three other English regiments, a Scottish regiment and a Welsh regiment, the 'Minden regiments' – through a misunderstanding of orders advanced directly at the French cavalry. Observers expected them to be annihilated but on the contrary they decimated their French opponents with their disciplined firing and carried the day. The French commander that day, the Marquis de Contades, said, *'I never thought I would see a single line of infantry break through three lines of cavalry lined up for battle and utterly defeat them.'*

During the American War of Independence the regiment were sent to Canada in 1776 fighting under the command of General Burgoyne. In 1777 they were part of the army that surrendered at the Battle of Saratoga burning their Colours to avoid them falling into enemy hands. Many of the men were taken prisoner and were only released when hostilities finally ceased.

The 20th fought in the Egyptian campaign against the French in 1801, then at the Battle of Maida in southern Italy, which was the first victory against Napoleon's troops on the mainland of Europe. In the Peninsular War, the 20th, over the space of five days, fought at both the Battles of Vimeiro and Rolica in Portugal in 1808. Early in the following year they were part of Sir John Moore's fighting retreat to Corunna against Marshal Soult. Two years later they were part of Sir William Myers's legendary Fusilier Brigade, whose counter-attack against the French helped to turn the tide at the Battle of Albuera in May 1811. In 1813 the regiment fought alongside its sister Fusilier regiments in the momentous victory at Vitoria, which effectively ended French resistance in Spain. After the pursuit over the Pyrenees the 20th gained further honours in battles with the French at Nivelle, Orthez and Toulouse. It was during the battle at Orthez that the regiment's commander, Colonel Robert Ross, who had led them at Maida and in the Peninsula battles was severely wounded. But he recovered and during 1814, now a Major General, led them in the successful campaign in America where, having won the Battle of Blandensburg, they proceeded to sack Washington. Ross was killed in a skirmish near Baltimore soon afterwards.

A contingent of the regiment formed Napoleon's guard at the time of his death on St. Helena on 5 May 1821. It was during this time that the Emperor became close to Surgeon Archibald Arnott of the 20th. On one occasion they were discussing the merits of British soldiers. While Napoleon mused that with French officers and British soldiers he could have conquered the world, he also said that he wanted to present to the regiment his three-volume history of the Duke of Marlborough, 'one of the best English generals'. After some diplomatic wrangling the volumes were presented and still reside in the care of the regiment.

Beyond Death's Starry West

Lieutenant G.B. Smith was a young poet and friend of J.R.R. Tolkien. He was killed in France on 3 December 1916, and was only 22 years old when he died. A volume of his poems was published after his death.

There is a place where voices
Of great guns do not come,
Where rifle, mine, and mortar
For evermore are dumb:
Where there is only silence,
And Peace eternal and rest,
Set somewhere in the quiet isles
Beyond Death's starry West.
O God, the God of battles,
To us who intercede,
Give only strength to follow
Until there's no more need
And grant us at that ending
Of the unkindly quest
To come unto the quiet isles
Beyond Death's starry West.

A soldier of the 20th at the Battle of Minden, 1759. (Tim Reese)

The regiment took part in the battles of Alma, Inkermann and Sevastopol in the Crimean War. They were also at the Relief of Lucknow three years later in India. They were named the Lancashire Fusiliers in 1881. They fought at the Battle of Omdurman in 1898 and were part of the force that relieved Khartoum after the death of General Gordon. In the Boer War they were in the battle of Spion Kop and the Relief of Ladysmith. After Spion Kop, in recognition of the regiment's extraordinary gallantry displayed there, and in acknowledgment of more than 200 years of service to the crown, the King granted the regiment the unique right to wear the bright yellow Primrose Hackle on their headdress. Permission was also given for the Red Rose of Lancaster to be worn on the Colours.

The regiment raised 30 battalions during the First World War starting out with the British Expeditionary Force in 1914 and fighting at Mons, Ypres, the Somme and Passchendaele. It was far from the Western Front that the regiment once more wrote its name in glory. It was at Suvla Bay on the Gallipoli peninsula in Turkey. On 25 April 1915, the expression *'Six VCs before breakfast'* was coined. Sergeant Alfred Richards was one of those fabled six. He, like the others, landed on W beach, rowed ashore by Royal Navy cutters straight into withering fire from the Turkish defences, which had clear sight from high ground of the whole landing area. As the men leapt out of the boats, many, weighed down by their equipment, drowned, others encountered wire under the water to impede them. As soon as he reached the beach, Sergeant Richards had his leg almost severed by a burst of machine gun fire. Realising that to stay in that exposed position would prove fatal, he crawled through more wire calling on his men to follow him and soon they secured some sort of foothold on the slope at the back of the beach. By the end of the day, despite casualties of more than 300 men, the Fusiliers had fought their way forward and had driven the enemy back. For his gallantry, Richards was awarded the VC. His leg was amputated a month later and he was invalided out of the Army after 29 years service.

In the Second World War the Lancashire Fusiliers were with the British Expeditionary Force in France in 1940 and later fought in Italy, Normandy and the Far East. On 16 May 1944 the 2nd battalion of the regiment were involved in heavy fighting against the Germans near Monte Cassino in Southern Italy. While the men were digging in, two German tanks put in a counter-attack causing heavy casualties. Fusilier Frank Jefferson grabbed an anti-tank weapon and ran forward. Unsighted, he moved into open ground despite drawing heavy enemy fire. He fired on the first tank and scored a direct hit, setting it on fire. As he was aiming for the second tank, it turned and fled and the attack was driven off. For *'his supreme gallantry and disregard of personal risk'* he was awarded the Victoria Cross.

On 23 April 1968, St. George's Day, the Lancashire Fusiliers amalgamated with the Royal Northumberland Fusiliers (5th), the Royal Warwickshire Fusiliers (6th) and the Royal Fusiliers (City of London Regiment) (7th) and to form the 4 battalions of the Royal Regiment of Fusiliers.

MUSEUM: Fusiliers Museum Lancashire, Wellington Barracks, Bolton Road, Bury BL8 2PL Tel 0161 7642208. (Planning to move to to the Arts and Crafts Centre, Bury.)

Above, from left
Officer of the 1st Battalion on Minden Day, Tientsin, China, 1937.

Fusilier Frank Jefferson of C Company, 2nd Lancashire Fusiliers, who won the Victoria Cross when he knocked out a Mark IV tank with his PIAT on 16 May 1944.

SOUTH WALES BORDERERS (24TH)

'Howard's Greens'

Dates	1689-1969 VCs 23
Motto	*Gwell angau na Chywilydd,* Better Death than Dishonour
Alumni	Saunders Lewis, poet and Welsh nationalist, Henry Mond, MP and Zionist, Lieutenant Colonel Henry Pulleine, Zulu War casualty, Christopher Burney, SOE agent, General Sir James Lyon, Barbados reformer, Eric Blore, actor
Anniversaries	22 January, Rorke's Drift, 1 March, St.David's Day
Battle Honours	Blenheim, Ramillies, Oudenarde, Malplaquet, Talavera, Busaco, Fuentes de Onoro, Salamanca, Ramanagar, Chillianwala, Rorke's Drift, Mons, Ypres, Loos, Somme, Gallipoli, Hindenburg Line, Norway, Normandy landings.

The Irish-born Lieutenant Nevill Coghill VC.

This is the regiment famous for the depiction of its heroic deeds in the epic film *Zulu*. It is also rightly famous for the part it has played in many other campaigns. It is without doubt one of the most famous regiments in the British Army. On 28 March 1689 a regiment of foot was raised by Colonel Sir Edward Dering in Kent in support of the new monarchs, William and Mary. The regiment fought in Ireland for King William III against the deposed James II and remained there for three years. In the following years they served loyally with King William in Flanders and the Low Countries.

But it was in May 1700 that the regiment began to make their mark on our island history. They crossed to the Low Countries once again, this time under the general command of John Churchill, Duke of Marlborough. During the following thirteen years in the War of the Spanish Succession they served in the Duke's army in numerous actions including his four epic and bloody victories at Blenheim, Ramillies, Oudenarde and Malplaquet. At the Battle of Blenheim on 2 August 1704 they were part of Brigadier Row's Brigade taking up the right of the line in the infantry advance against the numerically superior French defences. But their courage and tenacity prevailed and, though Row and his officers were killed, twenty-seven battalions of the French surrendered. In 1751 the regiments of the British Army were numbered, hitherto having just been named after their colonels, and the regiment became the 24th Regiment of Foot.

During the Seven Years War the 24th were one of the infantry regiments that fought well at the victories at Warburg on 31 July 1760, though the day was ultimately decided by the British cavalry who claim it as their victory.

The regiment was sent to Canada and fought with no loss of honour in the American War of Independence, losing their commanding officer Major Grant at the Battle of Hubbardton on 7 July 1777. The war ended badly for the regiment when they were part of the defeated army at Saratoga led by General Burgoyne, taken prisoner and held for three years before returning to the home country.

Lieutenant Teignmouth Melvill VC who, with Lieutenant Coghill, bravely defended the Queen's Colour of the 24th with their lives after the disastrous battle of Isandhlwana in January 1879. Their bodies were found on the banks of the Buffalo River and the Colour was retrieved. They were the first posthumous recipients of the Victoria Cross.

In 1804 a 2nd battalion was raised which took part in the Peninsular War until disbanded in 1814. During this decade the battalion fought at Talavera, Busaco, Fuentes de Onoro and Salamanca. In 1814 the 1st battalion fought in the Gurkha War. The fine qualities of the Gurkha soldiers resulted in their affiliation to this day with the British Army. The regiment fought in the Second Sikh War taking part in the bloody Battles of Ramnagar, Chillianwallah and Goojerat. At the Battle of Chillianwallah on 13 January 1849, though the regiment initially drove the enemy back, they were then counter-attacked and heavily outnumbered by the knife weilding Sikhs. It was at this point that their Brigade commander was killed as well as their commanding officer, Lieutenant Colonel Brookes, along with two other officers. Lieutenant Lloyd Williams received twenty-three sword and lance wounds, a fractured skull and a severed hand but survived to tell the tale. The regiment suffered 590 casualties. When people talk of the 24th in the Zulu War, they should be equally mindful of Chillianwallah, where brave men stood firm.

In 1875 the regimental headquarters were moved to Brecon in South Wales and the Welsh connection really began in earnest. In 1881 the 24th was renamed the South Wales Borderers.

VC in the Surf

Assistant Surgeon Campbell Douglas was one of the first Canadians to be awarded the VC. On May 7th 1867, with four privates from the regiment, he risked life and limb by guiding a boat through heavy surf to land on the Andaman Islands and rescue other members of the regiment who had gone ashore to ascertain the well-being of a merchant navy ship's captain and his men.

In 1879 the Zulu War began and both battalions of the regiment were stationed in South Africa. The 24th formed a significant part of Lord Chelmsford's invasion force when he crossed the Buffalo River into Zululand on 11 January. On 22 January Chelmsford left six companies of the 24th, under the command of Colonel Pulleine, camped near a place called Isandhlwana and set off with the rest of his force to look for the Zulu army. This was a disastrous decision and the camp was soon attacked by 22,000 Zulu warriors. The result was a massacre with the regiment losing 540 killed including their commanding officer. Lieutenants Coghill and Melvill were posthumously awarded VCs for their valiant attempt to save the Queen's Colour by escaping across the Buffalo River.

'Saving the Queen's', the painting by De Neuville of Lieutenants Melvill and Coghill seizing the Queen's Colour of the 24th from the Zulu army.

Two Nottinghamshire Lads

Caleb Wood and Robert Tongue were friends from the village of Ruddington in Nottinghamshire. In 1877, like many young men before and since, they enlisted together, joining the 24th Regiment of Foot. High hopes of adventure in foreign lands doubtless filled their heads as they marched away in their splendid new uniforms. Adventure they surely got. Within two years Private Wood and Private Tongue were part of the small unit that valiantly and successfully defended the outpost at Rorke's Drift against the relentless attack of the Zulu army. They survived the ordeal and went on to serve in the South Wales Borderers for many years. They then both retired to Ruddington and, when the time came, they were laid to rest in modest unmarked graves in the village churchyard. Robert died in 1918 and Caleb in 1935. On 18 July 2004 a service was held in their honour attended by more than five hundred people where two fine headstones, donated by the Nottingham Cooperative Society, were placed on their graves describing each of them simply as a 'Rorke's Drift Defender'. Relatives of the two men, as well as relatives of other defenders at Rorke's Drift, watched as the Band of the Prince of Wales's Division played the Last Post and Reveille, then sang 'Men of Harlech,' before a last volley was fired over their graves.

'Sleep of the Brave', the painting by Alphone de Neuville of Major Black finding the bodies of Melvill and Coghill.

Meanwhile at a place called Rorke's Drift, a small missionary post, a company of the 24th under Lieutenant Bromhead plus a number of other soldiers and civilians totalling 139, were attacked by about 5,000 Zulus fresh from their triumph at Isandhlwana. There followed one of the epic stands in British military annals with the tiny force holding off the attacks of the Zulu army for a day and a night, often in savage hand to hand fighting. In the morning the attacks finally wavered and the Zulus withdrew before the garrison was relieved by the arrival of Lord Chelmsford's army. Seventeen men had been killed and eleven of the defenders were awarded the VC, with seven going to men of the 24th.

During the First World War the regiment raised 19 battalions. The 1st battalion fought in the First Battle of Ypres where their bravery matched any of their forebears at Blenheim or Rorke's Drift. On 31 October 1914 at a pivotal point in the battle, the 1st battalion, Worcestershire Regiment and the 1st battalion, South Wales Borderers advanced, captured and held the village of Gheluvelt in Belgium. Some say that without this action, the Germans might have broken through the British lines altogether, advancing to the Channel ports, thereby potentially winning the war.

The 1st battalion spent the whole war on the Western Front, while the 2nd battalion had a number of postings. During 1914 they took part in the mainly Japanese-led siege and capture of the German territory of Tsingtao in China. The following year, on 15 April, they made a successful landing at Cape Helles on Gallipoli. A year later they were on the Western Front.

Medical attention at Buckingham Palace

Jack Williams (left) was the most highly decorated Welsh NCO of all time, winning the VC, DCM, MM and Bar. On 7 October 1918 at Villers Outreaux in France as the 10th battalion put in yet another attack on German defences, a machine gun was taking its toll on the advancing Welshmen. Sergeant-Major Williams ordered a Lewis gun to return fire while he single-handedly moved into attack. He put the machine gun out of action, taking fifteen of the enemy prisoner. After a few moments the prisoners, realising that they were being held by only one man, attacked him, grappling with his rifle. After a struggle in which he killed five of the enemy, he brought them under his control again. This act, for which he was awarded the VC, allowed the battalion's advance to continue. Ten days later, after being severely wounded by shrapnel in the right leg and right arm, he was medically discharged. Early in 1919 Williams attended at Buckingham Palace where he was decorated by King George V four times in the day. During the proceedings one of his wounds re-opened and he had to receive medical attention before he could leave the Palace. He made a full recovery and died in 1953. He is pictured here with Private John Williams VC of Rorke's Drift at Brecon Barracks, 1932.

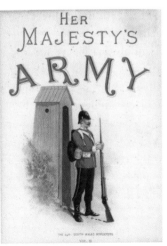

From far left
The Battle of Talavera, August 1809, where the 24th saved the Foot Guards.

A sentry of the South Wales Borderers on duty for Queen and Empress.

Seven holders of the VC of the 24th at Brecon on 23 January 1898. Rear left to right: Pte R. Jones VC, Pte A. Hook VC, Pte W. Jones VC. Sitting left to right: Pte D. Bell VC, Lt Col E.S. Browne VC, Pte F. Hitch VC, Pte J. Williams VC. Five of them had been defenders of Rorke's Drift, Bell had won his VC alongside Surgeon Douglas in the Andaman Islands in 1867 in a sea rescue, Browne during the Zulu campaign at Inhlobani Hill in January 1879.

In the Second World War the regiment raised five battalions, with the 1st battalion being virtually destroyed in North Africa while the 2nd battalion took part in operations in Norway in 1940; in 1944 as part of the 7th Armoured Division it was the only Welsh battalion to take part in the D-Day landings. They fought their way through to the German border by the end of the war in May 1945. In 1948 the 2nd battalion, in line with defence cuts, was disbanded. The 1st battalion served in Malaya during the Emergency in 1955. Field Marshal Sir Gerald Templer, commanding officer in this campaign, said of the regiment, '*There has been no better regiment in Malaya during the ten years of the emergency and very few as good.*'

In 1969 they amalgamated with the Welsh Regiment (41st) to form the Royal Regiment of Wales (24th/41st Foot). In 2006 this regiment amalgamated with the Royal Welsh Fusiliers (23rd) to form the Royal Welsh Regiment, in which it forms the 2nd battalion.

MUSEUM: South Wales Borderers Museum, The Barracks, Brecon, Powys LD3 7EB Tel 01874 613310

GLOUCESTERSHIRE REGIMENT (28TH AND 61ST)

'The Slashers'; 'The Old Braggs'; 'The Glorious Glosters'

Dates	1694 and 1758-1994 VCs 6
Motto	By Our Deeds We Are Known.
Alumni	Barry St. Leger, hero of American war, F. W. Harvey, poet, Colonel James Carne VC, the 'Manchurian Candidate', Sir Harry Wetherall, soldier, James Keir, pioneering scientist, Harold Lambert, Kenya and Swahili scholar
Anniversaries	21 March, Back Badge Day
Battle Honours	Ramillies, Quebec, Guadeloupe, Egypt 1801, Corunna, Vitoria, Toulouse, Quatre Bras, Waterloo, Chillianwallah, Alma, Inkerman, Sevastopol, Delhi 1857, Ladysmith, South Africa, Mons, Ypres, Loos, Gallipoli, Somme, Vittorio Veneto, Kut al Amara, Dunkirk, Burma, North West Europe, Imjin River.

The Glorious Glosters are as famous a regiment as any in the British Army. With battle honours from Ramillies to Korea, they stand second to none. The 28th Regiment of Foot was first raised in Portsmouth in 1694 by Colonel John Gibson. In 1697 they were sent to Newfoundland to protect British interests and in the winter that followed they lost 214 out of 300 men through illness and terrible living conditions. The regiment was then posted to the Low Countries as part of the Duke of Marlborough's army and saw action in 1705 during the forcing of the Lines of Brabant. Their first major engagement was in the Duke's army at the battle of Ramillies in 1706. This battle is considered by many to have been Marlborough's finest victory. Winston Churchill, comparing his ancestor with Frederick the Great and Napoleon, wrote,

Two officers make a toast after the battle of Barrosa, 5 March 1811.

'It will rank forever with Rossbach and Austerlitz as an example of what a general can do with men.' The regiment fought just as bravely in 1707 when they were sent to the Iberian peninsula and took part in the little known defeat at Almanza in Spain where they lost more than half their men in the bloody fighting, 300 out of 532 who started the day. By the time the War of the Spanish Succession was ended by the peace of Utrecht in 1713, the 28th had established a reputation for themselves as doughty fighting men. This was a reputation they would carry with them right up to modern times.

In 1734 Colonel Philip Bragg became the new colonel of the regiment and led them for the next twenty five years. They were numbered as the 28th Regiment of Foot during this period with their red coats keeping their original yellow facings. In the later years of Bragg's command they became known as the 'Old Braggs.' With other regiments gaining sobriquets such as 'King's' or 'Own', this ditty was compiled:

> Neither King's nor Queen's, nor Royal Marines,
> But 28th, Old Braggs: brass before, brass behind,
> Never feared a foe of any kind; shoulder arms.

In 1757 the 28th sailed to North America in the force under the command of General James Wolfe. They took part in the capture of Louisburg and were the first regiment to scale the Heights of Abraham at Quebec leading the British into the attack. Ensign James Henderson, a Volunteer during the battle, though wounded himself, helped Wolfe away from the field of fire and was at his side at his death in his moment of victory. He later wrote of Wolfe, '*Just then there came some officers who told him that the French had given ground and our troops were pursuing to the walls of the town. He was lying in my arms, just expiring, that great man whose sole ambition was his country's glory. Upon this news, he smiled in my face. 'Now' said he, 'I die contented.'* For his gallantry and devotion to duty Henderson was duly commissioned into Bragg's 28th.

The '*Slashers*' nickname comes from an incident in 1764 when the regiment was stationed in Montreal during a particularly cold winter. They were continually being harassed by a local magistrate named Thomas Walker. Eventually they took matters into their own hands and the tiresome gentleman was confonted in his own home. He put up a fight and during the melee part of his ear was slashed off. Nobody was ever charged with the assault and the perpetrators took their secret to the grave.

During the American War of Independence the Glosters fought in a number of actions including the Battle of Long Island in August 1776 which was an early victory for the British. In October of that year they took part in the inconclusive Battle of White Plains just outside New York against General George Washington. It was here they gained an alternative interpretation of their nickname. As they advanced through the long grass it is said they slashed it away to improve their line of sight.

In 1782 the 28th were renamed the 28th (North Gloucestershire) Regiment of Foot. The other part of the Gloucestershire Regiment, the 61st Regiment of Foot, had first been formed in 1756, as an additional battalion of the Buffs, but under their Colonel Granville Elliot they became an independently numbered regiment in 1758. In 1759 the 61st won their first battle honour at the capture of Guadeloupe. They were named the 61st (South Gloucestershire) Regiment of Foot in 1782. Both regiments would now be associated with the county but would follow their own paths for the next 99 years until they would become the 1st and 2nd battalions of the Gloucestershire Regiment.

It was at the Battle of Alexandria on 1 March 1801 that the 28th regiment first gained undying fame. They were sorely pressed by the French cavalry and, at a critical moment in the fighting, their commanding officer, realising that he was under attack from in front and behind, issued the famous order *'Rear rank, 28th! Right about face!'* The 28th duly obeyed and, waiting till the critical moment, fired a devastating volley into the attacking French cavalry thereby breaking up their onslaught. In honour of this the regiment was granted the right to always wear a cap badge on the back as well as the front of their caps. Sergeant Joseph Coates recalled, *'The French charged in three columns, the left of which came round the left flank of our regiment, over the ground which the 42nd regiment had left, to charge it in the rear, whilst it was warmly assailed by the infantry in front, and just as this column was making the turn to come upon our rear, they overtook me. At that time Colonel Paget ordered the regiment to the right about, and firing a volley as the enemy came within a few horse lengths, occasioned a most dreadful carnage. After the volley the 28th faced about again and resumed their fire on their assailants.'*

Below, from left
Private of the 28th in full marching order, Crimea, 1855. Photograph by Roger Fenton.

The Gloucestershire Regiment, arms drill *c.*1895.

28th Regiment
fighting back to back
at Alexandria,
21 March 1801.

The 61st also served in the latter part of the Egyptian campaign having been diverted there from South Arica while on their way to India. They had been in the strategically important port of Cape Town, South Africa since 1799 taking part in operations against the Boer farmers as well as the local Africans. After Egypt the 61st were based in Sicily and two companies crossed the Straits of Messina with the small British force under General Sir John Stuart that on 4 July 1806 met and defeated a French force of similar size under the command of General Jean-Louis Regnier, at Maida on the Italian mainland.

In 1808 the 28th were with Sir John Moore during the Retreat to Corunna. The 61st fought at Talavera in 1809. The 28th were at the Battle of Barrosa on 5 March 1811 where, by the end of the day, only two of their officers remained unwounded. At Albuera on 16 May their 2nd battalion also fought with great discipline while losing 164 out of 390. At the Battle of Salamanca a year later the 61st lost 366 men out of 546, more than any other regiment in the battle. A witness wrote, *'The 61st, which was almost annihilated in this severe action, was by far the finest regiment in the 6th division.'*

The 28th were at the battle of Vitoria in 1813. During the late summer and autumn of that year both regiments were involved in engagements with the retreating French over the Pyrenees and into France itself. In February 1814 they fought alongside each other at the battle of Orthez and on 10 April were involved in the Battle of Toulouse where the 61st suffered badly gaining the name the *'Flowers of Toulouse'* in reference to their red-coated bodies left on the field of battle where they had fought so valiantly, losing nearly 200 officers and men. The 28th were also at the battles of Quatre Bras and Waterloo. It was a matter of great pride in the regiment that they were the only English infantry regiment mentioned in the Duke of Wellington's despatches written immediately after the battle. *'The troops of the 5th Division, and those of the Brunswick corps, were long and severely engaged, and conducted themselves with the utmost gallantry. I must particularly mention the 28th, 42nd, 79th, and 92nd Regiments, and the battalion of Hanoverians.'* The 42nd, 79th and 92nd were of course Scottish regiments, the Black Watch, the Cameron and the Gordon Highlanders.

The 61st arrived in India in time to take part in the Second Sikh War when they fought both at the Battle of Chillianwallah and the battle of Gujerat in the early part of 1849. General Sir Charles Napier, the new commander in chief in India ordered that the following message be sent to London to the Secretary of State for War, the Duke of Wellington: *'Nothing in the whole of the British Army ever was more distinguished that the conduct of the regiment, the 61st, throughout the late campaign, but more particularly at the battle of Chillianwallah, where the conduct of the regiment was the admiration of the whole army.'*

The 28th took part in the Crimean War and had a presence at both the Alma and Inkerman as well as the siege of Sevastopol. Though they lost more than a hundred in combat, their main casualties totalling nearly 400 were the result of disease and the insanitary and harsh conditions.

The 61st were stationed in India when the Mutiny broke out in 1857 and they played a heroic part in its being brought under control. During the savage campaign the men's uniforms began to fall apart, so they wore whatever they could lay their hands on and took to dyeing their clothes a mud colour, khaki. They were the first regiment to do so in the British Army.

The 28th amalgamated with 61st (South Gloucestershire) Regiment of Foot to form the 1st and 2nd battalions of the Gloucestershire Regiment in 1881. One of the main bones of contention was the matter of the back badge of '28' which the 61st, quite naturally, were reluctant to wear, not having earned it. The matter was resolved by the new regiment wearing the back badge with the 'Sphinx' on it, which both regiments had been awarded after the Alexandrian campaign.

Officers' shako plate 1816–29.

The regiment raised 25 battalions during the First World War fighting on the Western Front, in the Middle East, in Italy and at Gallipoli. During the Gallipoli campaign in Turkey in 1915 the Gloucesters fought valiantly at the Battle of Chunuk Bair in early August in support of the Wellington Regiment from New Zealand. The New Zealanders lost 711 men out of a total of 745, while the Gloucesters suffered 350 casualties, including all their officers. In the Second World War battalions of the regiment took part in the Dunkirk campaign, in North Africa, Italy, Greece, Burma, and North West Europe from D-Day to the end of the war in Germany.

The most modern of their nicknames stems from the Korean War when the regiment took part in heavy fighting on the Imjin River in 1951. From 22 April for three days 750 Gloucesters and a Troop of the Royal Artillery kept approximately 10,000 attacking Chinese at bay at what became called Gloster Hill. By the end of the battle the Gloucesters were completely surrounded, out of ammunition and reduced to fighting hand-to-hand. When the final order was made to break out only 40 men made it, the rest were either captured or killed. Their bravery enabled the rest of the United Nations forces to regroup to defend Seoul. The Gloucestershire Regiment won the U.S. Distinguished Unit Citation and the South Korean Distinguished Unit Citation, as well as their nickname, the *'Glorious Glosters'*. The US Citation reads: *'Their sustained brilliance in battle, their resoluteness, and extraordinary heroism are in keeping with the finest traditions of the renowned military forces of the British Commonwealth, and reflect unsurpassed credit on these courageous soldiers and their homeland.'*

Drum-Major and Drummer, 28th Regiment, 1844. Illustration by A.C. Lovett.

In 1994 the Glosters amalgamated with the Duke of Edinburgh's Royal Regiment to form the 1st Battalion the Royal Gloucestershire, Berkshire and Wiltshire Regiment. In 2007 this regiment in turn amalgamated with the Devonshire and Dorset Regiment to become the 1st Battalion, the Rifles.

MUSEUM: Soldiers of Gloucestershire Museum, Custom House, 31 Commercial Road, Gloucester GL1 2HE Tel 01452 522682

BLACK WATCH (42ND AND 73RD)

'Come Near Who Dares'

Dates	1725–2006 VCs 15
Motto	*Nemo me impune lacessit,* No one assails me with impunity.
Alumni	Adam Ferguson, Ian Fleming, novelist, Field Marshal Lord Wavell, scholar and soldier, Eric Newby, writer, General Sir Neil Ritchie, Rory Stewart, diplomat, Fergus Bowes-Lyon, the Queen's uncle.
Anniversary	5 January, Red Hackle Day
Battle Honours	Fontenoy, Ticonderoga, Alexandria, Corunna, Busaco, Fuentes de Honoro, Salamanca, Orthez, Toulouse, Quatre Bras, Waterloo, Alma, Relief of Lucknow, .Boer War, Mons, Loos, Somme, Ypres, Mesopotamia, Dunkirk, El Alamein, Sicily, Chindits.

When we talk about Scottish regiments, be they from the Highlands or the Lowlands, from the cavalry or the infantry, it is important to remember this: on the outbreak of War in August 1914, Field Marshal Herbert Horatio Kitchener, Earl Kitchener of Khartoum, called for 100,000 recruits to join the New Army. The nation responded, and that number was reached by Scotland alone.

The name of this regiment alone has menace in it. It comes from their duty to 'watch' or police the highlands and the dark coloured tartan they wear. Their motto is more dramatically loosely translated as 'Come Near Who Dares.' From the beginning the 42nd (Royal Highland) Regiment of Foot, the senior Highland regiment, were known as the Black Watch and, even after their amalgamation with the 73rd in 1881, the name continued in use. They were established to control inter-clan fighting. Their origins can be traced back to 1624 as trustworthy Independent Companies employed by the authorities to keep order in the highlands. During the reign of King George I, the Independent Companies were disbanded since the idea of armed highlanders was not tolerated after the first Jacobite uprising.

An officer of the Black Watch at Ticonderoga, 1758. (Tim Reese)

In 1724 General Wade raised six Independent Highland Companies from the Campbell, Munro, Grant and Fraser families, totalling about five hundred officers and men. They were allowed to bear arms and became known as the Highland Regiment of Foot. A Highland Regiment of Foot was to be formed for the British Army in 1739 and John Lindsay, Earl of Crawford, the regiment's first colonel, mustered the new regiment on the banks of the river Tay near Aberfeldy in May 1740 only from those *'native of that country and none other to be taken'*. The regiment marched to London where three of her officers were presented to the King. He gave them each a sovereign, which they gave to the doormen on the way out of the Palace.

During the War of the Austrian Succession they fought bravely and cleverly at the Battle of Fontenoy on 11 May 1745. A French officer likened them to *'Highland Furies who rushed in on us with more violence than ever did the sea driven by tempest'*. Instead of marching, like the English regiments, line abreast into the hail of enemy fire, they lay down when a volley was about to be fired, then got up and continued the attack. The only person not to take cover was their commanding officer,

Sir Robert Munro, who was too corpulent to take such avoidingl action, so he stood firmly in front of the Colours. His three brothers, George, John and James, presumably kept their heads down with the men. All five officer casualties that day went by the name of Campbell. Another Campbell, a Sergeant, is reputed to have killed nine Frenchmen and was just about to make it ten when his arm was blown off. The Duke of Cumberland, commander that day offered him a reward *'of a value equal to the arm'*.

The Black Watch, as the 42nd, took part in the setback of the Battle of Ticonderoga in America in 1758. Therein lies the story of a dream. Major Duncan Campbell of Inverawe some years earlier had been involved in concealing a fugitive. When it turned out the man had murdered his cousin, Campbell turned him out in breach of a promise he had made. The fugitive appeared in a dream to Campbell and said, *'I will see you at Ticonderoga.'* Campbell had been with the Black Watch for many years when they arrived in America. There he heard the name of Ticonderoga for the first (or rather, second) time. The bloodstained figure of the fugitive appeared again to him in a dream the night before the battle, predicting his death. The next day Major Campbell was severely wounded and had to have his arm amputated. He died at Fort Edward shortly afterwards.

The 42nd were granted the title Royal soon after, and a second battalion was raised. In 1786 this battalion became a regiment in its own right, the 73rd Highland Regiment of Foot. They later were to serve in India at Seringapatam and Mysore. Meanwhile in 1759 the 42nd won battle honours for Guadeloupe, Martinique and Havana in the West Indies. In the American War of Independence they were transferred to New York where they took part in the successful action against the rebels at Brooklyn and other skirmishes.

Major General David Stewart of Garth, who joined the 42nd at the age of 16 and wrote the famous *Sketches of the Highlanders*.

The red hackle worn exclusively by the regiment since 1822 and before that from 1795.

Above, from left
The Battle of Corunna where Sir John Moore managed to hold the French army enabling the British Army to escape by sea. Men of the 42nd carried the mortally wounded Moore from the battlefield.

The 42nd at Quatre Bras. 'Surrender. you know you are beaten,' shouted the French cavalry commanding officer to the remains of the square. 'The General [Pack] raised his hat … a most destructive fire was opened … men and horses mixed together in one heap of indiscriminate slaughter.' Sergeant James Anton.

In 1795 while stationed in England, the 42nd started to wear the distinguishing red hackle in their bonnets. In 1822 an Army order went out declaring that it was *'to be used exclusively by the 42nd Regiment'*.

At the Battle of Alexandria in March 1801 the British fought an uncompromising exchange with the French. The 42nd, fighting in the ruins of the ancient city of Nicopolis, captured the Colours of Napoleon's *'Invincibles,'* winning the right for the Sphinx insignia to be worn on their cap badge and Colours. They also took severe losses when attacked by the French cavalry and were present when General Sir Ralph Abercromby was mortally wounded in his moment of victory.

During the Peninsular War the regiment fought from the retreat to Corunna, where men of the regiment carried the mortally wounded General Sir John Moore out of the line of fire, to the final victory at Toulouse, winning ten battle honours in the process. At Toulouse by the end of the day only sixty men of the Black Watch were left standing.

In the summer of 1815 another important chapter in the history of the regiment was written when the 42nd and 73rd fought side by side at the Battle of Quatre Bras on 16 June. Mistaking French Lancers for allies they had not formed a defensive square when the enemy attacked and had to literally fight for their lives. Two days later at Waterloo the 73rd, as part of the 5th Brigade, likewise took heavy casualties from French canon fire. A figure of a Black Watch soldier stands under the Duke of Wellington's statue at Hyde Park Corner in London in honour of their contribution to his reputation.

It was nearly forty years before the Black Watch came under fire again. In September 1854 the 42nd were in action at the Battle of Alma in the Crimea where, on the right of the Highland Brigade, their charge with the cry *'Forward the 42nd!'* drove the enemy back. This was followed by a grim eighteen months in the trenches before Sevastopol.

Two years later the regiment was in India during the Indian Mutiny fighting at Cawnpore and the Relief of Lucknow. They were also involved in sweep operations in pursuit of rebels, which involved marches over long distances in conditions of extreme heat and deprivation.

In 1881 the 42nd was merged with the 73rd becoming the two battalions of the Royal Highland Regiment (The Black Watch). The 1st battalion in 1881 fought at the Battle of Tel-el-Kebir and in 1884 in the Sudan against the followers of the Mahdi at the Battle of Tamai where Private Thomas Edwards was awarded the VC for conspicuous gallantry in saving his naval gun team though wounded several times.

During the Boer War both battalions of the regiment were in action. The 2nd battalion, as part of the Highland Brigade suffered badly on 11 December 1899 at the battle of Magersfontein when they were caught advancing in broad daylight by accurate enemy fire. Major General Andrew Wauchope, who had been commissioned in the Black Watch, was killed commanding the 3rd Highland Brigade, which incorporated the 2nd Black Watch, the 1st Highland Light Infantry, 2nd Seaforth Highlanders and the 1st Argyll and Sutherland Highlanders. As he died, he murmured, *'What a pity.'* He must have realised the murderous fire they were under was due to delays in their attack, which was intended to be before dawn. His decision to keep them in close order in the darkness became fatal in the daylight. This from a seasoned soldier who had fought, and been wounded twice, in the Ashanti War of 1873-4 and the Sudan campaigns of 1884-5 where he was again severely wounded. The Highland Brigade lost 53 officers and 650 men that fateful day, a bitter blow for Scotland. Ten weeks later they took part in the victory over the Boers at Paardeberg.

During the First World War twenty-five battalions were raised by the Black Watch. Fighting of course in their kilts, they were known by the Germans as the 'Ladies from Hell', as they attacked to the skirl of their pipes. By the end of hostilities they had lost 8,000 men killed. They had fought with tenacity and courage through the terrible battles of Mons, Loos, the Somme and Passchendaele. They had also fought and died in the campaigns in Mesopotamia and Palestine. Their efforts to relieve the Siege of Kut-al-Amara resulted in them suffering high casualties in a number of savage engagements with the Turkish enemy. Private Melvin won the VC at the Battle of Istabulat, near Baghdad on 21st April 1917, like Sergeant Campbell at Fontenoy, personally taking out nine of the enemy. His citation reads: *'Private Melvin's company had advanced to within fifty yards of the front-line trench of a redoubt, where, owing to the intensity of the enemy's fire, the men were obliged to lie down and wait for reinforcements. Melvin, however, rushed on by himself, over ground swept from end to end by rifle and machine-gun fire. On reaching the enemy trench, he halted and fired two or three shots into it, killing one or two enemy, but as the others in the trench continued to fire at him, he jumped into it, and attacked them with his bayonet in his hand, as, owing to his rifle being damaged, it was not 'fixed'. On being attacked in this resolute manner most of the enemy fled to their second line, but not before Melvin had killed two more and succeeded in disarming eight unwounded and one wounded. Melvin bound up the*

Private Charles Melvin VC.

wounds of the wounded man, and then driving his eight unwounded prisoners before him, and supporting the wounded one, he hustled them out of the trench, marched them in and delivered them over to an officer. He then provided himself with a load of ammunition and returned to the firing line where he reported himself to his platoon sergeant. All this was done, not only under intense rifle and machine-gun fire, but the whole way back Melvin and his party were exposed to a very heavy artillery barrage fire. Throughout the day Private Melvin greatly inspired those near him with confidence and courage.'

In the Second World War battalions of the Black Watch were involved in almost every theatre: from Dunkirk and back to Normandy, Holland and Germany, where they were the first British troops to set foot inside the Reich, North Africa, the breakout from Tobruk and El Alamein, the defence of Crete against airborne attack, the Sicily landings and Italy, as Chindits in Burma with the 14th Army, even Greece against Communist insurgency, the Black Watch were there, always to be trusted by friend and feared by foe.

After the War, the Black Watch took part in a number of historic actions. They were the last British regiment to leave Pakistan after the Partition in 1947. In Korea they fought in the Battle of the Hook in 1952, their 151st battle honour, where they held the line against waves of the Chinese army, often fighting hand-to-hand. In Malaya, Kenya and Cyprus they took part in difficult operations against the growing tide of independence movements in a declining Empire. They were even the last British regiment to leave Hong Kong at the handover to China in 1997. In recent times they have conducted operations in the Iraq War of 2003 and 2004.

The First VC

On 9 March 1858 at Lucknow, India, Lieutenant Edward Farquharson led a portion of his company and stormed a bastion mounting two guns and then spiked them. This meant that the advance positions held during the night were rendered secure from artillery fire. Lieutenant Farquharson was severely wounded while holding an advanced position the following morning. He was awarded the Victoria Cross, which was the first, but by no means the last, won by the regiment.

After 266 years as an independent regiment, on March 28th 2006 the Black Watch became The Black Watch (3rd Battalion, Royal Regiment of Scotland) losing their status as an individual regiment but at least retaining their name and, with it, their unique character.

MUSEUM: The Black Watch Regimental Museum, Balhousie Castle, Hay St, Perth PH1 5HS Tel 0131 3108530

DURHAM LIGHT INFANTRY (68TH AND 106TH)

'Faithful Durhams'

Dates	1758, 1839-1968	VCs 11
Motto	Faithful.	
Alumni	Sir Malcom Sargent, musician, Charles Laughton, Hollywood star, Bill Nicholson, football manager, Leslie Phillips, actor, Sir Peter de la Billière, soldier, William Cox, Australian pioneer, George Butterworth, composer, Gilbert Norman, SOE hero, Harold Orton, academic and authority on English dialects	
Anniversaries	9 August, Hooge Day, 5 November, Inkerman Day.	
Battle Honours	Salamanca, Vitoria, Orthez, Inkerman, Sevastopol, New Zealand, Relief of Ladysmith, Ypres, Hooge, Somme, Dunkirk, Mareth, Tobruk, El Alamein, Sicily, Salerno, Normandy, Kohima, Korea.	

It was in 1758, during the Seven Years War, that Colonel John Lambton, grandfather of the first Earl of Durham, raised the 68th Regiment of Foot in the county of Durham and became their first Colonel. This established a connection with the county that continues to this day. In 1764 the regiment was sent to Antigua and St Vincent in the West Indies where they distinguished themselves against a local uprising, operating in difficult conditions. It was in this campaign that they gained their nickname and were exempted from drinking the Loyal Toast as a sign of their loyalty to the Crown.

The concept of Light Infantry was originally conceived by General James Wolfe and Lord Amherst during the North American Wars against the French and their native American allies. The concept of close order advances in the highly conspicuous red uniforms of the British infantry regiments was deemed impractical. They decided that a force with good marksmanship, individual initiative, toughness, speed of action, lighter equipment and better training would be better suited to this type of guerrilla warfare. The bugle (rather than the drum), now the recognised symbol of light

LIEUT GEN! SIR JOHN MOORE. K.B.

Sir John Moore, who developed the concept of Light Infantry.

infantry, became the best form of communication since the soldiers would be spread over a wider area. Sounding the Retreat (the word is from the French *retraite,* meaning *'going to bed'* rather than the English, meaning *'go back'*) with the bugle became the norm in Light Infantry regiments at the end of the day. It was the legendary General Sir John Moore who developed the idea further with his motivational training methods and light infantry regiments were formed from 1802, fighting together as the Light Division in the Iberian Peninsula with singular success.

In 1770 a company of Light Infantry had been raised in America and in 1780 the prefix Durham was attached since many of the men were being recruited from that area. So in 1808 the regiment was officially designated as a light infantry regiment, a signal honour in recognition of their ability, only the third after the 43nd and 52nd. They were posted to Portugal in 1811 joining Wellington's army and fighting at Salamanca where they fought in the 7th Division under Major General Hope. In 1813 they fought again at the Battle of Vitoria, and over the Pyrenees into France with further engagements with the enemy at Orthez and Nivelle.

In 1839 the East India Company raised the 2nd Bombay European Light Infantry. In 1862 it became the 106th Bombay Light Infantry, which recruited in Durham. In 1881 the 68th and the 106th became the 1st and 2nd Battalions of the Durham Light Infantry.

The 68th fought in the Crimean War where on 5 November 1854 at the Battle of Inkerman they famously threw off their greatcoats, the better to fight and get at their ammunition, and fought in their scarlet tunics. The British were holding strategic heights and had heard the Russians, who outnumbered them, assembling at the foot of the hill. At dawn, the Durhams led by Sir George Cathcart prepared to counter-attack and charged down the slope at the Russian Yakutsk Regiment who, after holding a while, broke and fled. Cathcart was killed and the regiment lost half of their original line up of 16 officers, 15 sergeants, 14 buglers and 168 light infantrymen, but nevertheless it was a fine victory. The battle is remembered every year when the senior NCOs of the regiment wear a whistle and Inkerman chain on their sashes to commemorate their leadership on that day when so many of their officers fell.

A numbers of veterans of the Crimea took part in the less well known Second Maori War in New Zealand where on 21 June 1864 at Te Ranga Sergeant John Murray was awarded the VC for singlehandedly overcoming more than half a dozen men in an enemy trench. The regiment played its part in the Boer War and the 1st battalion fought at Colenso and Spion Kop and were at the Relief of Ladysmith.

In the First World War the Durham Light Infantry raised 43 battalions, many of them Territorial, manned by men not normally soldiers, of which 22 served overseas, losing more than 12,500 officers and men killed.

Left
A charming depiction of the regiment on foreign service, 1820.

Far left
The regiment at the trot, 1800s.

The Bradford Brothers

'*In the long roll of the young dead Roland Bradford is in some ways the most conspicuous figure.*' So said John Buchan writing after the First World War. The Bradford brothers were the most highly decorated British family of the War. Three of the four served in the Durham Light Infantry. Amongst them they won two VCs, one DSO and two MCs. Roland (right) and George both won VCs, a unique distinction in one family. James won the MC in March 1917 and was killed two months later near Arras. Lieutenant Commander George, serving in the Royal Navy, won his VC posthumously in the famous raid on Zeebrugge in 1918. (For the most complete account of that extraordinary effort to block the German submarines at Bruges, see *The Zeebrugge Raid: 'The Finest Feat of Arms'* by Paul Kendall.) Roland won the MC at Armentières in 1914, and the VC on the Somme in 1916 when he was already a Lieutenant Colonel. The following year he became the youngest Brigadier General in the British Army at the age of 25 but was killed three weeks later, probably by stray shrapnel. His VC citation reads '*Raked by machine-gun fire the situation of the battalion was critical. At the request of the wounded Commander, Lieutenant Colonel Bradford asked permission to command the exposed battalion in addition to his own. Permission granted, he at once proceeded to the foremost lines. By his fearless energy under fire of all description, and his skilful leadership of the two battalions, regardless of all danger, he succeeded in rallying the attack, captured and defended the objectives, and so secured the flank.*' Bradford was a compassionate and inspirational leader of men. He also firmly believed in the Almighty and before they went into battle and every evening the officers and men under his command would sing at least one verse of the hymn 'Abide With Me' accompanied by the assembled band whenever possible.

Sir George Cathcart
leads the Durhams at
the battle of Inkerman.

Left to right
A private of the
Durham Light Infantry
in the Crimea.

An officer of the
Durham Light Infantry
on the Western Front,
1916. (Tim Reese)

68

In the Second World War 18 battalions were raised by the Durham Light Infantry. The 1st battalion were in North Africa and Italy winning the battle honours of El Alamein, Mersa Matruh and Salerno. The 2nd battalion were part of the British Expeditionary Force that ended up at Dunkirk. During the fighting Second Lieutenant Richard Annand became the first British soldier to be awarded the VC in the war due to his heroic actions on 15 May 1940.

After the rigours of Dunkirk, they were posted to join the 14th Army in Burma where they distinguished themselves in the bloody fighting against enormous odds at the decisive Battle of Kohima, which effectively blocked the Japanese advance into India. Lord Mountbatten later described it as *'the British-Indian Thermopylae'*.

Sticking it Out

'The Durham Light Infantry Brigade fought under my command from Alamein to Germany... it is a magnificent regiment, steady as a rock in battle, and absolutely reliable on all occasions. The fighting men of Durham are splendid soldiers; they excel in the hard fought battle and they always stick it out to the end.'
Field Marshal Bernard Montgomery

In the post-war world the DLI continued to play its part in trouble spots from Korea to Aden, Cyprus and Borneo, their role as one of the legendary regiments of the British Army coming to an end in 1968. In Durham Cathedral on 12 December 1968 the Durham Light Infantry laid up their regimental colours for the last time and became the 4th battalion, Light Infantry Regiment, alongside the Somerset and Cornwall Light Infantry, the King's Own Yorkshire Light Infantry and the King's Shropshire Light Infantry, all proud regiments with strong traditions who would from henceforth become brothers in arms. On 1 February 2007 this regiment in turn became part of the current Rifles Regiment.

MUSEUM : Durham Light Infantry Museum and Durham Art Gallery, Aykley Heads, Durham DH1 5TU Tel 0191 3842214

From top
Mitre style cap as worn in the eighteenth century, known as the Lambton cap.

Helmet worn by the regiment during the Boer War.

Forage cap as worn by the regiment during World War II.

HIGHLAND LIGHT INFANTRY (71ST, 73RD, 74TH)

'Hell's Last Issue'; 'My fighting regiment'

Dates	1758-1959 VCs 13
Motto	*Nemo me Impune Lacessit,* No one assails me with impunity.
Alumni	David Niven, actor, Air Chief Marshal Sir Charles Burnett, Chief of Australian Air Staff, Major General Roy Urquhart, Arnhem commander, 'Mad Jack' Churchill DSO, MC, war hero (and archer), Patrick Ferguson, British hero of American War of Independence.
Anniversaries	23 September, Assaye, 18 June, Waterloo.
Battle Honours	Carnatic, Hindoostan, Mysore, Gibraltar, Seringapatam, Assaye, Cape of Good Hope 1806, Corunna, Busaco, Salamanca, Vitoria, Waterloo, South Africa 1851-3, Egypt 1882, Modder River, South Africa 1899-1901, Mons, Ypres, Loos, Somme, Arras, Hindenburg line, Gallipoli, Palestine, Mesopotamia, North West Europe 1940, 44-45, Reichswald, Sicily Landings, Greece.

The Highland Light Infantry were the only Highland regiment to wear trews, the Scottish plaid trousers, rather than the kilt. In 1758 a 71st Regiment of Foot was raised from the 2nd battalion of the 32nd Foot, later the Duke of Cornwall's Light Infantry. During the Seven Years War this regiment took part in two raids off the French coast at Cherbourg in 1760 and Belleisle 1761. It was disbanded in 1768.

In 1775 two battalions of Fraser's Highlanders were raised in Scotland as the 71st (Highland) Regiment of Foot (Fraser's Highlanders). In 1776 they sailed to New York to fight in the American War of Independence. They took part in many of the actions during the ensuing years including the engagements at Brooklyn, Brandywine, Savannah, Charleston, Camden and Yorktown. After the last battle they were apprehended and only returned home three years later to be disbanded.

In 1777, also as a result of the rebellion in America, the first clan regiment was raised by John MacKenzie, Lord Macleod, as the 73rd Highland Regiment of Foot (Macleod's Highlanders). They saw action in the Gambia and Mysore as well as taking part in the Battle of Pondicherry in 1793 and the capture of Ceylon in 1795. A second battalion was raised in 1778, which was sent to Gibraltar two years later and fought as marines in the great naval victory off Cape St. Vincent in 1780. To this day the regimental Colours bear the insignia of the Castle and Keys of Gibraltar. In 1783 the two battalions merged and, while still in India in 1786, became the 71st Highlanders, wearing the MacKenzie tartan. In 1787 due to the need for more regiments in India, the 74th Highland Regiment of Foot was raised in the City of Glasgow.

In 1802-5 the 74th took part in the future Major General Arthur Wellesley's campaign against the Mahrattas winning enduring glory with their fearless advance against the enemy at the Battle of Assaye in 1803. Wellesley was later to call them *'my fighting regiment'* and they were awarded the insignia of the elephant on their Colour. During the battle they lost four hundred men out of five hundred, including all their officers either killed or wounded. The situation was so dire that the Quartermaster, James Grant, took command of the regiment alongside the only officer left standing, the wounded Major Swinton. For their remarkable service in the battle, Lord Mornington, Wellesley's elder brother and Governor General, awarded them a special Colour in commemoration. The 74th were henceforth known as the 'Assaye Regiment'. At the annual parade in memory of the battle, the Quartermaster always carried the Colour in honour of Quartermaster Grant.

In 1806 the 71st landed in South Africa and took part in the capture of Cape Town from the Dutch. They were then deployed to South America where they took part in the capture of Buenos Aires, though this action did not end so well, with the rebels forcing the whole British garrison to surrender. Soon after this the British force returned to Britain.

The 71st took part in the first part of the Peninsula campaign under both Wellington and Sir John Moore, playing their part at the Battle of Vimeiro and in the Retreat to Corunna. It was during this time they were re-designated as light infantry, as a sign that they were now considered an elite regiment, and took the name of Highland Light Infantry. At the Battle of Vimeiro on August 21st 1808, the 71st were brigaded alongside the 36th and 40th under the command of Major General Ferguson. In

Clockwise from top left
A patrol of the 2nd HLI in Vis Island, Yugoslavia, September 1944. The battalion assisted the partisans against German troops on the mainland.

The Highland Light Infantry crossing the Rhine, April, 1945.

Souvenir hunters of the 9th HLI; Ptes McIvor, Harton and Mills at the village of Kranenburgh, near the Siegfried Line, February 1945.

fierce fighting, the 71st, after initial success, were driven back, then counter-attacked and turned the enemy flank successfully but were ordered not to advance. This was one of the factors that allowed the French Army to escape from Portugal; the day nevertheless ended with a spectacular British victory. Piper George Clark of the 71st, though wounded, famously continued to play his pipes to encourage his comrades as they fought to recapture the French guns.

Discipline

In 1852 the troopship *Birkenhead* was sailing to South Africa with reinforcements for the Kaffir War. The main contingent on board was from the 74th commanded by Lieutenant Colonel Alexander Seton along with women and children. The ship foundered off rocks near Cape Town and many soldiers were immediately drowned in their cabins. The survivors, many of them young recruits, were ordered up on deck and formed up with immaculate discipline while the women and children were allowed to take to the boats. Even when that was achieved, the men were ordered not to jump in the water lest it should capsize the boats. As a result they went to their deaths in their ranks as the ship sank. Out of 75 men the regiment lost an officer and 48 men drowned. This story of heroism became front page news in Europe and the King of Prussia insisted on having the story read out to his regiments as an example of military discipline and self-sacrifice. (See also Queen's Royal West Surrey regiment.)

The Highland Light Infantry at the Battle of Assaye, 1803.

In 1810 both the 71st and the 74th returned to the Peninsula after the escape from Corunna. At Busaco on September 27th the 74th held their positions all day despite constant French attacks. During the next four years with Wellington's army they won 17 battle honours and took part in every major battle. No other regiments in the British Army won more in this campaign. The 71st were called the 'Heroes of Vitoria' for their defiant fighting in Cadogan's brigade, while the 74th were instrumental in the storming of the fortress of Badajoz.

In the summer of 1815 the 71st played their part in perhaps the most famous battle honour of the regiment, Waterloo, where their advance, alongside the 52nd and 95th in Major General Adam's 3rd Infantry Brigade, finally broke the French Imperial Guard. In the battle they lost nearly 200 officers and men killed or wounded. Allegedly the 71st fired the last shot of the day at the fleeing French with a French gun they had captured.

Above, from left
The 71st Highlanders
in action at Waterloo.

74th in action in South
Africa, 1851.

The 71st were posted to the Crimea in 1854 and served in the trenches at the Siege of Sevastopol, suffering greatly due to the adverse weather and bad sanitary conditions. Three years later both the 71th and 74th took part in suppressing the Indian Mutiny.

In 1881 the two regiments amalgamated to become the 1st and 2nd Battalions of the Highland Light Infantry, the 71st becoming the county regiment of Perthshire and the 74th designated finally as the City of Glasgow Regiment from 1923.

During the Egyptian campaign of 1884 the regiment distinguished itself in a night march and attack at Tel el Kebir when Lieutenant Edwards won the first Victoria Cross awarded to the Regiment, '*for the conspicuous bravery displayed by him during the battle of Tel-el-Kebir on the 13th September, 1882, in leading a party of the Highland Light Infantry to storm a redoubt. Lieutenant Edwards, who was in advance of his party, with great gallantry rushed alone into the battery, killed the artillery officer in charge, and was himself knocked down by a gunner with a ramrod, and only rescued by the timely arrival of three men of his regiment.*' In the Boer War of 1899-1902 the Highland Light Infantry fought in a number of actions including the battles of Modder River and Paarderberg.

Governor-General of Australia

Alexander Hore-Ruthven was a Captain in the Highland Light Infantry while they were on campaign in 1898 in the Sudan. During fighting at Gedarif, Hore-Ruthven saw an Egyptian officer lying wounded in open ground with the enemy advancing. He picked up the wounded man and carried him back towards the lines, stopping a number of times to fire at the enemy to slow them down. His actions saved the officer's life and Hore-Ruthven was awarded the VC. He continued his army career ending up as a Brigadier General. During the First World War he fought at Gallipoli where he was severely wounded. Later he became Governor of South Australia during the famous Bodyline cricket series, where he did much to defuse the tension between Australia and Britain, and finally the Governor-General of Australia during the Second World War.

Sartorial Considerations

When David Niven, the Hollywood movie star, graduated from the Royal Military Academy at Sandhurst he applied for entry to a highland regiment. At the bottom of the page he wrote *'Anything but the Highland Light Infantry'* because they were the only Highland regiment to wear trews rather that kilts. He was of course duly commissioned into the Highland Light Infantry. He could have done a lot worse.

A soldier of the 71st in India, c.1800. (Tim Reese)

The Highland Light Infantry raised 26 battalions during the First World War. From the early desperate defensive fighting at Mons and Ypres, through Loos to heroic deeds on the Somme, right to the Armistice in 1918 ,they fought in the trenches of Flanders and France, after which the 2nd Battalion of the Highland Light Infantry marched proudly into Germany with their Assaye Colours unfurled and their pipes playing. Their tenacious battalions had been part of the original British Expeditionary Force of 1914 and had dogged it through the pitiless war in the trenches giving no quarter and finally prevailing. The 1st Battalion Highland Light Infantry were transferred to Mesopotamia in 1915 fighting the Turkish army in equally pitiless conditions. Other battalions fought at Gallipoli and in Palestine.

In 1923 the regiment's name was modified to Highland Light Infantry (City of Glasgow Regiment). On the outbreak of the Second World War the 1st battalion, Highland Light Infantry were part of the British Expeditionary Force escaping from Dunkirk. They landed back in Normandy at the end of June 1944 as part of the 53rd Division and fought across North West Europe to Germany in the spring of 1945. The 2nd battalion fought in North Africa, Sicily, Italy and the Balkans.

Following the war, the regiment served in Malaya, Cyprus, Germany and Northern Ireland. On January 29th 1959 the Highland Light Infantry merged with the Royal Scots Fusiliers with the new name Royal Highland Fusiliers (Princess Margaret's Own Glasgow and Ayrshire Regiment), keeping the MacKenzie tartan for their trews from the Highlanders and the flaming grenade in the cap badge of the Fusiliers. In 2006 that regiment became the Royal Highland Fusiliers, 2nd Battalion, The Royal Regiment of Scotland.

MUSEUM: Royal Highland Fusiliers Museum, 518 Sauchiehall Street, Glasgow G2 3LW Tel 0141 332563

Gordon Highlanders (75th and 92nd)

'The Ladies from Hell'

Dates	1794-1994 VCs 19
Motto	*Bydand,* Steadfast
Alumni	George MacDonald Fraser, novelist, George Keppel, husband of Alice, King Edward VII's mistress, Jack White DSO, Irish patriot and trade unionist, General Sir Ian Hamilton, commander at Gallipoli, Field Marshal George White VC.
Anniversaries	18 June, Waterloo
Battle Honours	Mysore, Seringapatam, Corunna, Peninsular War, Quatre Bras, Waterloo, Delhi, Kandahar, Dargai, South Africa 1899-1902, Ypres, Somme, Dunkirk, Malaya, North Africa, Sicily, Italy, North west Europe 1940-44.

This is the Highland regiment that grabbed the stirrups of their fellow countrymen, the Scots Greys, as they moved forward to attack the massed French infantry and cavalry at Waterloo. The 75th Regiment of Foot was first raised in 1787 by Colonel Robert Abercromby for service in India. The 92nd were raised in 1794 on the outbreak of the French Revolutionary Wars by the 4th Duke of Gordon from his estates and the surrounding areas of Aberdeenshire, Banffshire and Kincardineshire. He and his son, the Marquess of Huntly, who was a colonel in the 3rd Foot Guards, took a keen interest in the well-being of the regiment. It is said that his wife, the Duchess Jean, offered a kiss to each recruit who joined up. They were known as the Gordon Highlanders and wore the standard plaid with a yellow strand in it.

They were originally numbered the 100th Regiment of Foot but, after disbandments of other regiments ahead of them in the Army List, they became in 1798 the 92nd Regiment of Foot. The 92nd first saw action against the French in 1799 in Holland at Egmont op Zee while the 75th were serving under Colonel Wellesley

A Gordon Highlander of 1794. Painting by M. Georges Scott.

A private of the Gordon Highlanders in India, 1897. (Tim Reese)

against Tipoo Sahib in India. The 92nd then formed part of the expedition to Egypt under General Abercrombie. In the early stages of the Peninsular War the 92nd took part in the retreat to Corunna and the defensive battle there under Sir John Moore. In his memory they traditionally wore black buttons on their spats.

They returned to the Peninsula in the spring of 1809 under Sir Arthur Wellesley fighting in the battles of Fuentes de Onoro in 1810, Salamanca in 1812, Vitoria in 1813 and finally over the Pyrenees into France. During the Battle of the Nive on the night of 12 December 1813, near a village called St. Pierre, the Gordons fought a valiant holding action, though hugely outnumbered by the French attackers. Two of their three regimental pipers were killed but as each one fell, the next one continued to play to encourage the men. The regiment returned to Ireland in 1814 but, on the escape of Napoleon from Elba, they were at once posted to the Low Countries. On the evening of 15 June 1815 four Sergeants of the Gordon Highlanders were dancing reels to entertain the guests at the famous ball given by the Duchess of Richmond, the eldest daughter of Jean, Duchess of Gordon. The Duke of Wellington and many of his senior officers were present, among them John Cameron of Fassifern, the commanding officer of the 92nd. News came of Napoleon's sudden advance on Brussels and the military guests had to leave. At dawn the regiment was on the march and within hours were involved in the savage fighting of the Battle of Quatre Bras where Colonel Cameron and nearly half his men met their deaths. That night the survivors ate their food from the breastplates of French Cuirassiers they had killed. The next day they moved a few miles to a place called Waterloo. Colonel John Cameron of Fassifern had served with them since their formation in 1794, twenty-one years before.

Colonel Cameron of Fassifern (1773–1815)

During twenty years of active military service,
With a spirit that knew no fear and shunned no danger.
He accompanied or led
In marches, sieges, in battle
The gallant 92nd regiment of Scottish Highlanders.
Always to honour, almost always to victory.

On the morning of 18 June the regiment formed up once more as part of the 9th Infantry Brigade. As D'Erlon's legions advanced in their thousands towards the British lines, Brigadier Pack called out *'Ninety-second, you must advance! All in front of you have given way.'* At this point the Gordons moved swiftly forward and fired a devastating volley into the French phalanxes. Minutes later the Union Brigade received orders to advance and moved through them to the attack. Many of the Gordons took the stirrups of the Scots Greys and charged with them at the advancing French. The attack was devastating and some said they could see the ghost of Colonel Cameron in their midst waving them on with his cap in the air. Before long they were recalled to the lines as the cavalry charge sped away. The men spent the rest of the long day in their squares repelling the continuous French attacks. By the end they had lost more than a hundred officers and men but had played a critical part in one of the great battles in British and world history.

The storming of the Asmai Heights during the Afghan War of 1879 by the Gordon Highlanders. Watercolour by W. Skeoch Cumming.

To Run the Gauntlet not Once, but Twice

Colour Sergeant Cornelius Coughlan was an Irishman serving in the Gordon Highlanders during the Indian Mutiny. On two separate occasions he showed remarkable bravery in the face of the enemy. On June 8 1857 Coughlan led three others, under heavy fire, into a house occupied by rebels and rescued a private of the regiment who was severely wounded. On July 18 he encouraged nervous soldiers to charge down a lane raked by cross-fire. With his men he then ran into a courtyard full of the enemy, killing every one of them. Later he braved the cross-fire for a second time to collect stretchers for the wounded. On hearing of his heroism, Queen Victoria wrote him a personal letter of thanks and congratulations. When he returned home, Coughlan joined the Connaught Rangers and served with them for twenty years. He died in County Mayo in 1915 and was buried in an unmarked grave. On August 7 2004 a special ceremony was held at Aughavale Cemetery in Westport, County Mayo when a headstone was unveiled in his honour. The service was conducted by a Catholic priest and an Anglican minister and was attended by the Sergeant's family as well as senior Irish and British representatives.

92nd Gordon Highlanders attack the French guns at the battle of Mandora near Alexandria in March 1801. Watercolour by R. Simkin.

Both the 75th and the 92nd took part in the suppression of the Indian Mutiny. The 75th took part in the siege and capture of Delhi in 1857, winning three VCs in the process, as well as the capture of Agra and the Relief of Lucknow.

Both the 75th and the 92nd returned home in 1862 but the 92nd returned to India in 1878 where they fought valiantly in the Second Afghan War at the battles of Charasiab and Kabul in 1879. It was at Charasiab that Major George White of the 92nd won the VC. Thirty years later, now General White, commanded the army that was besieged at Ladysmith during the Boer War. In 1880 the 92nd took part in the epic march from Kabul to Kandahar with General Roberts, a distance of more than 300 miles in just 23 days

The 92nd were soon sent to South Africa where they fought in what is known as the First Boer War with the

Above, from left
Waterloo, the Gordon
Highlanders led by
Wellington.

Waterloo, the Gordon
Highlanders defend
themselves against
French cavalry on
Mont-Saint-Jean.

disastrous defeat at Majuba Hill in 1881. While in South Africa news came that they were to merge with the 75th. The 75th heard the news when they were in Malta. Neither regiment greeted the news with enthusiasm! The 92nd gave a formal burial to a flag decorated with the figures '92', and the words *'No died yet'*. At the same time in Malta the 75th wrote an inscription:

> *Here lies the poor 75th*
> *But under God's protection*
> *They'll rise again in kilt and hose*
> *A glorious resurrection*
> *For by the transformation powers*
> *Of Parliamentary laws*
> *They go to bed the 75th*
> *And rise the ninety twas.*

These first reactions were soon forgotten and together they would match the glories they had achieved singly. In 1882 the Gordon Highlanders led the attack in a bayonet charge in the battle of Tel el Kebir which defeated the Egyptian army after a night march through the desert. They then took part in the Sudanese campaign to rescue General Gordon. At Dargai Heights on 20th October 1897 on the North West Frontier they won a stunning victory over the tribesmen, remembered for the heroism of Piper George Findlater who kept playing despite being severely wounded.

The 2nd battalion fought at the victory over the Boers at Elandslaagte in South Africa where they shouted 'Majuba' as they pursued the enemy to remind them of the revenge they were taking for the battle of eighteen years before, when they had been picked off by the Boer marksmen. But soon they were trapped at Ladysmith under the command of one of their own, their General White VC. The 2nd battalion fought with the Highland Brigade during the campaign at Magersfontein and at Paarderburg but most famously at Doorknop, where they advanced decisively through severe enemy fire to carry the day. Winston Churchill wrote: *'The honours, equally with the cost of victory, belong to the 1st battalion, Gordon Highlanders, more than to all the troops put together.'*

The Gordon Highlanders fought all through the First World War. Of fifty thousand men from twenty-one battalions who served during hostilities, more than twenty-five thousand were killed or wounded, with particularly high casualties on the Somme. They won 65 battle honours and a number of VCs. James Anson Otho Brooke was a Lieutenant in the 2nd battalion, Gordon Highlanders. During heavy fighting near Gheluvelt in Belgium on October 29, 1914, in the face of heavy enemy fire he coolly led two attacks to recapture and hold an over-run trench, which could have led to a complete German breakthrough. He then moved position to call up reinforcements but was killed as he moved back. For his supreme courage and good leadership in the face of enemy fire, without regard to his own safety, he was awarded the VC.

A Blinded Hero

Captain Ernest Towse won the VC in South Africa in April 1900 in heroic and tragic circumstances. At this time he was an experienced soldier having fought in the Chitral Relief Force and on the North West Frontier in India. He and twenty-two men were surrounded by about 150 of the Boer enemy who called on this small band to surrender. He refused and, though severely wounded and blinded in both eyes, poured fire onto the enemy which put them to rout. He received the Victoria Cross from the Queen herself who is said to have shed tears when she pinned the medal on his chest.

At the start of the Second World War four Gordon battalions were in France during the German invasion of 1940. Two were forced to surrender in Normandy while another two escaped via Dunkirk. The 2nd battalion, stationed in Singapore, suffered a similar fate in 1942. But the tables soon turned and the Gordons fought with the Eighth Army from El Alamein to the beaches of Salerno and from Normandy to the German borders in 1945, avenging their comrades of 1940. In the Far East two further battalions did likewise for the men who had been captured in Singapore, fighting at Kohima and in the expulsion of the Japanese from Burma. During those five years the regiment won 27 battle honours and lost 2,500 lives.

After the war they served in Malaya, Cyprus and Northern Ireland continuing to uphold their reputation as a fierce fighting regiment but with a tradition of good behaviour and sensible soldiering. In 1994 the Gordon Highlanders merged with the Queen's Own Highlanders (formerly the Seaforth Highlanders and the Queen's Own Cameron Highlanders, who themselves had merged in 1961) to form the Highlanders Regiment, which in turn became the 4th Battalion of the Royal Regiment of Scotland in 2006.

MUSEUM: The Gordon Highlanders Museum, St. Lukes, Viewfield Road, Aberdeen AB15 7HX Tel 01224 311200

THE QUEEN'S OWN CAMERON HIGHLANDERS (79TH)

'Fiercer than fierceness itself'

Dates	1793–1961 VCs 4
Motto	*Pro Rege et Patria*, For King and Country.
Alumni	Lord Lovat, war hero, Fitzroy Maclean, writer and adventurer, Robert Holmes, TV writer, Jimmy Speirs MM, won FA Cup as captain of Bradford City in 1911, killed 1917 at Passchendaele, Sir Thomas Lauder, Scottish academic, writer and friend of Sir Walter Scott.
Anniversaries	18 June, Waterloo.
Battle Honours	Egmont op Zee, Alexandria, Corunna, Busaco, Fuentes d'Onoro, Salamanca, Toulouse, Waterloo, Alma, Balaclava, Sevastopol, Lucknow, Tel el Kebir, South Africa 1900-2, Mons, Aisne, Ypres, Loos, Somme, Arras, Macedonia, Dunkirk, El Alamein, Normandy, Reichswald, Kohima, Mandalay.

In 1881, when the British Army was being reorganised under the Childers Reforms, the story goes that a telegram was sent to the Cameron Highlanders asking whether, if they joined with the 42nd Black Watch Highlanders, they would be prepared to adopt their tartan. The answer, with all its risk of disbandment, was negative. This was a proud regiment indeed. The question was not asked again and the regiment was left alone, becoming the only regiment in the army with just one battalion.

The regiment was first raised by Sir Allan Cameron of Erracht as the 79th Highlanders Regiment of Foot (Cameronian Volunteers) at Fort William in 1793. In 1794 they campaigned for the first time in the Low Countries and in the West Indies

Cameron Highlanders officer, 1914. (Tim Reese)

in 1795. In 1799 they took part in their first full battle in Holland at Egmont op Zee against the armies of revolutionary France. In March 1801 the regiment was sent to Egypt in the army of Sir Ralph Abercrombie where they fought in the victories over the French army at the Battle of Alexandria and Cairo. It was during this campaign that they won the right to wear the Sphinx and the word 'Egypt' on their badges and colours. They were only fully incorporated into the British Army in 1804 and were renamed the 79th Regiment of Foot (Cameronian Highlanders) in 1806.

Lieutenant General Sir Allan Cameron of Erracht first raised the 79th in 1793.

The Sincerest Form of Flattery

During the American Civil War admirers of the Cameron Highlanders raised a regiment to fight against the Confederates called the 79th New York Highlanders, even copying the regimental number. Presumably many of its number were men of Scottish extraction. At the end of May 1861 they proudly marched down Broadway dressed in their full highland uniforms including kilts with the Cameron tartan. They were soon to go through some of the most bloody fighting of the Civil War where, for the ensuing three years they acquitted themselves bravely in the true tradition of their brethren across the ocean. During the Second World War the 61st battalion of the Australian Army were officially the Queensland Cameron Highlanders. There is currently a distinguished regiment in the Canadian Army named the Cameron Highlanders of Ottawa.

From 1808 in the Peninsular War they fought in the army of Sir John Moore during the retreat across northern Spain and the holding victory against the French at Corunna. Evacuated in January 1809 they returned with the rest of the army, this time under Sir Arthur Wellesley, in May of the same year. They now played their part in a number of the major engagements of Wellington's campaign fighting at Busaco in 1810, Fuentes de Onoro in 1811, Salamanca in 1812 and finally marching over the Pyrenees into southern France. In 1813, they fought in the sharp engagements of Nivelle and Nive before completing the defeat of Marshal Soult in the bloody Battle of Toulouse on 10 April 1814, when more than seven thousand French, British, Spanish and Portuguese soldiers lost their lives unnecessarily, unaware that Napoleon had already surrendered in Paris.

Piper Kenneth Mackay at the Battle of Waterloo, 1815.

In the spring of 1815 the 79th, now stationed in Ireland, were deployed to the Low Countries when news spread that Napoleon had escaped from Elba. They arrived near Brussels in May and first went into action against the French Grande Armée at Quatre Bras on 16 June. A number of British regiments were badly mauled; two days later, the rain-soaked army, the 79th among their number, faced Napoleon again.

At the Battle of Waterloo, as the regiment formed their squares against the attacking French cavalry, Piper Mackay continued to play the piece called 'War or peace' on his bagpipes to keep their spirits up as the enemy approached. After the battle he was presented by King George III with silver pipes. The Cameron Highlanders had sustained casualties of nearly two hundred killed and wounded.

The 1st battalion in South Africa, 1900.

Corporal McGillivray, 1st battalion, France, 1940. Pastel by official war artist Eric Kennington R.A.

The regiment was part of the Highland Brigade in the Crimea at the Battles of Alma, Balaclava and the Siege of Sevastopol. At the crossing of the Alma River they advanced on the left of the Highland Division, comprising the Black Watch, the Camerons and the Sutherlands, who in the last phase of the battle put ten thousand Russian defenders to flight. When the Crimea ended the regiment returned briefly to Britain before being transported to India in the suppression of the Indian Mutiny. After the two terrible winters they had endured in southern Russia the heat of India must have been welcome. They were involved in the recapture of Lucknow and the Battle of Bareilly. The regiment spent fifteen years in the sub-continent.

Three Days in No Man's Land

Ross Tollerton was born in Ayr, Scotland on 6 May, 1890. After being educated at Maxwell Town School, he joined the 1st Cameron Highlanders when he was fifteen serving in South Africa and India. He left the British Army in 1912 but was recalled as a reservist to the Cameron Highlanders at the outbreak of war in August 1914. On 14 September during the Battle of the Aisne the Cameron Highlanders were involved in a counter-attack on German lines alongside the Coldstream Guards and the 1st Loyal North Lancashire Regiment. All three regiments suffered badly but the Highlanders came off worst, losing 600 men from the relentless machine-gun fire. Lieutenant Matheson, Tollerton's company commander, was severely wounded and was unable to move. Though himself wounded in the head, back and hand, Tollerton carried Matheson away from the field of fire into a shell hole. Surrounded by the enemy, he could only move under cover of darkness. Matheson was extremely heavy, so Tollerton simply lay down next to his officer until he could effect a rescue three days later and bring him back to the British lines.

Tollerton was awarded the Victoria Cross for his act of bravery and it was presented to him by King George V at a ceremony attended by 50,000 people at Glasgow Green on 18th May 1915. He then returned to the trenches, survived the War and it was he who unveiled the town war memorial in April 1921. He died aged only 41 on 7 May, 1931. Major Matheson, whose life had been saved sixteen years before, sent a wreath.

In 1873 after their return from India, Queen Victoria conferred on them the honour of the title, 79th, The Queen's Own Cameron Highlanders. In 1881 under the Army Reforms the Cameron Highlanders were the only regiment left with just one battalion and they were also made the county regiment of Inverness-shire. In 1882 the regiment, as usual part of the Highland Brigade, was sent to Egypt under the command of Sir Garnet Wolseley whose aim was to suppress the uprising under the Egyptian nationalist Colonel Arabi Pasha. On 13 September, after a silent night march of eight kilometres in dress order across a pitch-dark desert, the Cameron Highlanders and the Gordon Highlanders were the first to attack the surprised defenders at the

Egyptian stronghold of Tel-el-Kebir. The Highlanders were up against the toughest troops and for a while the struggle was in the balance before the enemy broke. They remained in Egypt and campaigned in the Sudan in 1884.

In 1897 a 2nd battalion was in fact authorised and duly raised. The 1st battalion fought from 1900 to the end of the Boer War in South Africa During the First World War, thirteen battalions were raised of which nine were in the front lines winning 62 battle honours in all the main actions of the war at Mons, Aisne, Loos, Somme, Arras and even Macedonia. They also won three VCs.

Colours presented to the 1st battalion, 1955.

The Cameron Highlanders formed four battalions during the Second World War. They were sent to France with the BEF exactly as their predecessors had been in 1914. They fought again not far from Mons and Ypres but this time, the line could not be held and they, with the rest of the British Army, had to be evacuated at Dunkirk.

Kilts in Combat

At Le Bassée, a small town near the Belgian border, Donald Callander, an officer aged only twenty one, was commanding the anti-tank platoon. With just three anti-tank guns he and his men knocked out twenty-one German tanks. It was one of the last occasions at which the Highlanders fought in their kilts. For his gallantry Callander was awarded the Military Cross. He escaped off the beaches of Dunkirk and later in the war returned to France for the Normandy breakout, winning a second Military Cross on the borders of Germany at the Battle of Reichswald.

The battalions of the Cameron Highlanders fought in North Africa where they were at El Alamein with the 4th Indian Division, in North Africa and Sicily with 51st Highland Division, then Normandy, from where they reached the borders of Germany, and Burma from where they hold the battle honours of Kohima and Mandalay.

After the war the regiment was once again reduced to one battalion serving in Egypt, Libya, Germany Aden and Korea. On 7 February 1961 the Queen's Own Cameron Highlanders amalgamated with the Seaforth Highlanders to form the Queen's Own Highlanders (Seaforth and Camerons), a regiment which itself was amalgamated with the Gordon Highlanders on 17 September 1994 to form the Highlanders (Seaforth, Gordons and Camerons). On 28 March 2006 this regiment became part of the Royal Regiment of Scotland bearing the name The Highlanders (4th battalion, Royal Regiment of Scotland). They are now attached to the 7th Armoured Brigade, the Desert Rats, as armoured infantry.

MUSEUM: The Highlanders Regimental Museum, Fort George, Ardersier, Inverness IV2 2TD Tel. 0131 3108701

James Beadle's famous depiction of Brigadier General Crauford with the 95th Rifles, the 43rd and 52nd Light Infantry during the retreat to Corunna, December 1808.

three

THE RIFLE
REGIMENTS

'…not only the officers but each individual soldier, knows perfectly what he has to do; the discipline is carried on without severity, the officers are attached to the men and the men to the officers.'

General Sir John Moore

'I consider the action that was fought by the Light Division against the whole of the French 2nd Corps at Sebugal to be the most glorious that British troops were engaged in.'

Duke of Wellington, Peninsula Commander, 1811

OXFORDSHIRE AND BUCKINGHAMSHIRE LIGHT INFANTRY (43RD AND 52ND)

'The Light Bobs'; 'The Ox and Bucks'

Dates	1741, 1755–1958 VCs 6
Motto	*Honi soit qui mal y pense,* Shame on him who thinks evil of it.
Alumni	Sir John Moore, general and hero, Wilfred Blake, pioneer aviator and travel writer, Den Brotheridge, first man killed on D-Day, Frederick Smith, Viscount Hambledon, tycoon, Bernard Weatherill, Speaker of the House of Commons, Sir Samuel Auchmuty, New York-born general.
Anniversaries	17 January, 43rd Regimental birthday, 18 June, Waterloo, 20 December, 52nd Regimental birthday.
Battle Honours	Hindoostan, Vimeiro, Busaco, Badajoz, Fuentes de Onoro, Ciudad Rodrigo, Salamanca, Vitoria, Nivelle, Toulouse Waterloo, Delhi, Relief of Kimberley, Paardeberg, Mons, Ypres, Festubert, Loos, Somme, Hindenburg Line, Cambrai, Kut al Amara, Vittorio Veneto, North West Europe 1940, 1944–5, Salerno, Anzio, Normandy, Arakan, Burma.

These two fine regiments had an existence separate from each other for 140 years, longer than they were one. But in matters of fighting regiments their names are inextricably linked, much like the Argyll and Sutherland Highlanders. Thomas Fowke's Regiment of Foot was first raised in Winchester in 1741, was renamed the 54th Regiment of Foot in 1747 but in 1751 their number was finally changed to the 43rd Regiment of Foot due to regiment disbandments. In 1755 another regiment was raised in Coventry numbered the 54th Regiment of Foot. This regi-

Bugler Robert Hawthorne VC.

ment was renumbered the 52nd Regiment of Foot in 1757, again due to regiment disbandments.

In 1759 the 43rd formed part of General Wolfe's army which captured Quebec from the French and in the next few years fought successfully against the French in Canada and the West Indies. In 1774 the two regiments joined forces for the first time in the American War of Independence and were involved in the early victories of Lexington and Bunker Hill, where the 52nd suffered many casualties. The 52nd returned to England in 1778 and the 43rd followed three years later, having been involved with the final British surrender at Yorktown under General Cornwallis, which brought the war to an end.

In 1781 the 43rd gained the new name of the 43rd (Monmouthshire) Regiment of Foot and the 52nd became the 52nd (Oxfordshire) Regiment of Foot. It was exactly one hundred years later in 1881 that they came together forming the two battalions of one regiment.

In 1803 both regiments, along with the 95th, underwent special training at Shorncliffe in Kent and were created as the Light Brigade under the legendary Sir John Moore who taught that mutual respect between officers and men was crucial to any successful unit: a new concept at the time. As Captain John Kincaid said of Sir John Moore and his commanding officers in his famous memoir *Adventures in the Rifle Brigade*, '*The beauty of their system of discipline consisted in their doing everything that was necessary and nothing that was not, so that every man's duty was a pleasure to him, and the esprit de corps was unrivalled.*' It was at this point that they became Light Infantry with the emphasis on speed and individual initiative. Even their marching pace was quicker than line regiments at 140 paces per minute. In effect they were the infantry elite of the British Army. Both regiments now raised a 2nd battalion and both regiments were sent to Portugal with Sir Arthur Wellesley in 1808. At the Battle of Vimeiro, all four regiments, the 43rd, 52nd, 60th and 95th, which later formed the Green Jackets, were involved in the victory over the French. The 43rd encountered some tough hand-to-hand fighting during the battle before driving off the French grenadiers. At the end of the day the body of Sergeant Patrick was found bayoneted next to the French grenadier he had also bayoneted at his moment of death. The following year the Light Division served under Sir John Moore in his fighting retreat to Vigo and Corunna in North West Spain.

During the rest of the Peninsula campaign the two regiments were involved in most of the major actions. In the summer of 1809, hearing that Wellington needed reinforcements, they made the historic march to Talavera, a distance of over 400 kilometres. They covered the last 70 kilometres in 48 hours but arrived the morning after the battle with bugles playing. They then had to march for another 16 hours to reach the Alamarez Bridge, threatened by the French, which was a vital link for the British back to Lisbon. At the Battle of Busaco on 27 September 1810 the 43rd, 52nd and 95th of the Light Division were led into battle by General Robert Crauford with the cry, '*Now 52nd! Avenge the death of Sir John Moore!*' It was the grim-faced Crauford who some say was the cause of the regimental nick-name, the 'Light Bobs,' in ironic reference to their glowering commander, though the name had been given to light

Private Henry Addison VC.

The 52nd advancing at
Bunker Hill, 1776.

companies within infantry regiments some years before this. On 3 April 1811 at the Battle of Sebugal the Light Division made contact with the French 2nd Corps, a force ten times their strength, and drove them into retreat. At the capture of Ciudad Rodrigo, Lieutenant John Gurwood, one of the Forlorn Hopes of the 52nd, who had broken into the fortress and been severely wounded in the process, was presented with the sword of surrender from the French governor of the city by the Duke of Wellington. As part of the Light Division, both the 43rd and the 52nd were in the vanguard of Wellington's triumphant advance, which included the victories at Salamanca and Vitoria, across Spain and into Southern France in the coming months.

During the lull when Napoleon was exiled on Elba, the 43rd were posted to America and involved in the successful campaign culminating in the burning of the White House. They returned too late to take part in the Waterloo campaign. But the 52nd were brigaded with the 95th and the 71st at the Battle of Waterloo and under the command of Sir John Colbourne, made the decisive flank attack on the Chasseurs of the Guarde Imperiale of Napoleon, which turned the battle and shaped the history of Europe.

The 43rd became famous in 1852 as one of the brave and disciplined regiments on the transport ship *Birkenhead* which was shipwrecked off the South African coast. The regiment, with others, formed up on deck, while women and children were saved, before they were stood down to make their attempts at escape. (See Queen's Royal West Surrey regiment.)

Both the 43rd and the 52nd distinguished themselves during the Indian Mutiny. On 14 September 1857 Bugler Robert Hawthorne of the 52nd was one of the party assembled to rush the Kashmir Gate and blow it open in full view of the enemy in broad daylight. Under murderous and heavy fire from the rebels Hawthorne sounded the advance and the task was successfully completed, while he also tended to one of the wounded. For his bravery he was awarded the VC. Private Henry Addison of the 43rd won the VC for his brave action on 2 January 1859 when he rescued an officer who was under attack from rebels. Despite being severely wounded in both legs, one of which later had to be amputated, Addison managed to drag the stricken officer to safety.

In 1881 the two regiments were amalgamated into one regiment, the Oxfordshire Light Infantry. 'Buckinghamshire' was only added in 1908, so the 'Ox and Bucks' name, so famous in military circles, was only in existence for fifty years.

During the First World War the regiment raised twelve fighting battalions plus further support battalions. They won a further fifty-nine battle honours and were involved in combat on the Western Front, in Italy and Macedonia, and in Mesopotamia winning two VCs as well as many other decorations.

The 2nd battalion arrived in France with the British Expeditionary Force and fought in all the pivotal battles between September and December of 1914. On 11 November during the First Battle of Ypres in 1914 the regiment routed the elite Prussian Potsdam Guard almost exactly 100 years after they had routed the French Imperial Guard at Waterloo. At the Battle of Festubert in May 1915 the battalion lost 400 men, which again harked back to the Waterloo campaign, the last time they had taken so many casualties in a battle. Battalions of the regiment took part in most of the major actions during the First World War including Loos, the Somme, Passchendaele, the Hindenburg Line and Cambrai.

Forlorn Hope

During the Peninsular War, the 52nd were often involved in fortress assault parties. They, along with the 43rd, still wore their infantry red coats with black shakos. The companies that made these assaults were known as the 'Forlorn Hope'. It was considered an honour to be part of these storming parties who dared to brave severe casualties with the potential reward, if you survived, of instant battlefield promotion. The 52nd were part of the Forlorn Hope at a number of sieges and the regiment, by order of its commanding officer, had its own system of honouring their heroes. Those who survived at Ciudad Rodrigo and Badajoz were entitled to wear on their right arm a badge with a laurel wreath and the letters 'V.S.' standing for 'Valiant Stormer'.

The 1st battalion fought as part of the 6th Indian Division in the 1915 campaign against the Ottoman Empire at the Battle of Ctesiphon and the capture of Baghdad. But then they were part of the army besieged at Kut al Amara. The siege continued for nearly five desperate months before the British and Indian Army, with many men sick, surrendered.

Of the three hundred men of the regiment who were captured only 90 survived. Of the whole army of ten thousand men, nearly half died in captivity. Replacements for the 1st battalion were converted into the new 1st battalion and took part in the victorious end to the Mesopotamian campaign in October 1918. In April 1919 they were posted to Archangel in Russia to take part in the Russian Civil War on the side of the White Russians against the Bolsheviks but were withdrawn later in the year. Two battalions of the regiment fought with the Italian Army at the Battle of Vittorio Veneto against the Austro-Hungarians and a further two fought in Greece against the Bulgarians.

The Lost VC Winner

Until recently, Lance Corporal Alfred Wilcox, of the 2nd battalion, Oxfordshire and Buckinghamshire Light Infantry, was the only winner of the VC whose burial place was unknown. On 12 September 1918 near Bethune in France, his company was held up by enemy machine-gun fire. Wilcox rushed the nearest enemy position, threw a grenade and killed the gunner. Then, attacked by the enemy, he picked up German grenades and led his men to attack the next gun, capturing and destroying it. He then captured a third gun with the only other man left standing. Fighting his way forward in the trench, throwing grenades as he went, he captured a fourth gun and then returned to his platoon. For his supreme gallantry in the face of the enemy he was awarded the VC. In 2006 his grave was located at the graveyard of St Peter and St Paul Church in Aston, Birmingham. A proper gravestone was erected and a memorial service was held in his honour on 12th September 2006, 88 years to the day from when he captured the enemy machine gun nests.

During the Second World War the battalions of the regiment saw action as part of the British Expeditionary Force in France in 1940, North Africa and Italy, taking part on the Salerno and Anzio landings, in North West Europe and the Far East. On D-Day they pioneered the highly dangerous glider landings to capture Pegasus Bridge and Horsa Bridge hours prior to the Normandy landings. The 2nd battalion of the Ox and Bucks were in fact the first Allied forces to land in France that day. At the end of March 1945 they also were part of Operation Varsity, which was a glider-borne attack across the Rhine. Here they met stiff opposition and took many casualties. The battalion ended the war in April 1945 meeting up with the Russians in Northern Prussia and providing the Guard of Honour when General Montgomery met his Russian opposite number, General Rokossovsky.

After the war the regiment was deployed in numerous trouble spots around the world including Palestine, Egypt, Cyprus, Borneo and Northern Ireland. In 1948 the 1st and 2nd battalions were merged into one as a result of government troop reductions. In 1958 they became 1st battalion, Green Jackets Brigade. In 1966 this Brigade was transformed into the Green Jackets Regiment with the Ox and Bucks becoming the 1st battalion. In 1992 this battalion was disbanded and amalgamated with the 2nd battalion to form a new 1st battalion, with the 3rd battalion becoming the 2nd battalion.

MUSEUMS: Museum of the Oxfordshire and Buckinghamshire Light Infantry, Slade Park, Headington, Oxford OX3 7JL Tel 01865 780128
The Rifles Museum, Peninsula Barracks, Romsey Road, Winchester SO 23 8TS Tel 01962 828549

THE KING'S ROYAL RIFLE CORPS (60TH)

'The Americans'

Dates	1756 –1958 VCs 23
Motto	*Celer et Audax,* Swift and Bold.
Alumni	Henry Bouquet, Swiss tactician and first battalion commander, John Christie, opera impresario, Anthony Eden, prime minister, Bill Deedes, journalist, General William Gott, killed before taking up post as commander of the Eighth Army, John Standing, actor, Nigel Patrick, actor, Major Monte Radlovic, Yugoslav patriot, journalist and businessman.
Anniversaries	25 December, Regimental birthday
Battle Honours	Quebec, West Indies, Vimeiro, Talavera, Fuentes de Onoro, Salamanca, Vitoria, Toulouse, Peking, Delhi, Afghanistan , South Africa 1899-1902, Mons, Somme, Messines, Calais 1940, Greece, Tobruk 1941, El Alamein 1942, Italy 1943-4.

Originally the 62nd Royal American Regiment of Foot was raised from settlers in America by the Earl of Loudoun in 1756. This was in response to the debacle earlier in the year when General Braddock and his red coats had been ambushed by the French and their Native American allies on their way to Fort Duquesne. Braddock's dying words, *'We shall learn better how to do it next time,'* indicated his realisation, too late, of the need for camouflage and a different tactical approach. Since much of the recruitment was from German settlers a special Act had to be passed through Parliament to allow commissions for foreigners. The regiment even recruited in Europe and Germany. They could easily have become known as 'the Germans.' It was at this time that Henry Bouquet, a Swiss officer, and fellow countryman Frederik Haldemand, were recruited. They soon became commanders of the 1st and 2nd battalions of the regiment.

Officer's silver pouch-belt plate, bearing the battle honour 'Martinique' and those for the Peninsular War.

The French Swiss Henri Bouquet.

The idea of a rifle regiment is speed into action and individuality in battle. In the eighteenth century this was contrary to the norm of harshly disciplined soldiers advancing en masse. It was largely based on Bouquet's ideas about fighting the Native Americans in wooded country.

After two years they became the 60th (Royal American) Regiment when two more senior regiments were disbanded. They fought in the Seven Years War against the French at Louisburg in 1758 and at Quebec in 1759 under General Wolfe where they earned their motto *Celer et Audax* – Swift and Bold. This was followed by Pontiac's Native American rebellion against the British, which resulted in the decisive victory at Bushey Run in 1763 where Bouquet's men fought for two successive days in desperate straits but eventually drove off their attackers. At the same time other battalions were in action in the capture of Havana and Martinique in the West Indies.

The Baker Rifle

Ezekiel Baker, a London gunsmith, designed a new rifle that aimed to fulfil military rather than hunting requirements. The British rifle had similar accuracy as the German rifle, but greatly reduced the rate of fouling allowing more shots between cleaning. A well-trained rifleman could fire it at a rate of approximately one shot per minute. For this reason the rifles were far more suited for skirmishers than line troops, as accuracy, not rate of fire, was the key to light infantry tactics, and riflemen had to be deadly proficient at their task. Along with their brother rifle regiments, the 'Americans' were of course the first to use rifles as opposed to muskets.

Two battalions fought in the American War of Independence and, operating in Georgia as mounted infantry, met with some success, capturing the Carolina Regiment's Colours. They were not present at the humiliation of Yorktown and after hostilities ended they withdrew to Canada.

In 1797 the 60th became the first British Army unit to wear the familiar dark green uniform and carry the Baker rifle. This was with the formation of the regiment's 5th battalion under the aegis of Baron Francis de Rottenburg, who wrote a book on the subject, which became the basis of Sir John Moore's plans. This battalion, and the 6th battalion which was formed soon after, fought through the Napoleonic Wars.

They performed with distinction throughout the Peninsular War under Sir Arthur Wellesley, landing with him in Portugal in 1808, always fighting in the vanguard in pivotal battles such as Ciudad Rodrigo, Salamanca and Vitoria, often alongside their future comrades in arms, the 43rd, the 52nd and the 95th. During this campaign they won 16 battle honours.

After the Napoleonic Wars the 60th Americans were re-named the Duke of York's Own Rifle Corps in 1824 and, in 1830, on the accession of King William III, the King's Royal Rifle Corps, the KRRC. The regiment was stationed in India, fighting in the Sikh Wars, China, Egypt and South Africa during the reign of Queen Victoria.

In 1857 they were stationed in Meerut when the Indian Mutiny broke out. Having narrowly escaped a plot to massacre them as they attended church, they were in the vanguard of the attack on Delhi fighting alongside the Sirmoor Gurkhas in recapturing the Kashmir Gate and the Royal Palace. During this campaign they won seven VCs. Following the Mutiny, they formed an Elephant Corps to enforce the peace after the uprising, maintaining the tradition of innovation within the regiment in unmissable style.

In the Boer War of 1899-1902 needing to cover large distances they proved successful, often operating as mounted infantry to increase their speed to points of contact with the enemy. They fought during the first action of the war at the Battle of Talana Hill where they took a number of casualties, alongside the Dublin Fusiliers and the Irish Fusiliers, and lost their commanding officer, Colonel Gunning, attempting to capture a Boer defensive position.

A sergeant of the King's Royal Rifle Corps, South Africa, 1881. (Tim Reese)

The regiment supplied 22 battalions during the carnage of the First World War, winning eight VCs at a price of nearly 13,000 killed in action. Among many stories the following stands out. Arnold Jackson won the Gold medal in the 1,500 metres at the 1912 Olympic Games in Stockholm. His Olympic record breaking feat formed part of what many considered to be the greatest race ever run. During the First World War, having risen from the rank of 2nd Lieutenant to become the youngest Brigadier-General in the British Army, he also became the most highly decorated officer of the war winning the DSO and three Bars and being mentioned in dispatches a further six times. He was wounded three times and left lame at the end of the war so was unable to continue his athletic career.

A fashionably dressed officer of the 60th, (the one on the right), 1810.

Machine-gun
detachment, 3rd
Battalion, *c*.1895.

In 1926 the regiment was one of the first units to become mechanised infantry in accordance with their traditions of speed into action. The regiment raised six battalions during the Second World War. In 1940 two battalions suffered badly in France with the British Expeditionary Force, losing almost half their number they made a heroic fighting retreat to Dunkirk. As part of the 7th Armoured Division the 1st battalion took part in the spectacular successes against the Italian army in Libya during the early part of the North African campaign. Battalions of the regiment were later in action in Sicily and Italy, then in Normandy and North West Europe fighting with the 8th Armoured Brigade, liberating Lille and ending the war inside the borders of Germany. It is interesting to note that the 'American' connection was kept alive during this difficult time for Britain with the joining up of sixteen United States citizens as volunteers into the regiment

Three Generations of the VC

Lieutenant Frederick Roberts of the KRRC won the VC at the Battle of Colenso on 15 December 1899 when as one of a group of four men he rescued two abandoned horse-drawn guns that were under enemy fire. He was mortally wounded and died two days after the incident but was awarded the highest prize for bravery under fire. His father, Field Marshal Roberts, had won the VC during the Indian Mutiny. He was one of the commanders during the South African War and was devastated when brought news of his only son's death. There have only been three occasions when a father and son have both won the VC and, extraordinarily, another of Robert's heroic party at Colenso was Captain Walter Congreve, who also was awarded the VC that day and whose son also won the bronze medal 'For Valour' during the First World War.

In 1958 the KRRC became the 2nd Battalion of the Green Jackets Brigade, which in 1966 transformed into the Royal Green Jackets Regiment with three battalions, the Oxfordshire and Buckinghamshire Light Infantry (43rd and 52nd), the King's Royal Rifle Corps (60th) and the Rifle Brigade (95th). In 1992 this regiment was reduced to two battalions, the 2nd battalion becoming the 1st battalion. In 2007 they amalgamated with a number of other Light Infantry regiments to form the Rifles Regiment.

MUSEUM: The Rifles Museum, Peninsula Barracks, Romsey Road, Winchester SO 23 8TS Tel 01962 828549

Above, from left
Private and officer, 60th Regiment, 1801. Illustration by P.W. Reynolds.

H.R.H. Frederick Duke of York, KG, Colonel-in-Chief, 1797–1827. Illustration by P.W. Reynolds.

THE RIFLE BRIGADE
(PRINCE CONSORT'S OWN)
(95TH)

'The Rifles'; 'The Grasshoppers'

Dates	1800-1958 VCs 27
Motto	*Audax et Celer,* Bold and Swift.
Alumni	Quintin Hogg, Lord Hailsham, politician, Sir Harry Smith, chronicler of the Peninsular War and General in India, Boyd Alexander, explorer, Sir Alec Coryton, Air Chief Marshal, Percy Creed, author and businessman, Tony Rolt, Le Mans winner, Field Marshal Sir Henry Wilson, assassinated by the IRA, Richard Sharpe, fictional hero.
Anniversaries	18 June, Waterloo
Battle Honours	Copenhagen, 1801, Montevideo 1807, Vimeiro, Badajoz, Salamanca, Vitoria, Waterloo, Alma, Balaclava, Sevastopol, Indian Mutiny, South Africa 1900-2, Ypres, Mons, Somme, Hindenburg Line, Calais, Tobruk, El Alamein, North West Europe 1940, 1944-5.

In 1800 the British, following other European armies such as the French with their *voltigeurs*, formed a special unit, handpicked from other regiments, of infantry for skirmishing and reconnaissance in front of the main army – the key factors being speed of foot, accurate shooting and individual initiative. Buglers rather than drummers were to be used for communication and Colours were not to be carried. The unit was named the Experimental Corps of Riflemen in 1802 and officially numbered as the 95th Regiment of Foot, dressed in dark green with black facings and armed with the Baker rifle. The regiment's first commanding officer was Colonel Coote Manningham, who firmly believed in the potential of these new infantry tactics gleaned from the

60th in America. They, along with other senior officers such as Sir John Moore, realised the value of intelligent, individual infantrymen working as a unit. This notion had grown out of the experience of the British Army during the American War where the massed advances of red-coated infantry had not always worked in country where cover and cunning had been used by the enemy to great effect. Within its first year of existence the regiment made an ambitious but only partially successful assault on Ferrol in Spain and was gazetted under the title of the Rifle Corps.

In 1801 units of the regiment served as marksmen on warships under the command of Vice Admiral Nelson at the Battle of Copenhagen. This action gave the regiment the unique distinction of wearing a naval crown on their cap badge and carrying the battle honour of Copenhagen, one of Nelson's triumvirate of great victories. Shortly after this they were transferred to Shorncliffe in Kent where they underwent Light Infantry training alongside the 42nd and 53rd, later the Oxfordshire and Buckinghamshire Light Infantry, under the watchful eyes of Manningham and Sir John Moore.

In 1807 the 95th, as they now were, posted under General Auchmuty to South America where they took part in the capture of Montevideo and numerous successful actions against the Spanish allies of the French. They were then caught up in the disastrous attack on Buenos Aires under the command of Lieutenant General Whitelocke, which resulted in the British surrender and Whitelocke himself being drummed out of the army.

Colonel Coote Manningham.

Sir John Moore

'Moore's contribution to the British Army was not only that matchless Light Infantry who have ever since enshrined his training, but also the belief that the perfect soldier can only be made by evoking all that is finest in man - physical, mental and spiritual.'

Sir Arthur Bryant

The regimental Copenhagen medal.

The 95th landed with the army of Sir Arthur Wellesley in Portugal in 1808 and on August 15 fired the first shots of the Peninsular War near Obidos during a skirmish with the French. In the same incident Lieutenant Ralph Bunbury was the first British officer to be killed in the campaign. Two days later the regiment, as part of the 6th Division, fighting alongside the 60th, played a significant role in the Battle of Roliça. The regiment were soon to play a major part in the Peninsular War making an effective fighting retreat with Sir John Moore's outnumbered army to Corunna. Here they formed, alongside the 43nd and 52nd, the Light Brigade, which was to build up such a formidable reputation in the following years.

Returning to the Iberian Peninsula under Sir Arthur Wellesley in 1810, they fought with his army for the following four seasons gaining sixteen such truly legendary battle honours as Vimeiro, Ciudad Rodrigo, Fuentes de Onoro, Salamanca, and Vitoria before crossing the Pyrenees into Southern France in 1813. At the Battle of Nivelle on 10 November 10th, the 95th, again fighting alongside the 43rd and 52nd as the Light Division, stormed the French defences defeating a whole French Division and inflicting nearly two hundred and fifty casualties at the price of their commanding officer, Captain Daniel Cadoux and thirteen other men of the regiment.

Sniper Plunket

During the Retreat to Corunna in 1808, Rifleman Thomas Plunket shot the French General Colbert from a distance of something between 200 and (a frankly unbelievable) 600 yards. Plunket then moved position and proceeded to hit a French sergeant who had gone to the General's help, proving the first shot was not a fluke. This marksmanship with the newly introduced Baker rifle must have been staggering to those accustomed to the Brown Bess muskets used by the rest of the infantry, which had an effective range of little more than 50 yards.

Three battalions of the Rifle Brigade fought at the Battle of Waterloo, one holding the farm of La Haie Sante for the whole day against relentless French attacks, while the other two battalions brigaded with the 52nd to make the final destructive charge on the Garde Imperiale. A year later, in 1816, in honour of the three battalions who had fought at Waterloo, the regiment was taken out of the numbered list of foot regiments and renamed the Rifle Brigade.

The regiment sent two battalions to the Crimean War where they fought at the Battles of Alma and Inkerman and at the Siege of Sevastopol winning eight of the newly instigated medals for valour, the Victoria Cross. This number was more than any other regiment on this campaign. During the Indian Mutiny during 1857 they won a further four VCs.

Shortly after the death of Prince Albert in 1861, the Brigade was named after their former Colonel in Chief as the Prince Consort's Own Rifle Brigade.

Father and Son

On 15 December 1899 Captain Walter Congreve (pictured) of the Rifle Brigade was one of four men who made a spectacularly heroic attempt to rescue four artillery pieces that had been abandoned by their crews under enemy fire during the Battle of Colenso during the Boer War in South Africa. They managed to hitch up and rescue two of the guns. Then, though already wounded, Congreve with one colleague again braved the hail of enemy fire and dragged the mortally wounded Lieutenant Freddie Roberts to safety. For his remarkable valour he was awarded the VC. Sixteen years later, on 20 July 1916 his son, Major Billie Congreve, also in the Rifle Brigade, was killed fighting on the Somme during the First World War. For the two weeks leading up to his death he had constantly tended to the wounded in the face of enemy fire and had guided his men into position in the front line. For his courage in the face of the enemy with no regard for his own safety, only for that of his men, he also was awarded the VC. Despite this tragedy, Walter Congreve, now a senior officer in the Army, continued to serve on the Western Front, losing a hand after being severely wounded and rising to the rank of General before becoming the Governor of Malta where, at his own request, he was buried at sea in 1927. (See also King's Royal Rifles.)

During the First World War the Rifle Brigade formed more than twenty battalions and lost eleven and a half thousand men, winning ten VCs as well as nearly two thousand other medals for gallantry.

In the Second World War the regiment was part of the British Expeditionary Force sent to France early in 1940, making a heroic defence of Calais which did much to divert German forces encircling Dunkirk, thereby ensuring the escape of a large part of the Expeditionary Force. Battalions of the Rifle Brigade fought with outstanding success against the Italians in the Western Desert and at the Battles of Adam El Halfa and El Alamein. The regiment played a major role in turning back the German counter-attacks with deadly use of their anti-tank weapons.

Above, from left
Napoleon's *Voltigeurs*, skirmishers trained in marksmanship, were defined as units within each battalion in 1804. They were in part the inspiration for the British Rifle regiments.

November 1914, France.

Two battalions of the Rifle Brigade fought with the Eighth Army across North Africa to Tunisia, then to Sicily and through the Italian campaign. The 1st battalion was later withdrawn from Italy and, with other battalions, took part in the post D-Day sweep across North West Europe into Germany in the spring of 1945.

The 1st battalion of the Rifle Brigade, which traced its roots directly back to the formidable 95th, became the 3rd battalion, the Green Jackets Brigade in 1958 and in 1966 this became the Royal Green Jackets Regiment. In 1992 the 1st battalion was disbanded and now the descendants of the 2nd battalion have become the 4th battalion of the 2007 regiment, The Rifles.

Incident at Snipe Ridge

On 27 October 1942 during the Battle of El Alamein, Lieutenant Colonel V.B. Turner was commanding a battalion which came under heavy counter-attack from tanks – about ninety. The battalion knocked out more than fifty enemy tanks and at one point in the battle Turner, though wounded, worked as a gun loader for two other members of the regiment who, with the last remaining artillery piece, a 6-pounder, knocked out another five enemy tanks. For his gallantry in the face of the enemy during the sixteen-hour battle Turner was awarded the VC. His elder brother, 2nd Lieutenant A.B. Turner, had won the VC serving with the Royal Berkshire Regiment on the Western Front on 28 September 1915.

MUSEUM: The Rifles Museum, Peninsula Barracks, Romsey Road, Winchester SO23 8TS Tel 01962 828549

ROYAL GURKHA RIFLES

'Non-stop Gurkhas' (4th battalion 1943, The Times*); (Though no one seems to have risked appending a general nickname, for fear of offence)*

Dates	1815 to present	VCs 26
Motto	*Kaphar hunnu bhanda marnu ramro,* Better to Die than Live a Coward.	
Alumni	John Nott, politician, Gordon Corrigan, military historian, Field Marshal Sir John Chapple, former CGS, Field Marshal Lord Bramall, former CGS, Brigadier E.D. 'Birdie' Smith, author of *Valour: A History of the Gurkhas.*	
Anniversaries	1 March, Meiktila, 16 April, Medicina, 7 August, Gallipoli, 14 September, Delhi Day.	
Battle honours	Bhurtpore, Sobraon, Delhi, Kabul, Kandahar, Loos, Mesopotamia, Gallipoli, Kut al Amara, El Alamein, Tunis, Monte Cassino, Slim River, Malaya, Arakan, Chindits, Burma.	

The Gorkha people trace their name from the Guru Gorakhnath, an 8th-century Hindu warrior and priest.. If you had to choose a regiment to fight for your life this might well be it. The Gurkhas' ferocity is legendary. Their war cry has put the fear of god into many enemies of the British Army, *'Glory be to the Goddess of War! Here come the Gorkhas! Ayo Gurkha!'* Many flee before the Gurkhas even come into sight.

As the East India Company expanded in India during the early part of the 19th century they came up against the fearsome King Prithwi Narayan Shah from Gorkha who controlled most of what is now Nepal. War was declared, which continued from 1814 for two years. During this time a mutual respect for the two nations' fighting qualities grew up, which continues to this day. In the peace treaty signed at Sugauli it was agreed that Gurkhas could volunteer in the East India Company's Army. They fought in the 3rd Anglo-Maratha War a year later, the first of a long list of conflicts through a period nearing 200 years where they would display their loyalty, courage and steadfastness alongside the British. They were to win their first battle honour at Bhurtpore in 1826.

The Truncheon presented by Queen Victoria to the 2nd Gurkha Rifles in 1863 in recognition of valiant service during the Indian Mutiny.

A Gurkha officer and
Sepoys of the Sabarho
Battalion in 1834.

They fought valiantly in the 1st and 2nd Sikh Wars of 1846 and 1848, during the Indian Mutiny and on the North West Frontier on a number of occasions. During the Mutiny in 1857 the Sirmoor battalion held the stronghold of Hindu Rao's house, alongside the 60th Rifles, for three months against continual and determined enemy attacks. They had casualties of 327 out of a total number of 490. General Tucker later wrote, *'If the Main Picquet had fallen, India would have fallen.'* The 60th Rifles were so impressed by their fighting qualities that they insisted they should wear their distinctive dark green uniforms, call their men 'riflemen' and adopt their customs and traditions, which they do to this day. Queen Victoria honoured them with a third honorary colour but, as it was inappropriate for a rifle regiment to carry colours, The Queen's Truncheon was designed and is carried to this day. It has precedence over all other units' colours.

At the outbreak of the First World War one hundred thousand Gurkhas joined regiments of the Gurkha Brigade. They fought and died in France and Flanders, Mesopotamia, Persia, Egypt, Gallipoli, Palestine and Salonika. A battalion of the 8th Gurkhas greatly distinguished itself at Loos, fighting to the last, and in the words of the Indian Corps Commander, *'found its Valhalla'*. The 6th Gurkhas gained immortal fame at Gallipoli during the capture from the Turks of the feature later known as 'Gurkha Bluff'. At Sari Bair they were the only troops in the whole campaign to reach and hold the crest line and look down on the Straits, which was the ultimate objective.

Slim

'I first met the 6th Gurkha Rifles in 1915 in Gallipoli. There I was so struck by their bearing in one of the most desperate battles in history that I resolved, should the opportunity come, to try to serve with them. Four years later it came, and I spent many of the happiest, and from a military point of view the most valuable, years of my life in the Regiment.'
Field Marshal Sir William Slim.

There was little respite after the First World War, with fighting in the Third Afghan War in 1919 followed by numerous campaigns on the North-West Frontier, particularly in Waziristan.

In the Second World War there were forty Gurkha battalions in British service totalling some 112,000 men. Gurkha regiments fought in Syria, the Western Desert, Italy and Greece, from North Malaya to Singapore and from the Siamese border back through Burma to Imphal and then forward again to Rangoon.

After the fall of France in 1940, when Britain stood alone, permission was sought to recruit an additional 20 battalions for the Gurkha Brigade. This was granted by the Nepalese Prime Minister who said, *'Does a friend desert a friend in time of need? If you win, we win with you. If you lose, we lose with you.'*

The Nusseree Battalion, c. 1857 (which would become the 1st Gurkha Rifles).

Gurkha patrol in Afghanistan, 2006.

A Stolen VC

Lance Corporal Rambahadur Limbu was a 26-year-old member of the 2nd Battalion 10th Princess Mary's Own Gurkha Rifles, British Army, during the Indonesian Confrontation when, on 21st November 1965 in Sarawak, Borneo, he was in an advance party of 16 men who encountered about thirty Indonesians holding a position on the top of a jungle-covered hill. The lance-corporal went forward with two men, but when they were only ten yards from the enemy machine-gun position, the sentry opened fire on them, whereupon Limbu rushed forward and killed him with a grenade. The remaining enemy then opened fire on the small party, wounding the two men with the lance-corporal who, under heavy fire, made three journeys into the open, two to drag his comrades to safety and one to retrieve their automatic weapon, with which he charged down and killed many of the enemy. For his actions while under fire he was awarded the Victoria Cross. His original medal was stolen, along with all his other possessions, while he was on a train journey in India to his native Nepal in 1967. It has never been found. Fortunately he was issued with a replacement. The painting of the action is by Terence Cuneo.

In the two World Wars the Gurkha Brigade had suffered 43,000 casualties. After Indian Independence in 1947, four Gurkha Regiments joined the British Army. They were the 2nd King Edward VII's Own Gurkha Rifles (The Sirmoor Rifles), 6th Queen Elizabeth's Own Gurkha Rifles, 7th Duke of Edinburgh's Own Gurkha Rifles, and 10th Princess Mary's Own Gurkha Rifles. The six remaining regiments, 1st, 3rd, 4th, 5th, 8th and 9th remained in the Indian Army. This was known as 'The Opt' and many British and Gurkhas simply crossed over to the barracks of the regiment of their choice.

Bravest of the Brave

'As I write these words, my thoughts return to you who were my comrades, the stubborn and indomitable peasants of Nepal. Once more I hear the laughter with which you greeted every hardship. Once more I see you in your bivouacs or about your camp fires, on forced marches or in the trenches, now shivering with wet and cold, now scorched by a pitiless and burning sun. Uncomplaining you endure hunger and thirst and wounds; and at the last your unwavering lines disappear into the smoke and wrath of battle. Bravest of the brave, most generous of the generous, never had a country more faithful friends than you.'

Sir Ralph Turner MC, 2nd battalion, 3rd Queen Alexandra's Own Gurkha Rifles

Crest of 6th Queen Elizabeth's Own Gurkha Rifles.

After 1945 the Brigade of Gurkhas operated throughout the Malayan Emergency, for twelve years, 1948 to 1960 and from December 1962 when the 1st Battalion, 2nd KEO Gurkha Rifles arrived within 12 hours in Brunei, in the Indonesian confrontation.

By 1972 the Brigade of Gurkhas had been reduced from 14,000 to about 8,000 men. In 1994 the four Gurkha regiments were disbanded and were reformed into one large Regiment, the Royal Gurkha Rifles (RGR), which initially consisted of three battalions but was reduced to two battalions in November 1996. There are also Gurkha engineer, signals and transport corps.

During its nearly two hundred years of service the Gurkhas have won 26 Victoria Crosses, 13 by Gurkhas and 13 by British officers. This simple fact exemplifies the mutual respect that the British and Gurkhas have for each other. When young officers join the Gurkhas they have to learn Gurkhali, the Gurkha language and some go to the Hills to assist with recruiting or to pay pensions. Young officers are encouraged to go trekking in the Himalayas, to better understand the extraordinary men they will have the honour to lead.

Crest of 7th Duke of Edinburgh's Own Gurkha Rifles.

In recent years the Gurkhas have served in the Falklands, Kosovo, Afghanistan and Iraq and their military prowess has in no way diminished. They say that the imminent attack by the Gurkhas on Port Stanley in the Falklands in 1982 brought about the immediate surrender of the Argentine forces.

MUSEUM: Gurkha Museum, Peninsula Barracks, Romsey Road, Winchester, Hampshire SO 23 8TS Tel 01962 842382

Crest of 10th Princess Mary's Own Gurkha Rifles.

Soldiers of 3 Para prepare to storm a compound during Operation *Snakebite*, Musa Qaleh, Afghanistan, August 2006.

four

THE NEW REGIMENTS

'Never forget that no military leader has ever become great without audacity. If the leader is filled with high ambition and if he pursues his aims with audacity and strength of will, he will reach them in spite of all obstacles.'

Karl von Clausewitz

'Where is the prince who can afford so to cover his country with troops for its defence, so that ten thousand men descending from the clouds might not, in many places, do an infinite deal of mischief before a force could be brought together to repel them?'

Benjamin Franklin

ROYAL TANK REGIMENT

'Tankies', 'Cav', 'Chavalry'

Dates	1917 to present	VCs 6
Motto	'Fear Naught', 'From mud, through blood, to the green fields beyond.'	
Alumni	Chris Bonnington, mountaineer, Keith Floyd, chef, John Le Mesurier, actor, Basil Liddell Hart, military strategist and author, Jack Hargreaves, broadcaster, Field Marshal Lord Carver, J.K. Stanford, writer, Marcus Cunliffe, academic, Thomas Armour, professional golfer.	
Anniversaries	20 November, Cambrai.	
Battle Honours	Cambrai 1917, Arras 1940, Tobruk 1941, El Alamein, Salerno, Anzio, Normandy, Caen, Falaise, Rhine, Burma, Korea, Iraq.	

The Queen sits for an official photograph with the Royal Tank Regiment after presenting them with their new Standards at Buckingham Palace, 25 June 2008.

The name 'tank' comes from 'water tank', since the code word used by Intelligence during the development of this revolutionary vehicle was 'water carrier'. Despite a difficult birth, the tank has now become the most decisive weapon on the battlefield replacing the centuries-old idea of the cavalry charge breaking through defensive lines swiftly and decisively. The concept of an armoured vehicle that could operate with impunity against the devastating effect of the machine gun was the brainchild of General Ernest Swinton who had originally conceived the idea during the Boer War along with South African engineer Hugh Merriot, who had seen the potential of armoured tractors. William Tritton, a designer of agricultural tractors with caterpillar tracks and engineer Walter Wilson are credited with the invention of the tank under the aegis of the Landships Committee set up by Winston Churchill while he was First Lord of the Admiralty. The naval connection with

the tank is evident with the names of tank parts such as hull, deck, bow and hatches. Swinton was made responsible for the training of the original tank units.

British tanks were first used in battle on 15 September 1916 when they attacked German positions during the Battle of the Somme. A newspaper at the time reported, *'A tank is walking down the main street of Flers with the British Army cheering behind it.'* They were slow and unreliable vehicles with just 32 making it to the start line and only 21 actually going into combat. But it was the beginning of armoured warfare.

They were initially manned by men of the Machine Gun Corps, known as the Heavy Section. In July 1917 they were officially named the Tank Corps. They were commanded by the dynamic Brigadier Hugh Elles who, in his own tank called *'Hilda'*, personally led three hundred and fifty tanks of the regiment at the Battle of Cambrai on 20 November 1917 with great success, breaking through the hitherto impregnable Hindenburg Line and nearly taking the town of Cambrai. Eight thousand prisoners were taken and more than one hundred artillery pieces captured. When news of this innovative and revolutionary method of battle reached England the church bells rang out.

The Pennant

The regimental pennant of the Royal Tank Regiment has horizontal stripes of brown, red and green signifying mud, blood and green grass. It is their unofficial motto. The story goes that just before the battle of Cambrai in 1917 the tank commander personally went out and bought material of different colour silk to make a distinctive pennant to mark his tank. Only three colours were available, brown, red and green, so he took them and had them sewn together in horizontal strips with the green uppermost. It was Colonel John Fuller of the Tank Corps who later added the words.

In April 1918 the first ever tank battle took place when a German tank took on three British tanks and was knocked out by one commanded by Lieutenant Frank Mitchell. During the First World War four members of the regiment were awarded the VC. On 29 August 1918 at Fremicourt in France Lt. C. H. Sewell was leading a group of light Whippet tanks into an attack on the enemy, one of his tanks overturned in a shell hole and the crew became trapped while the tank caught fire. With no regard for his own safety, in the face of shell and machine gun fire, Sewell went to the aid of his comrades, forcing open the jammed door and releasing them. He then saw that one of his own men was wounded and returned across the open ground, being hit in the process. Despite his wounds he tended the wounded man and was fatally wounded by hostile fire a few moments later.

In 1923 the regiment became the Royal Tank Corps and started to wear the black beret, then, in 1939, the Royal Tank Regiment. Field Marshal Bernard Montgomery often wore the distinctive black beret of the Royal Tank Regiment. It is said that the black beret came about when General Elles was discussing headwear with Colonel

Fuller early in 1918. It was decided that peaked caps of any sort would not be practical inside a tank, particularly when trying to look through the viewing positions. Elles was positioned near some French 70th Chasseurs Alpins who wore berets. He tried one on and so it was decided to go for this Gallic form of headwear. The black was chosen since it would not show oil stains. This was made official in 1924 when it was given royal approval by King George V.

At the end of the First World War, with the Russian Civil War still in progress, a detachment of tanks were sent to support the White Russian Army and was involved in the capture of Tsaritsin, later Stalingrad, now Volgograd.

By the outbreak of the war in 1939, there were eight battalions of the Royal Tank Regiment and units of the regiment had been responsible for the training of the cavalry regiments as they were inexorably converted to armoured units. Old fashioned as it may sound, there were strong feelings about this at the time and a number of cavalry officers resigned in protest rather than give up their horses in favour of metal machines. Technology won out over horse power and both Winston Churchill and Montgomery, vigorously endorsed the growth of armoured units, as indeed did their opponents in the German *Wehrmacht,* who pioneered the concept of *Blitzkrieg* or *Lightning War* with their Panzer units. If the First World War had seen the tank as a revolutionary new weapon, the Second World War confirmed it critical importance as a battlefield weapon, alongside air power, which would win or lose future wars. This has remained so since 1940.

The Royal Tank Regiment's first engagement of the Second World War was against General Erwin Rommel's 7th Panzer Division in the Battle of Arras in northern France on 21 May 1940. The 4th and 7th Royal Tank Regiment supported by two battalions of the Durham Light Infantry blunted the German advance driving them back with considerable success before being overwhelmed by sheer weight of numbers. The subsequent German delay was one of the factors that allowed the British Expeditionary Force those extra hours to embark from the beaches of Dunkirk.

Below, from left
Royal Tank Corps in action with an officer using a probing stick. This looks like a Mk I or Big Willie, later known as 'Mother'.

A Grant tank of Eighth Army advancing after the Alamein breakthrough, 1942.

The regiment then saw action against the Italians in North Africa and at El Alamein in 1942 where many were involved in anti-mine operations in the Scorpion tank. Units of the Royal Tank Regiment formed part of the British 1st Army in Operation Torch under the general command of General Dwight Eisenhower, which landed in Algeria and advanced into Tunisia at the end of 1942. In their Churchill tanks the regiment gave a good account of themselves against the formidable tanks of the Afrika Korps.

In 1944 General Percy Hobart commanded the 79th Armoured Division, made up largely of Royal Tank Regiment battalions, in the landings on D-Day. They were equipped with a number of specifically designed armoured vehicles for use in river or canal crossings, mine clearing and a variety of other battlefield tasks, including the 'Funnies', which were specially modified amphibious tanks. The division played a major role in the taking of Le Havre and the breakout from Normandy to the Belgian border in the autumn of 1944. They finally crossed the Rhine into Germany in March 1945 having been at the sharp end of Allied operations throughout the War.

At the end of the War there were twenty-four regiments within the Royal Tank Regiment. This was soon reduced to the eight that had existed before the outbreak of hostilities and has been further reduced in the ensuing years.

The original members of the Tank Corps were described as men *who cheerfully went to war in tin cans, closely surrounded by a lethal mixture of petrol and ammunition'*. Though technology has changed and improved in the ensuing years, this truth is still essentially the same and it is highly trained and brave men who take the Royal Tank Regiment into battle. Ash plant sticks are still carried by officers on parade to commemorate the First World War when officers would walk in front of the tanks probing the ground to see if the mud was too deep for the machines. Methods of operation may have changed but the ethos remains the same.

MUSEUM: The Tank Museum, Bovington, Dorset BH20 6JG Tel 01929 405096

Above, from left
One of the many variants of the highly adaptable Churchill tank shown at Juno Beach, serving with an Assault Engineer unit, Normandy 1944.

Tank crews mounting before an advance against enemy positions in Tunisia, March 1943.

PARACHUTE REGIMENT

'The Red Devils'

Dates	1941 to present VCs 5
Motto	*Utrinque Paratus*, Ready for Anything.
Alumni	Richard Todd, actor, Innes Ireland, motor racing driver, John Ridgeway, sailor, Tim Healy, actor, Frank Carson, comedian, Oliver Reed, actor and roisterer, Ian McKay VC, soldier, Milos Stankovic, Yugoslav patriot, Johnny Johnson, D-Day commander of 12th Parachute battalion, Dick Rubinstein, SOE operative in France and Far East
Anniversaries	6 June, D-Day, 17 September, Arnhem.
Battle Honours	Normandy Landings, Arnhem, Rhine, North Africa 1942-3, Sicily, Falkland Islands, Basra.

The 'Paras' is one of the élite regiments of the British Army, by virtue of the tough selection process and rigorous training. Its traditions are of fighting in difficult conditions, often against a numerically superior enemy; so aggression is their watchword, attack being the best form of defence. Their battle record is fearsome.

Some say the colour of their beret, which incidentally, has been taken up by many airborne troops around the world, was chosen by the novelist Daphne du Maurier, the wife of General Robert 'Boy' Browning, commander of the Parachute Regiment during the Second World War. It is known as the red beret but in army circles as the cherry beret.

Paratroopers were first used in warfare by the Germans in the invasion of Norway in April 1940. The British Army tried their hand for the first time, very much encouraged by Winston Churchill, in November 1940, when 50 men jumped out of four Whitley bombers that had been adapted for paratroopers by the removal of the aft gun turrets.

The first British use of paratroopers in combat was on 10 February 10 1941 when 37 men from 2 Commando, under the leadership of Major T.A.G. Pritchard, were

Above, from left
Memorial at Goose Green to the men of the 2nd Battalion's Battle Group who were killed in the first action of the Falklands War.

A Pathfinder comes into land.

dropped at night into southern Italy to blow up a water aqueduct. The mission, known as Operation Colossus, was initially successful but within hours the escaping men were rounded up and imprisoned. Their interpreter was an Italian waiter from the Savoy Hotel in London. He was tried and executed; an unsung hero.

As a result of this raid, the 1st Parachute Brigade was formed. Almost exactly a year later, on 27 February 1942, Major John Frost led 116 men of the Parachute Regiment in a successful raid known as Operation Biting on a German radar installation in northern France, with relatively low casualties despite a dangerous and difficult exfiltration. In July 1943 the Parachute Regiment took part in Operation Husky which was an airborne attack during the invasion of Sicily in concert with American airborne troops.

On D-Day, June 6 1944, the Parachute Regiment operated on the flank of the British landing beaches Juno, Sword and Gold. They effectively put the German defensive guns out of action. On August 15th they also made a drop into Southern France at the start of Operation Dragoon opening the way for the unopposed landings of the American Seventh Army.

The most famous of airborne operations was the attack on Arnhem in Holland, entitled Operation Market Garden, which took place in September 1944 as the Allied armies advanced across the Low Countries. A daring plan to speed up the advance

Above, from left
Lt Col John Frost,
Commanding Officer
of 2Para during
Operation Market
Garden.

Major Frost, right, who
led the Bruneval raid,
briefs a colleague, 1942.

towards Germany was decided upon; to drop 35,000 airborne troops 100 miles ahead of the advancing Allied armies, well behind the German lines, to open up the road for their armoured columns. British, American and Polish paratroopers took part in what was initially a successful landing. But intelligence had not seen that there were two German Panzer divisions secreted in the woods around the Dutch town of Arnhem and the British and Poles found themselves up against three times the opposition they had anticipated. Heroically they held out for a week, when they had been told that they would be relieved after a few hours. The British paratroopers fought virtually to the last man. When a small group were forced to surrender, a German officer said, *'I fought at Stalingrad on the Eastern Front but I have never fought against such good street fighters as you. Where did you learn this?'* The British officer replied *'It was our first time! But we'll try to do better next time.'* After the battle, Montgomery said, *'So long as we have officers and men who will do as you have done, then indeed we can look forward with complete confidence to the future. In years to come it will be a great thing for a man to be able to say "I fought at Arnhem."'* Too many paratroopers would not get the chance.

Operation Varsity was the last and biggest of the Allied Second World War airborne actions. It took place at the end of March 1945 to secure the bridgeheads over the Rhine into Germany itself and was a complete success. The Parachute Regiment dropped alongside Canadian and American airborne units as part of the 6th Airborne Division a force of about 8,000 men, made up of battalions of 750. Losses were substantial but the objectives were achieved.

MIA, VC

Twenty-four-year old Captain Lionel Queripel won the VC at the Battle of Arnhem on September 19th 1944. He was leading a company of paratroopers that came under heavy machine gun and anti-tank fire from a German strongpoint. He carried a wounded sergeant to a medical post and was wounded in the face. He then led his men into the attack and suppressed the machine guns and captured the anti-tank gun. Later in the battle he held out against heavy German attacks, though wounded in both arms, with grenades and small arms fire. Finally realising his position was no longer tenable, he ordered his men to withdraw and he covered them. He was not seen again and it was only after the war was it confirmed that he had been killed fighting to the last.

Between 1971 and 1991 the Parachute Regiment completed a number of tours in Northern Ireland, losing 40 men in the process including Sergeant Michael Willetts who was awarded the George Cross for his gallantry in saving the lives of others while sacrificing his own. On 25 May 1971 an IRA man dropped a fused bomb into a police station where Sergeant Willetts was working. Realising the immediate danger, he

The Nijmegen railway bridge taken from the north of the Waal.

The World War II grave of a British paratrooper, prepared by German soldiers at Arnhem, 1944.

cleared the room of women and children amongst others and held the door against the blast. He was killed as a result of his actions. If this had been in war, he would have been awarded the Victoria Cross.

In recent years the Paras have fought in the Falkland Islands and both Iraq and Afghanistan where they have suffered a number of casualties. Colonel H. Jones's heroic charge against the Argentines at the Battle of Goose Green on 28 May 1982, is well documented and many commentators have questioned the sense of a regimental commander leading his men into battle and exposing himself to mortal fire. This is to misunderstand the whole ethos of the Parachute Regiment, where officers and NCOs lead from the front and where impetus in attack is all important: a little like the cavalry charges of old.

More recent is the story of Corporal Bryan Budd who was awarded the VC posthumously for counter-attacking the Taliban on 20 August 2006 when his patrol came under intense fire. His commanding officer wrote, '*Bryan died doing the job he loved, leading his men from the front, where he always was. He was proud to call himself a paratrooper and we were proud to stand beside him.*' This is a regiment of true warriors.

MUSEUM: The Parachute Regiment and Airborne Forces Museum, Browning Barracks, Aldershot, Hants GU11 2BU Tel 01252 349619
Imperial War Museum Duxford, Duxford, Cambridgeshire CB22 4QR Tel 01223 835000

SPECIAL AIR SERVICE REGIMENT

'The Chicken Stranglers'

Dates	1941 to present	VCs 1
Motto	*Who Dares Wins.*	
Alumni	David Stirling, soldier, General Sir Peter de la Billière, Mike Calvert, Chindit leader, Randolph Churchill, journalist, Eric Newby, travel writer, Sir Ranulph Fiennnes, adventurer, Bear Grylls, TV presenter, Fitzroy Maclean, diplomat and adventurer, Alfred de Chastelain, Canadian soldier and entrepreneur.	
Anniversaries	22 July, Foundation Day.	
Battle Honours	North Africa 1940-3, Tobruk 1941, Benghazi 1942, Sicily 1943, Landing in Sicily 1943, Termoli 1943, Italy 1943-5, Valli di Comacchio 1945, Greece 1944-5, Adriatic 1943, Middle East 1943-4, Normandy and North West Europe 1944-5, Falkland Islands 1982, Western Iraq 1991, Western Iraq 2003.	

This is of course one of the most famous fighting units in the world, with countless books written about it, and with probably the most famous motto. There is almost an SAS media industry. An inscription at SAS HQ, Hereford, reads:

> *'We are the pilgrims, master; we shall go*
> *Always a little further; it may be*
> *Beyond that last blue mountain barred with snow*
> *Across that angry or that glimmering sea.'*

The SAS were originally founded in 1941 in North Africa to conduct operations behind enemy lines. On the British Army's expulsion from the mainland of Europe

David Stirling.

in June 1940, a number of units evolved with the purpose of striking at the enemy in small groups in covert operations. Thus the Commandos, the Parachute Regiment and the Glider Pilot Regiment evolved. In the Middle East Colonel Robert Laycock, a Commando, led a number of raids including a successful attack at Bardia on the Libyan coast. This unit was called Layforce. In June 1941 a costly attack was made on Vichy forces in Lebanon as a result of which Layforce was discontinued.

Second Lieutenant David Stirling, Scots Guards kept the concept alive when he presented the idea of the SAS to Major General Neil Ritchie in Cairo, Egypt. The idea was for small raiding groups to operate deep behind enemy lines, a concept which had originally been worked out by Lieutenant John Lewes of the Welsh Guards. Many of the recruits had been with Commando or Layforce units. 'L' Detachment, as it was called, worked in conjunction with the Long Range Desert Group, commanded by Lieutenant Colonel Guy Prendergast. The name Special Air Service was used in an effort to deceive the enemy into thinking that the Allies had more airborne troops than they did. In a speech made in 1984 when opening the new regimental barracks in Hereford, David Stirling said, *'I have always felt uneasy in being known as the founder of the regiment. I would like it to be recognised that I have five co-founders – Jock Lewes and Paddy Mayne of the original 'L' Detachment, SAS, Georges Berge, whose unit of the Free French joined the SAS in 1942, Brian Franks, who re-established 21 SAS Regiment after the SAS had been disbanded at the end of the Second World War, and John Woodhouse, who created the modern 22 SAS Regiment during the Malayan campaign.'*

The unit started with 65 officers and men called *'that band of vagabonds'*, the basic rank being Parachutist, which was changed to Trooper in 1944. The first mission in the desert, Operation Squatter, on 16-17 November 1941 went badly wrong and out of the force of 65 only 21 returned in one piece. But the regiment continued their missions and destroyed in excess of 400 enemy aircraft and miscellaneous equipment, which did much to impede the Afrika Korps. Many of the later insertions were made with the support of the Long Range Desert Group and with the newly designed Jeeps with Lewis machine guns mounted on them. In 1942, Hitler issued the infamous *Kommandobefehl* order that any Allied operatives captured while on Special Forces missions should be shot. Fortunately the 'Phantom Major' Stirling, captured in January 1943 did not suffer this fate and spent the rest of the war in prison camps, making four escape attempts before being sent to Colditz Castle until the end of the war.

It was Major 'Paddy' Blair Mayne who took over command of 1SAS. In a list of Irish heroes of the British Army he must be close to the top. An outstanding sportsman, he was a good golfer, boxer and played rugby for Ireland and the British Lions on their tour of South Africa in 1938. He played in 17 of the provincial matches and all 3 Test matches. When war broke out the qualified lawyer joined the Ulster Rifles and then 11 Commando. In June 1941 he led his men in the fateful Litani River crossing against Vichy French forces. Around a third of the unit, 130 officers and men, were killed or wounded. It was shortly after this action that he was recruited by Captain David Stirling for the SAS. During the ensuing months he took part in a number of operations deep behind enemy lines in North Africa destroying many German aircraft on the ground. When Stirling was captured in January 1943 1SAS was divided into two units, the Special Raiding Squadron and the Special Boat Squadron, which would expand to regimental status as the Special Boat Service. Mayne took command of the Raiding Squadron and operated in Italy for most of 1943. In January 1944 he was promoted to Lieutenant Colonel and took command of 1SAS leading them in numerous actions in Norway, France, Belgium, Holland and Germany. He had already won the DSO three times, the Légion d'Honneur and the Croix de Guerre when his unit was held up by enemy fire on 9 April 1945 in Oldenburg, North West Germany. They had taken a number of casualties and Mayne pro-ceeded under fire to carry the wounded into his

Inspection by the Duke of Gloucester of SAS stripping Spandau machine guns and Schmeissers in the Western Desert.

Jeep and take them to safety. Firing from the hip, he then single-handedly attacked the enemy positions putting them out of action. He was at once recommended for the Victoria Cross, which was signed for by the British commander in Chief, Field Marshal Montgomery. For some reason this recommendation was downgraded to a fourth DSO. His former commanding officer in Layforce, Major General Sir Robert Laycock, wrote to Mayne, *'You deserve more and, in my opinion, the appropriate authorities do not really know their job. If they did, they would have given you a VC.'*

Mayne ended the war as the most highly decorated Allied officer. He died in a motor accident on 14 December 1955 aged only 40 years. The lobbying for his VC continues to the present day. In 2005 a motion in the House of Commons was proposed: *'This House recognises the grave injustice meted out to Lieutenant Colonel Paddy Mayne, of 1st SAS, who won the Victoria Cross at Oldenburg in North West Germany on 9 April 1945 and notes that this was subsequently downgraded, some six months later, to a third bar DSO, that the citation had been clearly altered and that David Stirling, founder of the SAS, has confirmed that there was considerable prejudice towards Mayne and that King*

SAS jeep, heavily armed with Browning and Vickers K machine guns.

George VI enquired why the Victoria Cross had 'so strangely eluded him'. The House further notes that on 14 December it will be fifty years since Colonel Mayne's untimely death in a car accident, and this will be followed, on 29 January 2006, by the 150th anniversary of the signing of the Royal Warrant to institute the Victoria Cross; and therefore calls upon the Government to mark these anniversaries by instructing the appropriate authorities to act without delay to reinstate the Victoria Cross given for excep-tional personal courage and leadership of the highest order and to acknowledge that Mayne's actions on that day saved the lives of many men and greatly helped the Allied advance on Berlin.'

In 1943 SAS units were the first ashore during the invasion of Italy and took the first prisoners of the campaign. As they progressed with their operations into the interior of Italy, they were joined by Italian guerrillas and escaped Russian prisoners who formed an Allied SAS Battalion. Major Anders Lassen was a 24-year-old Danish citizen fighting with the British Army in Italy when he earned the only VC won by (or rather, awarded to) the SAS. This was his citation, '*In Italy, on the night of 8/9 April, 1945, Major Lassen was ordered to take out a patrol and raid the north shore of Lake Comacchio. His task was to cause casualties, capture prisoners and give the impression of a major landing. The patrol was challenged and came under machine-gun fire. Major Lassen himself attacked with grenades and silenced two enemy posts, capturing two prisoners and killing several Germans. The patrol had suffered casualties and was still under fire. Major Lassen moved forward and flung more grenades into a third enemy position, calling upon the enemy to surrender. He was then hit and mortally wounded, but whilst falling he flung a grenade, wounding more of the enemy and enabling his patrol to capture this last position. Finally, he refused to be evacuated lest he should impede the withdrawal and endanger further lives. His high sense of devotion to duty and the esteem in which he was held by the men he led, added to his own magnificent courage, enabled Major Lassen to carry out with complete success all the tasks he had been given.*' Major Lassen was first cousin of the German officer, Major Axel von dem Bussche, Knights Cross, Iron Cross, who was a co-conspirator with Count Claus von Stauffenburg in the July Plot against Hitler.

In June 1944 following the Allied invasion in Normandy, SAS operations on the European mainland were stepped up with troops of the regiment's operatives being parachuted into France, often in groups of nine. They operated in alliance with the French underground disrupting German troop movement, blowing up ammunition dumps, railheads and bridges to impede enemy action. On one occasion, well behind enemy lines, nearly 150 men were dropped into the Burgundy region near Dijon along with Jeeps. When missions went wrong the price paid was high. On one occasion 24 men were executed when captured.

Gravestone of the Mayne family showing Blair Mayne's name.

By the end of hostilities there were five SAS Regiments with 3 SAS and 4 SAS made up from French volunteers and 5 SAS from Belgians. In the Middle East there was an SBS (Special Boat Service) Regiment and also one Italian SAS Regiment. It is estimated that perhaps 2,500 individuals served with the SAS during the Second World War. After the War the SAS was officially disbanded. But as the Malayan Emergency became more critical the SAS (Malayan Scouts) were formed in 1950 from units originally raised by Colonel Mike Calvert, formerly the Chindit commander in Burma, combined with troopers from the Korean War and from members of the Territorial 21 SAS Regiment. These jungle-trained squadrons remained in Malaya until 1958.

SAS units operated in Sarawak, Malaysia and Indonesia, Oman, Aden and South East Asia during the following years, often in un-named and secret operations. Their outstanding bravery against overwhelming odds in the Battle of Mirbat in Oman on 19 July 1972 has only recently come to light. There, just nine SAS operatives resisted an attack by 250 rebels. In recent times the SAS are perhaps best known for the Iranian Embassy Siege in London in 1980, an action uniquely brought into every living room as it unfolded, and the Falklands War. In this campaign SAS officer Captain Gavin Hamilton, formerly of the Green Howards (Alexandra, Princess of Wales's Own Yorkshire Regiment), was awarded a posthumous Military

British member of the SBS at the Qali-e-Jhangi fortess, Afghanistan, 2006. Like the SAS, the SBS was originally born out of HQ Layforce in the Middle East in 1941.

Cross, which some thought should have been a Victoria Cross. He had already led his Troop in a number of extremely dangerous operations, surviving two helicopter crashes in appalling weather conditions on South Georgia and losing half his men when their helicopter crashed into the sea. Shortly after dawn on 10 June 1982 on East Falkland, Hamilton realised that he and his radio operator had been surrounded. Although heavily outnumbered, he gave the order to engage the enemy, telling his signaller that they should both attempt to fight their way out of the encirclement. After the resulting exchange of fire he was wounded in the back. Nevertheless, he told his signaller that he would continue to hold off the enemy whilst the signaller made good his escape, and then proceeded to give further covering fire. Shortly after this he was killed. Captain Hamilton displayed outstanding determination and an extraordinary will to continue the fight in spite of being confronted by hopeless odds and being wounded. He furthermore showed supreme courage and sense of duty by his conscious decision to sacrifice himself on behalf of his signaller. His final, brave and unselfish act will be an inspiration to all who follow in the SAS.

In the past few years the SAS have been involved in a number of operations in the Gulf War, the Iraq War and Afghanistan, some of which we know of, and some we may learn about in the future. Traditionally, members of the SAS who receive military honours are identified in Army lists by their name, their original regiment and where the decoration was won. Citations are rarely published, except in the case of a posthumous award, to avoid giving details of SAS activities. The SAS is an elite and famous regiment of the British Army made up of men who have come through their own regiments to serve in this renowned body of men.

MUSEUM: Imperial War Museum London, Lambeth road, London SE1 6HZ Tel 0207 416.5000

Charge of the Heavy Cavalry Brigade, October 25, 1854. Lithograph by William Simpson.

five

THE LINE CAVALRY REGIMENTS

'Without cavalry, battles are without result.'

Napoleon Bonaparte

'At this critical and awful moment, Lord Uxbridge galloped up to the 2nd Heavy Brigade (Ponsonby's), when the three regiments were wheeled up in the most masterly style, presenting a beautiful front of about thirteen hundred men; and as his Lordship rode down the line, he was received by a general shout and cheer from the brigade. After having taken a short survey of the troops, and the threatening attitude of the enemy, his Lordship determined upon a charge, which, for the wonderful indrepidity of its execution, and its complete success, has rarely been equalled.'

William Hamilton Maxwell, *Stories of Waterloo*, 1833

'The British cavalry never know when to stop charging.'

Duke of Wellington

1st The King's Dragoon Guards

'The Bland Dragoons'; 'The Trades Union'

Dates	1685-1959 VCs 1
Motto	*Honi Soit Qui Mal y Pense,* Shame on him who thinks evil of it.
Alumni	Francis Younghusband, explorer of Tibet, Pitt the Elder, prime minister, Banastre Tarleton, cavalry leader extraordinaire, Walter Wingfield, father of lawn tennis, General Sir David Dundas, commander in chief of the British Army, 1809-11, Richard Temple, Lord Cobham, founder of the Foundling Hospital, N.H. Gibbs, historian.
Anniversaries	18 June, Waterloo.
Battle Honours	Namur, Blenheim, Ramillies, Oudenarde, Malplaquet, Dettingen, Fontenoy, Warburg, Beaumont, Waterloo, Sevastopol, Taku Forts, South Africa 1879-81, 1901-2, Flanders 1915-17, Aghanistan 1919, Tobruk, El Alamein, Salerno, Italy 1943-4.

The regimental badge of the King's Dragoon Guards, the KDG, was the double-headed Imperial Eagle of the Hapsburgs, in honour of Franz Joseph, Austro-Hungarian Emperor, who was colonel in chief of the regiment between 1896 and 1914. This unusual honour came about because Queen Victoria was staying in Nice in the spring of 1896. There she met the Emperor of Austria, Franz Josef. She presented him with his appointment as colonel-in-chief of the 1st King's Dragoon Guards. This he duly accepted and later wrote to the Prince of Wales, *'I am delighted with this beautiful present, which will always remind me of its kind donor, but also of the gracious disposition of the Queen, your noble mother, who did me a single honour when she appointed me Colonel-in Chief of the King's Dragoon Guards.'* The new colonel must have been more than happy with the regimental quick march, the Radetsky March by Johann Strauss, the famous Austrian composer, named after the famous Austrian General Radetsky.

The regiment was one of two Regiments of Horse raised by King James II against the Duke of Monmouth's rebellion in 1685, and numbered as the 2nd, the Queen's Regiment of Horse since the 1st Regiment of Horse was already in existence, later to become the Blues. It was named for King James's consort Queen Mary of Modena but, as was the practice throughout most of the period, was commonly referred to as Lanier's Horse, after its first colonel's name, Sir John Lanier.

A private of the King's Dragoon Guards.

Lanier's regiment's first job was to escort the forlorn Duke of Monmouth back from Winchester to London for his trial and execution after his defeat at the Battle of Sedgemoor. The regiment first saw action on King William III's winning side at the Battle of the Boyne in Ireland in 1690 and subsequent engagements in that campaign. In 1693 at the Battle of Neer Landen in the Low Countries they made two gallant charges at the French army thereby saving their new King from being captured. The regiment also fought in all of the four great victories of the Duke of Marlborough over the French, thus carrying Blenheim, Ramillies, Oudenarde and Malplaquet as battle honours. The great general, Prince Eugene of Savoy, on seeing Marlborough's cavalry at Mondelheim for the first time, said, *'I have heard much of the English cavalry, and find it to be the best appointed and finest that I have ever seen.'*

In 1714 the regiment changed its name from the 2nd, the Queen's Regiment of Horse to the 2nd, the King's Regiment of Horse, in honour of King George I. In 1743 the regiment took part in the Battle of Dettingen where they held the line in the face of superior numbers of French cavalry. In 1745 they also took part in the Battle of Fontenoy. Three years later, following the suppression of the second Jacobite rebellion, to save money it was decided by the government to downgrade the regiment from a Regiment of Horse to a Dragoon regiment, since members of such regiments were paid a little less. They thus became the 1st King's Regiment of Dragoon Guards, the Blues having been upgraded to the Royal Horse Guards.

King's Dragoon Guards charging French Dragoons, 1815.

King's Dragoon Guards
patrolling Benghazi,
1941.

During the Seven Years War the regiment was in attendance at the Battle of Minden but was denied the chance of attack when Lord George Sackville disobeyed orders, for which he was later court martialled. They fought well at Corbach and just three weeks later they served under the dashing Marquis of Granby in the cavalry triumph at the Battle of Warburg where he lost his wig in the cavalry charge, giving rise to the expression *'going at it bald headed'*. It was there in Germany that they fought alongside the 2nd Dragoon Guards, their first action together since the Battle of the Boyne, and not their last.

At the Battle of Waterloo the King's Dragoon Guards were included in the Household Cavalry Brigade, making up forty per cent of its number. In the early afternoon of the battle the French launched a massive attack in the centre with about ten thousand infantry supported by the heavy cavalry Cuirassiers. The Household Cavalry Brigade under Major General Lord Edward Somerset was ordered to respond. And respond they did. Their charge utterly routed both the French infantry and cavalry but despite going too far, and sustaining excessive casualties fighting their way back to the Allied lines, they had established a precedent of dominance over the enemy that would in the end carry the day. Starting out with 240 members of the regiment, after more than a dozen frantic charges, only about thirty were left standing in a total of one hundred left in the brigade. It was Captain Naylor of the King's Dragoon Guards who ended the day commanding the whole brigade. The Duke of Wellington personally rode over to them and thanked them. After the battle the King's Dragoon Guards were awarded the honour of having 'Waterloo' emblazoned on their colours and every survivor was awarded a silver medal in memory of the battle, and an extra two years pay. Every year on 18 June the officers and sergeants of the regiment dine together.

During the years that followed Waterloo the regiment was often used in the quelling of civil disturbances in times of social and economic unrest. They thus gained their nickname, 'the trade unionists', for their calm and efficient approach to these situations.

The King's Dragoon Guards were sent to China in 1860 where they took part in the capture of the Taku Forts on August 21 and Peking itself a month later. The two squadrons of the regiment acquitted themselves well and in one incident charged Tartar cavalry with success, making them the only British cavalry to have faced the descendants of Ghenghis Khan in battle. An observer wrote, *'The charge of the king's Dragoon Guards was an act of horsemanship most remarkable.'* During this Chinese campaign in 1860, Trooper Phipps escorted some envoys into the Chinese rebel lines. They were promptly taken prisoner, transported to Peking, and severely maltreated. But Phipps remained brave under torture and cheerful to the end. He, a French officer, the *Times* correspondent and an Indian trooper all died. General Wolseley, an officer on the campaign wrote, *'Up to the day of his death, he never lost heart, and always endeavoured to cheer up those around him when any complained or bemoaned their cruel fate. Even to the last moments of consciousness he tried to encourage them with words of hope and comfort. All honour to his memory: he was brave when hundreds of brave men would have lost heart. Nothing except the highest order of courage, both mental and bodily, will sustain a man through the miseries of such barbarous imprisonment and cruel torture as that which Private Phipps underwent patiently, his resolute spirit living with him up to the very last moments of his existence.'* As a result of this act of barbarity the leaders of the expedition resolved to burn the Summer Palace and enforce their authority over the Chinese government.

The King's Dragoon Guards arrived in South Africa in April 1879 in response to the Zulu victory at Isandlwana. It was a patrol of the King's Dragoon Guards that discovered the body of the unfortunate Prince Imperial, the son of the exiled French Emperor Napoleon III, and brought it back for proper burial. It was another KDG patrol led by Major R.J. Marter that tracked down and captured the Zulu King, Cetawayo, after his defeat at Ulundi. A unit of the King's Dragoon Guards was still in South Africa two years later when trouble began to break out with the Boers who were objecting to the British annexation of the Transvaal.

The regiment spent the next ten years stationed in India and it was during this time that they were paid an official visit by Nicholas, the Tsarevitch of Russia while he was on a tour of the Far East. On his departure he presented the regiment with a beautiful gold and enamel punch bowl. He ascended the Russian throne a few years later as Czar Nicholas II.

The regiment were in South Africa when the First World War broke out and were posted to France as part of the Indian Expeditionary Force, arriving in November 1914, fighting for three years in the trenches before returning for further duty in India in October 1917. During their time in France, they had moved twenty-two times, with nine spells of duty in the trenches, each of which averaged ten days. The regiment then took part in the three-month 3rd Afghan War in 1919 making the last recorded charge by a British cavalry regiment at a village called Dakka where they galloped at the enemy across more than a thousand yards of difficult terrain.

The King's Dragoon Guards held their last mounted parade at Secunderabad in 1937 before becoming mechanised and on the outbreak of the Second World War were deployed to Egypt where they operated in armoured cars fighting at El Agheila, Beda Fomm, Tobruk and El Alamein. They next took part in the Salerno landings and were the first troops to liberate Naples. During the long and arduous Italian campaign, often in mountainous terrain, the regiment operated with their armoured cars as infantry. But they also managed to organise some horses, which they used in mounted patrols across difficult country with some success. This again was probably a 'last' for the British cavalry. As the War went into its last winter, the regiment was deployed to Greece in December 1944, then Egypt, then Syria, followed by Palestine, to police conflicts as they arose in these territories. In the following years they served in Malaya, Borneo, Aden and Cyprus as well as Northern Ireland.

In 1959 the 1st The King's Dragoon Guards merged with the Queen's Bays, the 2nd Dragoon Guards, to form the senior cavalry regiment of the Line in the British Army, the 1st The Queen's Dragoon Guards. They are sometimes known as the Welsh Cavalry, since they recruit mainly from Wales, Herefordshire and Shropshire. These two regiments, whch had been created at the same time 274 years before and had forged such proud separate histories, would now serve side by side as one regiment. What had started in the heat of battle on July 1 1690 near the River Boyne in Ireland, when Lanier's Regiment of Horse and Peterborough's Regiment of Horse fought side by side, would continue into the future.

Laing's Nek

Private John Doogan was a 27-year-old Irishman serving in the King's Dragoon Guards during the First Boer War. On 28 January 1881 at Laing's Nek, a small pass in the Drakensburg Mountains of South Africa, a small detachment of the KDG led by a Major Brownlow and supplemented by mounted infantry from the 58th and 60th , were attacking a Boer position. Within moments they were mown down by accurate Boer fire. Private Doogan, Major Brownlow's batman, saw the Major fall, when his horse was shot beneath him, and immediately went to his aid despite ferocious enemy fire. Though he was himself severely wounded, he at once dismounted and persuaded the officer to take his horse, being wounded again at that moment. Fortunately a ceasefire was called later in the day to allow medical attention for the British wounded and Doogan was treated and recovered from his ordeal. He was awarded the Victoria Cross. He lived another sixty years, to the ripe old age of eighty-seven. He was buried with full military honours at the Shorncliffe Barracks Military Cemetery, near Folkestone where he lived.

MUSEUM: 1st The Queen's Dragoon Guards Museum, Cardiff Castle, Cardiff CF10 2RB Tel 02920 781213

Queen's Bays
(2nd Queen's Dragoon
Guards)

'The Bays'

Dates	1685-1959 VCs 4
Motto	*Pro rege et patria,* For King and Country.
Alumni	Mark Phillips, Gold medal equestrian, (1st the Queen's Dragoon Guards), John Le Marchant, founder of Sandhurst Military Academy, Sir Percy Sykes, diplomat, writer and scholar, Sir Benjamin d'Urban, Governor of Cape Colony, Field Marshal John Campbell, 2nd Duke of Argyll.
Anniversaries	1 June, Gazala.
Battle Honours	Namur, Almanza, Dettingen, Warburg, Indian Mutiny, South Africa 1901-2, Mons, Marne, Somme, Gazala, Alamein, Argenta Gap, Gulf War, Iraq.

Queen's Bays trooper in India, 1854. (Tim Reese)

Along with the Scot's Greys, the Queen's Bays are the only regiment known by the colour of their horses. There was also a Chestnut Troop of the Royal Horse Artillery during the Peninsula War.

Though officially the 2nd Regiment of Horse, after they returned from campaign in the Seven Years War they began to be known as the Queen's Bays, since the regiment were mounted exclusively on bay horses with the reddish brown body and black mane and tail. The Bays cap badge was the word 'Bays' surrounded by a laurel wreath and surmounted by a crown.

The Bays were one of the Regiments of Horse raised by King James II against Monmouth's rebellion in 1685, becoming the 3rd Regiment of Horse, known as Peterborough's, after their first colonel, the Earl of Peterborough. The new regiment

The Earl of Peterborough, first colonel of the regiment.

Lieutenant Robert Blair VC.

first saw action under King William III at the Battle of the Boyne in Ireland where they fought alongside the 2nd Regiment of Horse, with whom they would merge 169 years later. Peterborough's then took part in a famous cavalry charge against the French in Portugal at the Battle of Almanza in 1707 routing two regiments of the enemy but ending up on the losing side. They fought well in other actions at Alcantara in 1706 and Balaguer in 1709 but the campaign ended in failure and surrender and the regiment returned to England in 1711. Defeats in battle, let alone defeats in campaigns, merit small attention from historians on the losing side, but often regiments have displayed the same courage, discipline and good soldiering in defeat as much as in victory. The Bays enhanced their reputation in these little known encounters.

In 1715, following the regiment's creditable performance at the Battle of Preston, where they played an important part in defeating the Jacobite rebels, the new King George I rewarded them with the title of the Princess of Wales Own Royal Regiment of Horse, which in due course became the Queen's Own Royal Regiment of Horse in 1727 when her husband King George II succeeded to the throne. In 1746, though the regiment had played a key part in the suppression of the second Jacobite rebellion at Clifton Moor in the previous year, it was decided to downgrade the regiment from Regiment of Horse to Dragoons, who were paid less money. So the 2nd Regiment of Horse became the 2nd Dragoon Guards, the Queen's Regiment of Dragoon Guards.

In 1760 the 2nd Dragoon Guards fought alongside the 1st Dragoon Guards, the King's Dragoon Guards, charging together under the dashing leadership of the Marquis of Granby at the Battle of Warburg where he famously lost his wig in the cavalry charge. It was in 1767, after their return from the battlefields of Germany, that the 2nd gained their nickname, the Queen's Bays, due to the fact that they were mounted only on bay horses rather than the more usual black or dark bays used by the rest of the cavalry.

The regiment next fought in the Flanders campaign of 1793 against the French revolutionary armies winning the battle honour of Willems, under the general command of the grand old Duke of York.

In 1857 the Indian Mutiny broke out and the Bays were dispatched to India. They first saw action at Nusrutpore in January 1858 where they charged the enemy successfully. Two months later they charged again at the Relief of Lucknow. The regiment now became involved in a number of mopping up operations against the rebels and for eighteen months acquitted themselves with efficiency and courage.

Robert Blair was a lieutenant in the Queen's Bays attached to the 9th Lancers during the Mutiny. On 28 September 1857 he was ordered to take a party of one sergeant and twelve men to retrieve an abandoned ammunition wagon. As they approached the wagon, sixty of the enemy surrounded them. Without hesitation Lieutenant Blair formed up his men and charged the rebels. A number were killed but Blair was severely wounded in the action when one of the rebels nearly severed his arm at the shoulder. He was rescued by Private Patrick Donohoe, 9th Lancers who went to his aid. The patrol returned safely. Both Blair and Donohoe were awarded the VC, but Blair sadly died of his wounds six months later at Cawnpore on March 28 1858.

The Queen's Bays served in South Africa during the closing stages of the Boer War and remained there for a number of years after the cessation of hostilities. In 1914 the

regiment were to be deployed to France with the 1st Cavalry Division, alongside the 11th Hussars and the 5th Dragoon Guards. Lieutenant Colonel H. W. Wilberforce and his men were seen off by King George V and Queen Mary on 11 August, arriving in France on 16 August, and were in the front line by 21 August. They endured the retreat from Mons and in the ensuing four years served on the Western Front, paying with the rest of the British Army a terrible price for victory. One action illustrates what they had to endure. In the early morning mist of 1 September 1914 they were involved in the defence of Nery alongside the heroic 'L' battery of the Royal Horse Artillery. They came under heavy shell fire and many of their horses were killed but they held the line with Lieutenant Lamb bringing the regiment's machine guns into effective action. As the dying Captain Bradbury of the RHA was brought back on a stretcher, he remarked to Colonel Wilberforce of the Bays, *'Hello, Colonel, they've been giving us a warm time, haven't they?'* By mid morning the battle was over and the Bays had lost eighty horses killed and many stampeded. Colonel Wilberforce was awarded the Légion d'Honneur while Lieutenant Lamb won the DSO and his men were decorated or mentioned in despatches. A week later, when the retreat from Mons had ended, the regiment took stock to find they had casualties of seven officers and more than a hundred men either killed, wounded or missing, out of a roll call of seventeen officers and just over four hundred men. They had also lost more than 350 of their 600 horses. The Bays had fought gallantly in the true traditions of the regiment.

The Bays like many of the other cavalry regiments on the Western Front spent the war filling in when necessary in the trenches and keeping their horses prepared to follow through on attacks when the ever-elusive breakthrough was made. Finally, with the Armistice in position, the regiment led the 1st Cavalry Division across the border into Germany in December 1918. There they formed part of the army of occupation until transferred to India the following year.

Once there they were deployed in a relatively lesser known operation, the Malabar campaign in 1921 against the so-called Moplah Rebellion in South West India, a corner of the sub-continent not often associated with military action.

In 1935 the Bays gave up their horses for the last time and began the process of

Above, from left
Bays Regimental Band, 1899.

B Squadron of the Queen's Bays being replenished with ammunition, World War II.

A sergeant major of the Bays, c. 1900.

The Bays charging at Lucknow, 1858.

mechanisation. In the Second World War the Bays were sent to France in May 1940 to support the beleaguered British Expeditionary Force, but after some fierce fighting in an attempt to break through, were withdrawn soon afterwards. The regiment was then posted to North Africa where they fought at Gazala and in the Battle of Knightsbridge where alongside the Royal horse Artillery and the Rifle Brigade they were in continuous action for nearly three weeks. They later were part of the Alamein victory and the advance across Libya to Tunisia. In May 1944 the regiment landed in Italy fighting their way up the east coast until the war ended. After the war the regiment served in Egypt, Germany, Jordan and Libya.

In 1959 the Queen's Bays, the 2nd Dragoon Guards merged with the 1st The King's Dragoon Guards to form the senior cavalry regiment of the Line in the British Army, 1st The Queen's Dragoon Guards. They are sometimes known as the Welsh Cavalry, since they recruit mainly from Wales, Herefordshire and Shropshire.. Within a short time the two former regiments had been on operations in Borneo, Aden, Cyprus and Northern Ireland.

The Irishman and the Welshman

On 8 October 1858 near Sundeela Oudh, India, the regiment was pursuing mutineers in a sugar cane plantation when they came under attack. Lieutenant Colonel W.H. Seymour, commanding the regiment, was wounded with sword cuts and fell from his horse. An Irishman Private Charles Anderson and a Welshman Trumpeter Thomas Monaghan immediately came to his aid, enabling him to get to his feet and together they saw off the enemy, some forty-strong. Both Anderson and Monaghan were awarded the Victoria Cross. Thomas Monaghan VC died on 10 November 1895, aged 56, and was buried in a common grave in Woolwich Cemetery, South East London. In 1967 his Victoria Cross came up for sale at auction and was purchased by an officer of the Bays. It was forty years later in 2007 that the Regiment received a letter from a visitor to Woolwich Old Cemetery, who had come across the grave of Trumpeter Monaghan, which was in a bad state of neglect and quite overgrown. The regiment took it upon themselves to rectify the situation and, with the Old Comrades Association, gained permission, since the Trumpeter had no living relatives, to maintain the upkeep of the hero's grave. The plot was purchased and the headstone restored.

MUSEUM: 1st The Queen's Dragoon Guards Museum, Cardiff Castle, Cardiff CF10 2RB Tel 02920 781213

SCOTS GREYS (2ND DRAGOONS)

'Les Terribles Chevaux Gris'

Dates	1678-1971 VCs 3
Motto	*Nemo me impune lacessit*, No one assails me with impunity; *Nulli secundus*, Second to None.
Alumni	Geoffrey Keyes, VC, war hero, Lieutenant-General Sir Ralph Abercromby, Charles Douglas-Home, editor of *The Times*, Sir Ranulph Fiennes, adventurer, Colonel James Hamilton, killed leading the charge at Waterloo, Field Marshal Sir John Stanier.
Anniversaries	18 June, Waterloo, 25 October, Balaclava Day.
Battle Honours	Blenheim, Ramillies, Oudenarde, Malplaquet, Dettingen, Waterloo, Balaclava, Sevastopol, Delhi, Afghanistan, South Africa, Mons, Ypres, Hindenburg Line, El Alamein, Salerno, NW Europe 1944-5, Gulf War.

The Scots Greys have been immortalised by the painting of their epic charge at the Battle of Waterloo by Lady Elizabeth Butler. The uncontrolled impetus of heavy cavalry charging straight at you painted from the perspective of a waiting French infantryman is dramatically depicted and takes the breath away.

The regiment, originally raised in 1678, can claim to be the oldest surviving Cavalry of the Line regiment in the British Army. They were raised by the crown, along with the 21st Regiment of Foot, later the Royal Scots Fusiliers, to control unrest in Scotland. Their first colonel was the formidable Lieutenant General Dalziel who had seen service in Russia against the Tartars. In 1681 they became the Royal Regiment of Scots Dragoons but took second place in precedence behind the two Regiments of Horse raised in 1685, which later became Dragoon Guards and were allowed to take precedence over the already existing Royal Dragoons and Scots Greys. The regiment was numbered the 4th Dragoons in 1694 and that year went

Troopers of the Scots Greys.

Machine-gun squadron of the Scots Greys during the Somme offensive, 1916.

on campaign in Flanders for the first time. Before they departed they were inspected in Hyde Park by King William III and it was noted that *'they made a fine sight, for the entire regiment rode grey horses'*. By 1702 they had already become known as the Grey Dragoons or the Scots Regiment of White Horses, due either to the grey uniforms that Dalziel ordered for them from England, or perhaps for the grey horses they inherited from King William's Dutch Life Guards, who had departed from England to go home when no longer needed and had left their horses to the 2nd Dragoons. In any event the name stuck. It was not unusual for elite cavalry regiments of the time to be mounted on monotone horses. The Life Guards, for example, rode black horses exclusively.

The regiment took part in the taking of the heights of the Schellenburg before the Battle of Blenheim in 1704. At Blenheim they attacked the enemy in several magnificent charges led by the Duke of Marlborough himself. Some time after the battle when the British Army was visited by the Holy Roman Emperor, his honour guard was formed by the Scots Greys with Marlborough himself at their head.

An Amazon

Mrs Welch, giving her name as Christian Welch, joined the Scots Greys when pursuing her errant husband who had run away to join the army in the War of the Spanish Succession. At the Schellenberg she was wounded, not for the first time. After the battle of Hochstedt, she finally found her husband who had by now joined the 1st Regiment of Foot but they again went their separate ways. At the battle of Ramillies the redoubtable Mrs Welch had her skull fractured, and she was discovered to be a woman. This, of course, ended her fighting career, but the Colonel of the Greys sent for her husband and persuaded the couple to re-marry. Mrs Welch then became a camp follower and soon afterwards her husband was killed. She was then befriended by a Captain Ross, and when their closeness became known she was nicknamed *'Mother Ross'*. She later married yet another soldier, who was killed during a siege. When she returned to England she received a payment of £50 and a pension from Queen Anne of one shilling a day. She married yet again and became Mrs Davies, following her husband's regiment until he was admitted as a pensioner into Chelsea Hospital. She died in 1739, and was granted a funeral with full military honours at Chelsea Hospital and laid to rest in the graveyard there.

The Scots Greys were the only cavalry regiment in the British Army to wear the bearskin. This unique honour was awarded to them after the Battle of Ramillies in

1706 where under the leadership of Lord John Hay they had defeated the French grenadier Regiment du Roi. Up to that point they had worn the traditional mitre head-dress and only grenadier regiments in the French army wore the bearskin. It was only about seventy years later that the Scots Greys began the tradition with full dress. The bearskin also had a white plume on the left side and on the back the White Horse of Hanover in silver, though this was later discontinued by officers.

‘A’ Squadron, firing a broadside on the outskirts of Torre Annunziata, with Mount Vesuvius in the background, September 1943.

In 1707 following the Act of Union uniting England and Scotland, the regiment was renamed the Royal North British Dragoons and with this name they fought at Oudenarde in 1708 and Malplaquet in 1709. In 1713 the regiment was numbered as the 2nd Dragoons, since only one English Dragoon regiment preceded them, the Royals. Two years later they fought at the battle of Dunblane during the Jacobite rebellion of 1715. It was at this time that some troops from the Greys and some from the Royals were taken out to form a new regiment of Dragoons, the 7th, known at the time as ‘the Black Horse’.

The Greys were on the Continent once more when they fought at Dettingen in 1743 under the command of King George II and led by the tenacious Sir James Campbell. They charged the French cavalry capturing the Standard of the French Household Cavalry, winning the day with no casualties. But at Fontenoy in 1745 they paid a heavy price for their luck at Dettingen. Colonel Campbell and a number of others were killed. At Lauffeldt in 1747 their charge was ambushed by French infantry and they lost more than a hundred men killed or wounded.

During the Seven Years War the regiment charged at the Battle of Warburg in 1760 under the command of the dashing Marquis of Granby. In the French Revolutionary Wars they fought at Beaumont and Willems in the Low Countries.

It was at the Battle of Waterloo that the Scots Greys won undying fame in their historic charge as part of the Union Brigade. The brigade, led by Major General Sir William Ponsonby, was named thus since it contained one English, one Scottish and one Irish regiment – the Royals, the Scots Greys and the Skins. As General D’Erlons’ Corps attacked, the Union Brigade responded. The Greys were on the left of the line led by their Colonel James Hamilton. The charge built up momentum and the British Heavy Cavalry dragoons launched themselves on the French infantry, the Greys shouting ‘Scotland for Ever.’ Sergeant Charles Ewart of the Greys rode at the eagle bearer of the French 45th Infantry of the Line, the Invincibles. He cut down the four escorts and the eagle bearer and grabbed the eagle; this from a regiment that had been victorious at Austerlitz and Jena. The Union Brigade cut through the French and, now out of control, continued to charge up the far incline to the French guns, where they disabled numerous pieces of the French artillery. The Emperor Napoleon, within a short distance of this heroic action, complained, *’Ces terribles chevaux gris. Comme ils travaillent!’*

At this point they were counter-attacked by the green-clad French Lancers of General Jaquinot’s division and suffered heavy casualties. Colonel Hamilton and

The charge of the Scots Greys at the battle of Waterloo.

General Ponsonby were both killed. As they had charged, Hamilton had lost both his arms and had ridden at the enemy with the reins in his teeth. Ponsonby, veteran of many a stern action in the Peninsula, probably died because he was not riding one of his war horses that day. His groom had been unable to reach him before the battle began and he was on a domestic hack. The Scots Greys' casualties that day were 122 killed, 93 wounded with the loss of 228 of the 416 horses that had started the day. But the Union Brigade had made a devastating impact on the French Grande Armée, driving them back on their heels, capturing two Imperial eagles, and putting much of their artillery out of action. The French had been mortally wounded.

After the battle, the Greys adopted the captured French eagle as the regiment's badge. It is still the badge of the present regiment, the Royal Scots Dragoon Guards. Sergeant Ewart was later personally congratulated by the Prince Regent and promoted. The rest of the British Army wryly gave the Scots Greys the nickname, 'the Bird Catchers'.

In the Blood

During the successful charge of the Heavy Brigade at the Battle of Balaclava Sergeant Major John Grieve of the Scots Greys saw that one of his officers was in trouble, surrounded by Russian cavalry. Grieve charged into them cutting the head off one and driving off the others. For his bravery he became one of the first recipients of the newly instigated medal simply engraved, 'For Valour'. On 26 June 1857 at a ceremony in Hyde Park in London he was one of the 62 first recipients of the Victoria Cross presented by Queen Victoria herself. Just over 60 years later, on 7 June 1917, his great nephew, Captain Robert Grieve, also won the supreme medal for gallantry at the Battle of Messines, fighting with the 1st Australian Imperial Force on the Western Front.

British military history has not restricted the Scots Greys fame to the battle of Waterloo alone. During the Crimean War the regiment was also part of an equally successful Heavy Brigade charge at the Battle of Balaclava on 25 October, 1854. The heavy brigade was drawn up in two lines, the Scots Greys and Inniskillings at the front and the 4th Royal Irish, the 5th Dragoon Guards and the 1st Royal Dragoons in the second line. The British heavy brigade accelerated from the trot to the charge and hit the Russians with enormous weight, driving right through them. The Adjutant of the Greys, Lieutenant Miller, then rallied the men and charged again as the Inniskillings did likewise and the day was won. The 2nd Dragoons that day were indeed '*Nulli Secundus*', 'Second to None' .

Old Sir Colin Campbell rode up, and cried out: *'Greys! Gallant Greys! I am 61 years old, and if I were young again I should like to have served with you.'* It is a little unfair that Balaclava is more remembered for the ill-fated Charge of the Light Brigade rather than the success of the Heavy Brigade. Unofficially the sergeants of the regiment celebrate Balaclava night on October 25th, since two of their number won VCs on that day.

The Scots Greys capturing the French guns at Waterloo.

In 1877 the regiment incorporated their nickname in their title, the 2nd Dragoons (Royal Scots Greys). In 1885 a detachment of the Scots Greys volunteered as part of the Heavy Camel Regiment with 2 officers and 44 men. They fought at the Battle of Abu Klea on 17 January against the Mahdists where they lost one officer and twelve men.

During the Boer War they formed part of French's Cavalry Division, which made the dramatic and costly charge across the veldt to relieve Kimberley. Units of the regiment were the first in to the beleaguered town. Two weeks later they took part in the victory at Paardeberg.

When embarking on active duty in 1914, an order was given that white horses would be too conspicuous, so the men would have to dye their mounts with permanganate. This was not altogether successful! A dull, messy colour resulted, but maybe it saved a few lives, both of man and horse. The First World War was an arduous time for the Greys, as it was for most of the cavalry regiments. They fought in the retreat from Mons, in the first Battle of Ypres, at Arras, Cambrai, the Somme in 1918 and the Hindenburg Line, ending the war only a few miles from where they had started; and of course facing a future in which their horses would play no part. Following the Armistice there was a rearrangement of many of the cavalry regiments. The Greys survived any amalgamation but had their name inverted to the Royal Scots Greys (2nd Dragoons). The regiment mechanised in the ensuing years and during the Second World War fought at Alam el Halfa, Alamein, in Italy, notably at Salerno, and Normandy.

In 1971 the Scots Greys amalgamated with another old and famous cavalry regiment, the 3rd Carabiniers who themselves had been formed in 1922 from the 3rd Dragoon Guards and the 6th Dragoon Guards (the Carabiniers). This new regiment was named the Royal Scots Dragoon Guards, the senior Scottish cavalry regiment in the British Army.

MUSEUM: The Royal Scots Dragoon Guards Museum, The Castle, Edinburgh EH1 2IT Tel 0131 3105100

3RD KING'S OWN HUSSARS

'The Moodkee Wallahs'

Dates	1685-1958 VCs 4
Motto	*Nec aspera terrent,* Rough Going Does Not Deter.
Alumni	General George Keppel, who captured Havana, James Easton, diplomat, Sir George Evans, MP and Peninsula and Crimea veteran, General George Ramsay, Earl of Dalhousie, Governor-General of North America 1820-8.
Anniversaries	23 October, El Alamein, 18 December, Moodkee.
Battle Honours	Dettingen, Salamanca, Vitoria, Toulouse, Kabul, Moodkee, Ferozashah, Sobraon, Ramnagar, Chillianwallah, Goojerat, South Africa, Mons, Ypres, Somme, Hindenburg Line, El Alamein, Italy.

An officer of the 3rd Hussars, c. 1890.

The 3rd King's Own Hussars, 'the Galloping 3rd', were first raised in 1685 as a Dragoon regiment by order of King James II to combat the threat of the Duke of Monmouth's rebellion. In honour of his wife, Mary of Modena, they were named the Queen Consort's Regiment of Dragoons. The blue colour still worn by the regiment comes from the Garter blue feathers they wore in their hats when they were first formed, the colour of their first patron. During the Glorious Revolution they fought successfully in Ireland under their Colonel Leveson and were known as Leveson's Regiment of Dragoons and in the subsequent reign of William and Mary they were renamed the Queens Regiment of Dragoons.

In 1707 at the Battle of Almanza in Spain the 3rd Dragoons fought the French alongside two of the regiments that would subsequently become their brothers in arms in the Queen's Own Royal Hussars, the 4th and 8th. The battle was a heavy defeat, but, if there is such a thing as glory in defeat, the 3rd earned it with their repeated brave charges, losing more than half their number. On the accession of King

3rd Hussars
Regimental
Headquarters after
El Alamein.

George I in 1714, the King, having no consort, the regiment was renamed the King's Own Regiment of Dragoons.

In 1715 they fought against the Jacobites at the Battle of Sherrifmuir in Scotland with the 7th, thus operating alongside all their current comrade's predecessors within the space of eight years and within thirty years of all their founding. After the suppression of the Jacobite rebellion King George I awarded to the 3rd the honour of wearing the White Horse of Hanover in their cap badge, which they have done ever since. After the second Jacobite rebellion in 1745 all British Army officers in their messes after dinner were required to toast the monarch, but King George II, on account of the unquestioned loyalty of the 3rd, allowed them to forego this symbolic action and to ignore the National Anthem when it was played by the band. The tradition is continued to this day.

During the War of the Austrian Succession King George II led the allied Pragmatic Army against the French at the Battle of Dettingen on 27 June 1743 where the 3rd and 7th fought side by side, along with the 4th. For the first few hours of the contact they had to endure winnowing French artillery fire but then were ordered to attack. In three charges they routed the French Household Cavalry, capturing two fine silver kettle drums, which are paraded on ceremonial occasions to this day. For this they were awarded their first battle honour. It is said that when the regiment was inspected by the King on their way back to England, the Monarch enquired who was the commander of this poorly manned regiment. General Bland, their Colonel, replied *'Please, your Majesty, it is my regiment, and I believe the remainder of it is at Dettingen.'* During the battle all the officers but two had been wounded and they had sustained nearly 150 casualties. Private Thomas Brown of the 3rd recaptured one of the regimental

A Gale and Polden 'Famous Regiment' card produced just before World War I.

3rd (KING'S OWN) HUSSARS.

BATTLE HONOURS.

The White Horse within the Garter.
"Neo aspera terrent."

"Dettingen,"
"Salamanca,"
"Vittoria,"
"Toulouse,"
"Peninsula,"
"Caboul, 1842,"
"Moodkee,"

"Ferozeshah."
"Sobraon,"
"Punjaub,"
"Chillianwallah,"
"Goojerat."
"South Africa, 1902."

HISTORY AND TRADITIONS.

The regiment was raised in 1685. It served in Flanders 1694-7, and took part in the siege of Namur. It took part in the Cadiz expedition, 1702, and witnessed the capture of the galleons in Vigo Bay. It went to Spain again in 1706, and fought at the fierce battle of Almanza the year after. It was in Flanders, 1742-5, and fought with much distinction at Dettingen and Fontenoy. It served in the Walcheren expedition, 1809. It went to Portugal, 1811, and served at Ciudad Rodrigo and Badajos, at Salamanca, Burgos, Vittoria, Pampeluna, and Toulouse. It landed at Ostend after the battle of Waterloo was fought, but marched to Paris, and served with the Army of Occupation until 1818. It formed part of the avenging army which entered Afghanistan in 1842, forcing the Khyber Pass, capturing Caboul, and effecting the release of the British captives. In 1845 it served in the first Sikh War at Moodkee, Ferozeshah, and Sobraon. In 1848-9 it took part in the second Sikh War at Ramnuggur, Sadoolapore, Chillianwallah, and Goojerat. It took part in the latter part of the South African War.

Standards during the battle in a heroic action, which in later years would surely have won him the Victoria Cross: *'He had two horses killed from under him, two fingers of ye bridle hand chopped off, and after retaking the standard from ye General D'Arms, whom he killed, he made his way through a lane of the enemy, exposed to fire and sword, in the execution of which he received eight cuts in ye face, head and neck, two balls lodged in his back, three went through his hat, and in this hacked condition he rejoined his regiment who gave him three huzzas on his arrival.'*

The Hungarian Connection

The word 'Hussar' is Hungarian in origin, describing light, fast-moving horsemen. The word 'corsair' from the Italian *'corsario'* is from the same root. It also means 'I in 20' alluding to the tradition in Hungarian villages of one in twenty of the men being selected for military service. The name spread slowly across Europe until the major nations began to use the term for light cavalry in the eighteenth century.

Another veteran of Dettingen was John Andrews. In 1811, at the age of 91, Andrews attended a review of the regiment near Colchester where he lived. The review was being attended by the Earl of Chatham in front of the Prince Regent and his brother the Duke of York, Commander in Chief of the Army. They enquired as to who was this old boy, dressed in his antique uniform sitting on his old hack. The Earl advised them that it was Andrews, the oldest man in the army, now on half pay. They invited him over and he told them he had served for seventy years, fighting at Dettingen where he attended on their grandfather, King George II, and at Fontenoy. When the

Prince Regent, always a man of fashion, felt the cloth of his uniform he commented *'They don't make material like this anymore.'* To which the old man replied, *'Nor men either.'* As a reward, he was put on full pay for the rest of his days.

In 1811 the regiment was sent to Spain and took part in Wellington's campaign. They were part of General Le Marchant's Heavy Brigade whose devastating charge at 6 o'clock in the evening on 22 July 1811 at the Battle of Salamanca, alongside the 4th and 5th Dragoon Guards, ensured Wellington's victory within the space of one hour. The battle honour of Salamanca was won and the three regiments of the brigade were also given the honour of calling themselves 'Salamanca Regiments'. The regiment fought in Portugal and Spain for the rest of the Peninsular War winning battle honours at Vitoria in 1813 and Toulouse in 1814, a battle, incidentally, which need never have been fought, since Napoleon had already resigned. In 1818 their name was changed once again to the 3rd King's Own Light Dragoons as they were now officially Light Cavalry.

'Sausage, Anyone?'

The story of Knowles the cook and Gurnham the waiter of B Squadron in the First World War is remarkable. They were outside Cambrai just as the regiment was moving into position to attack. The two Troopers set off on their bicycles and, unable to find their comrades, cycled on into the centre of the town. They saw a number of German soldiers but, thinking they were prisoners, leant their bicycles against a railing and went into a building, which turned out to be a German food depot. They helped themselves to as many provisions as they could and cycled back to their positions, not realising that they had cycled right through the British and German front lines and all the way back again. That evening their officers had a sumptuous meal courtesy of the Kaiser.

The regiment was posted to India in 1837 remaining there until 1853 and gaining a formidable reputation. In 1842 they rode with the army into Afghanistan to retake Kabul in the 1st Afghan War. In December 1845 the 1st Sikh War broke out and a series of bloody engagements took place in the Punjab, starting with the Battle of Moodkee, against the fearsome Sikh army. It was here that the regiment gained their nickname for their famous charge where they suffered casualties of nearly 100 officers and men out of a total of 500. The Sikhs called them 'the Devil's Children' as they had attacked in virtual darkness. Within the space of the next few weeks the regiment had distinguished themselves with further courageous charges at the Battles of Ferozeshah and Sobraon. In the 2nd Sikh War, which broke out 18 months later, they again performed gallantly in charges during the Battles of Ramnagar, Chillianwallah and Goojerat where they suffered considerable casualties and fearful wounds from the razor-sharp Sikh swords, the kirpans. It was said of the 3rd after the Sikh Wars, *'Few regiments of horse in the world can show a finer record of hardihood and endurance.'*

A trooper of the 3rd Dragoons at Dettingen, 1743. (Tim Reese)

The Fern Leaf insignia of New Zealand granted to the 3rd Hussars by General Freyburg VC for their heroic actions as part of the New Zealand Division of the Eighth Army.

In 1861 the regiment once more changed its name, becoming The 3rd King's Own Hussars under the Army reforms. The First World War saw them, like all the cavalry regiments, fluctuating between operating as cavalry waiting for the so-called 'gap' to appear in the enemy lines and being used as infantry support in the trenches. In four years they won 27 hard-earned battle honours, twice the amount they had won in the previous 200. During the early German onslaught in 1914, the 3rd were part of General Gough's 2nd Cavalry Division fighting to hold the line. General Sir John French wrote later in his account of those momentous events, *It is no disparagement to the other troops engaged if I lay stress on the fact that it was the cavalry alone who, for more than a fortnight previously, had been disputing foot by foot every yard of the ground. They had fought day and night with the utmost tenacity, and the battles of 31st October and 1st November were but the climax to a long and bitter spell of heroic effort.* An official history of the regiment underlines this, *Messines and Ypres are names that deserve equal pride in their history with Salamanca and Moodkee.*

During the Second World War the 3rd Hussars were deployed as part of the 7th Armoured Division in Egypt in 1940, taking part in Wavell's famously prolific victories over the Italians in Libya. But their finest hour was the role they played in the famous victory of El Alamein against the Afrika Korps. Fighting as part of the New Zealand Division, in the first days of the battle they made constant probes, all the while taking heavy losses, through the minefields and enemy defences, finally forcing a way through, which enabled following armoured units to break through and complete the victory. During the action the 3rd Hussars lost 47 tanks out of 51. For their heroic conduct, the symbol of New Zealand, the Fern Leaf, is painted on all 3rd Hussars', and their successors', armoured vehicles, an honour bestowed on them by General Freyburg VC, commander of the New Zealand Division. Withdrawn from the line to refit, the regiment returned once more in April 1944 in Italy and took part in fierce fighting in the Tiber Valley before being withdrawn once again to see out the war in Syria.

In 1958, after 273 years of valour, sacrifice and unique tradition, the 3rd King's Own Hussars were amalgamated with the 7th Queen's Own Hussars to become the Queen's Own Hussars, which existed as a regiment for a further 35 years. Then in 1993 the Queen's Own Hussars amalgamated again with the Queen's Royal Irish Hussars formerly the (4th Queen's Own Hussars and the 8th King's Royal Irish Hussars) to become the Queen's Own Royal Hussars, the senior light cavalry regiment in the British Army.

MUSEUM: The Queen's Own Hussars Museum, Lord Leycester Hospital, Warwick CV34 4BH Tel 01962 6492035

6TH (INNISKILLING) DRAGOONS

'The Skins'

Dates	1689-1922 VCs 1
Motto	Inniskilling.
Alumni	Captain Lawrence Oates, explorer, General John Le Marchant, founder of the Royal Military Academy, James Mouat VC, Surgeon General.
Anniversaries	27 June, Dettingen Day, Captain Oates Sunday, 17 March.
Battle Honours	Dettingen, Fontenoy, Warburg, Waterloo, Balaclava, Ypres, Somme, Dunkirk, Normandy, Caen, North West Europe 1940, 44-45.

This is a regiment that charged at the Boyne with King William III, fought at Dettingen under the command of King George II, charged with the Union Brigade at Waterloo and with the Heavy Cavalry at Balaclava.

When King James II landed in Ireland in 1689 the 6th Dragoons were raised in the town of Enniskilling by Gustav Hamilton, a Swedish baron who lived in Donegal, who had been made the governor of the town. Each man was compelled to take an oath of loyalty: *'I do hereby testify and declare, and upon the Holy Evangelists swear, that I will own and acknowledge Gustavus Hamilton, Esq., Chief Governor of this town of Enniskillen, and shall give due obedience to him and my superior officers in all his and their commands, and shall to the utmost of my power and ability defend him, them, and this place, with the country adjacent, together with the Protestant religion and interest, with my life and fortune, against all that shall endeavour to subvert the same. So help me God, and the holy contents of this book.'*

Sir Albert Conyngham was appointed to lead them, so they became known as Conyngham's Dragoons and joined with the Earl of Arran's Regiment of Cuirassiers (later to become the 4th Dragoon Guards) the Earl of Shrewsbury's Regiment of Horse (later the 5th Dragoon Guards) who had crossed the Irish Sea with their new King William III from England to face the threat of a Jacobite invasion led by the

The 6th Iniskilliing Dragoons would leave Ireland in 1708 and not return for a hundred years.

Right
Trooper *c*.1751.

Far Right
Trooper of the
Waterloo campaign.

deposed King James II: two claimants to the English throne fighting in Ireland. On July 1 1690 the three regiments fought alongside each other at the victory of the Battle of the Boyne.

They left Ireland for the first time in 1708, not to return to their homeland for another one hundred years. In 1715 they took part in the suppression of the first Jacobite rebellion in Scotland. During the War of the Austrian Succession they were posted to Flanders in 1743. Alongside the 7th Dragoon Guards they fought at the four major engagements of the War. At Dettingen, Fontenoy, Roucoux and Lauffeldt they enhanced their already formidable reputation as heavy cavalry. At Lauffeldt on 2 July 1747 the regiment lost more than a hundred men in the magnificent charges by the British heavy cavalry, led by the legendary John Ligonier, that saved the day from being a complete rout. In 1751 during the numbering of regiments the Skins became the 6th Inniskilling Dragoons, more often simply known as The Inniskillings.

In the Seven Years War, at the Battle of Minden in 1759 six immortal British infantry regiments broke the French cavalry, only for the cavalry commander, Lord George Sackville, not to charge and win the full victory that was deserved. The Inniskillings were one of those cavalry regiments so badly led. They fully redeemed themselves at the Battle of Warburg in the following year fighting alongside the 7th Dragoon Guards in the famous cavalry charge led by the Marquis of Granby.

During the French Revolutionary Wars the regiment was based mainly in England waiting for the call. It finally came with the news of Napoleon's escape from Elba in the early spring of 1815. The British Army had to be quickly mobilised. The Inniskillings, based in Northampton, were assembled and 450 men crossed to the Low Countries on 23 April 1815. Near Brussels they came under the general command of Sir William

Ponsonby, who had led the 5th Dragoon Guards at the Battle of Salamanca in 1812, and were brigaded with the 1st Royal Dragoons and the Scots Greys to form an English, Irish and Scottish heavy cavalry brigade, called the Union Brigade. On the wet morning of 18 June they were positioned in the centre of the Allied lines behind Sir Thomas Picton's 5th Infantry Division. Having watched events unfold during the course of the first few hours, at about two o'clock they were ordered forward to counter a massive French infantry onslaught. The Inniskillings moved through the 1st Royal Scots Regiment before moving into the attack. What followed is an epic event in British military history and one which established a dominance over the French army. If ever there was a predecessor to *blitzkrieg*, the shock effect of a heavy cavalry charge was it. Fortescue described the scene: *'The Union Cavalry Brigade was now ordered forward. The 6th Inniskilling Dragoons passed through the ranks of the Royal Scots and the Black Watch, and the Royal Dragoons, further to the right, went through the 28th Foot and passed the right flank of the Royal Scots. The Greys, who had been in a theoretical reserve position, moved straight to their front, which took them through the ranks of the Gordons. The head of the French Division was now only 20 yards away and the Greys simply walked into the 1st/45th Infantry of the Line. There was no gallop and no 'charge' It is clear from the French report that they did not expect to see British cavalry materializing through the ranks of the British infantry. When the cavalry hit them, the 45th were in the act of forming line, and their 1st battalion was at once thrown into violent confusion, already shaken by the fire of the 92nd. The regimental eagles were carried by the 1st battalion of all French infantry regiments, and in a few minutes the Greys were in the midst of the battalion, at which stage Sergeant Charles Ewart of Captain Vernor's troop captured the eagle of the 45th. He was ordered to take it to the rear, which he reluctantly did, but sat on his horse for some time watching the engagement before finally setting off for Brussels with his trophy. The rest of the French columns believed what they saw could only be an advance guard, and were now under the mistaken impression that they were being attacked by large numbers of cavalry. The Royal Dragoons and 6th Inniskilling Dragoons charged Donzelot's Division and the Eagle of the 105th Regiment was taken by the Royal*

A trooper of the 6th (Inniskilling) Dragoons at Balaklava, 1854. (Tim Reese)

From left
An officer of the 6th Inniskilling Dragoons, 1811.

Trooper in the Crimea, 1854.

Dragoons. These were the only two Eagles captured during the entire Waterloo campaign. At this point the divisions of Marcognet and Donzelot were not completely shaken, although contrary to romantic legend, the Union Brigade did not, and could not, defeat an Army Corps of some 16,900 infantry on their own. Having carried out a highly successful defensive action in support of infantry, the Union Brigade lost all cohesion and refused to recognize or hear any orders.'

Though the charge ended in some confusion, the effect it had on French morale was clearly devastating. Like a boxer hurt in an early exchange of blows, they began to doubt their ability to win the day. The Duke of Wellington, though somewhat exasperated, was also impressed by the charge that day. The Inniskilling Dragoons earned a place on his memorial at Hyde Park Corner.

In 1854 the regiment arrived in the Crimea, once more renewing their comradeship of the Battle of the Boyne 164 years earlier, riding with the 4th and 5th Dragoon Guards in the Heavy Brigade cavalry charge at the Battle of Balaklava, routing more than three thousand Russian cavalry and so denting their confidence that they took no advantage from the disastrous charge of the Light Brigade later in the day. Colonel Paget, of the Light Brigade, witnessed the charge: *'It was a mighty affair, and considering the difficulties under which the Heavy Brigade laboured, and the disparity of numbers, a feat of arms which, if it ever had its equal, was certainly never surpassed in the annals of cavalry warfare, and the importance of which in its results can never be known.'*

During the latter part of the 19th century, the Skins, like most cavalry regiments, split their time between Britain, India and Southern Africa. When the bad blood between the Boer farmers and the British authorities broke out into war, the regiment was deployed in South Africa. This time, alongside the 7th Dragoon Guards their fellow combatants at Dettingen and Fontenoy, they performed effectively on the veldt in sweep operations that were mainly carried out by the cavalry. One action during this campaign is interesting. A small reconnaissance unit of the regiment came under fire. Second Lieutenant Lawrence Oates instructed the patrol to withdraw to safety while with three men he held off the enemy. More of the enemy moved into the attack, twice calling on the wounded young officer to surrender. He replied, 'I've come here to fight, not to surrender.' For his gallantry he was mentioned in despatches. A decade later Oates was selected to be in charge of the ponies and dogs on Captain Scott's expedition of 1912 to the South Pole. He took part in the epic journey to the Pole and in the tragedy that ensued on their journey back. As they struggled back across the polar ice cap in extreme weather, he contracted frost bite and as a result could not walk very fast. Realising he was slowing his companions down, he decided to sacrifice himself for the sake of the others. On the night of 17 March, his 32nd birthday, when they were camped in a blizzard, he excused himself with the immortal words, *'I am going out. I may be some time.'* His body has never been found and his heroism only came to light when the diary of the dead Captain Scott and his companions was discovered some months later.

The Skins arrived in France from India in December 1914 to take their place on the Western Front. They spent the next four years often un-mounted in the trenches, then preparing for breakthroughs during attacks. On one occasion they made a costly and tragic cavalry charge at machine guns during the Battle of the Somme, when they were ordered to attack High Wood to take advantage of an advance. By the time they had reached their start position the Wood was bristling with German machine guns.

Four years later, in 1922 in Cairo, the 6th Inniskilling Dragoons and the 5th Dragoon Guards (Princess Charlotte of Wales's) amalgamated, taking the name of the 5th/6th Inniskilling Dragoon Guards. In 1927 this was changed to the 5th Inniskilling Dragoon Guards and in 1935 'Royal' was added to make them the 5th Royal Inniskilling Dragoon Guards.

The regiment, which had only been mechanised in 1938, alongside the 4th/7th Royal Dragoon Guards (which had been formed with the merging in India of the 4th (Royal Irish) Dragoon Guards and the 7th Dragoon Guards (Princess Royal's)) formed part of the British Expeditionary Force to France in 1940 and were the first armoured units to land, fighting shoulder to shoulder in the retreat to Dunkirk, often over ground they had contested two decades earlier. A composite regiment was then made up and re-equipped, and numbered after the sum of the four regiments, the 22nd Dragoons. As part of the 8th Armoured Brigade they were the first tanks to land on Gold Beach in Normandy where they encountered stiff resistance. Units of the regiment fought their way across France and the Low Countries, playing a leading role in the liberation of Lille and taking part in the drive towards Arnhem, right to the borders of Germany in the spring of 1945.

After the war the composite regiments served in Palestine, Korea, Suez, Cyprus, Aden, Northern Ireland and Iraq. On 1 August 1992 the 4th/7th Royal Dragoon Guards and the 5th Royal Inniskilling Dragoon Guards came together to become the present regiment, the Royal Dragoon Guards. The four original Dragoon regiments, founded within a four-year period during the reign of King William III, each one of which had written its own impressive chapter in British military history – sometimes separately, sometimes alongside each other – would now be banded together and would bear the name 'The Skins', after the men of Enniskilling.

Regimental Quick March

A beautiful damsel of fame and renown,
A gentleman's daughter near Monaghan town;
As she rode by the barracks, this beautiful maid,
She stood in her coach to see Dragoons on parade.
Fare thee well, Inniskilling! Fare thee well for a while
To all your fair waters and every green isle!
And when the war is over we'll return again soon,
And they'll all welcome home the Inniskilling Dragoon.

MUSEUM: Royal Dragoon Guards Museum, 3 Tower Street, York YO1 9SB
Tel 01904 642036

9TH QUEEN'S ROYAL LANCERS

'The Delhi Spearmen'

Dates	1715-1960 VCs 14
Motto	*Vestiga nulla retrorsum,* We do not retreat; *Dieu et Mon Droit,* God and my right.
Alumni	Derek Allhusen, 1968 Olympic equestrian medal winner, Colonel John Gurwood, Peninsula hero and Wellington's secretary, Thomas Wildman, schoolfriend of Lord Byron who bought and preserved Newstead Abbey, Prince Francis of Teck, brother of Queen Mary, Francis Pym, Foreign Secretary under Margaret Thatcher.
Anniversaries	18 June, Waterloo.
Battle Honours	Peninsula, Waterloo, Sobraon, Chillianwallah, Delhi, Lucknow, Kandahar, Kimberley, Paardeberg, Mons, Ypres, Somme, Arras, Cambrai, Dunkirk, El Alamein, Argenta Gap.

French Lancer of Napoleon's army after whom the newly created Lancer regiments modelled their uniforms.

This cavalry regiment has won the most VCs. The regiment dates from the raising of seventeen Dragoon Regiments and thirteen Regiments of Foot in anticipation of a Stuart rebellion in Scotland following the death of the last Stuart monarch, Queen Anne. All were disbanded three years later with the exception of six of the Dragoon regiments, the 9th to 14th. Major General Wynne, a veteran of Marlborough's campaigns, was their first colonel and as such saw action against the Scottish rebels at the Battle of Preston on 12 November 1715. They were not to see action again for a number of years and spent the latter part of the 18th century posted in Ireland. We have a glimpse of them in 1751 when their uniforms were described as scarlet with buff facings and breeches. When they changed to Light Dragoons in 1783 their uniforms changed to blue.

Charge of the 9th Lancers at Badli-Ki-Serai, 8 June 1857. The British victory would lead ultimately to the prolonged siege and then capture of Delhi.

The regiment was next involved in two difficult and ultimately unsuccessful military expeditions in 1806 and 1809. The first was to the River Plate in South America, where, because their horses were either unfit or dead, they had to fight as infantry in the defence of Monte Video. Fighting bravely alongside the 6th Dragoon Guards (the Carabiniers), also operating as infantry, their endeavours were unsuccessful. They were shipped back to England and almost at once sent on the ill-fated Walcheren Island expedition where most of the casualties succumbed to fever.

They then took part the Peninsular campaigns 1811–13 claiming the Peninsula battle honour. In 1816 the regiment was appointed Lancers, in the manner of the Polish Lancers of Napoleon's grand army who had earned so much admiration from their British opponents during the Napoleonic wars. In 1830 the regiment was given the sobriquet 'Queen's Royal' from Queen Adelaide, the consort of King William IV.

During the following years the regiment was stationed in India winning numerous battle honours in different campaigns. During the Sikh Wars they took part in the battles of Sobraon and Chillianwallah.

In 1857 they became known as the Delhi Spearmen, a name which was given to them by the mutineers. They were present at the three main military actions of the emergency, the capture of Delhi and the Siege and Relief of Lucknow, during which they won no less than 12 VCs. To recall just one is to indicate the desperation of the fighting and the courage of all the combatants on both sides. Lieutenant Alfred Jones virtually single-handedly captured a gun in one engagement and in another at Agra some weeks later, was wounded no less than 22 times, including being blinded in one eye, but still continued to fight.

During the Second Afghan War they took part in General Roberts's epic march to Kabul and Kandahar and with other cavalry units of the Indian Army at the Battle of Kandahar putting the Afghan rebels to flight.

A trooper of the 9th Lancers, India, 1840. (Tim Reese)

9th Lancers advancing during the Italian campaign, 1944.

During the Boer War another cavalry charge won the day at Klip Drift. It is recorded by the regiment that they travelled more than 8,000 miles during their months in Southern Africa, a testament to the mobility of light cavalry in open country.

The Irish Aristocrat and the Sergeants

Lord William Beresford was the son of the 4th Marquis of Waterford. He was a captain in the 9th Lancers during the Zulu War, seconded to the 17th Lancers. His own regiment was deployed on the North West Frontier fighting in the Second Afghan War. On 3 July 1879 at Ulundi in Zululand while on patrol Beresford went to the help of Sergeant Fitzmaurice of the 24th Regiment, whose horse had fallen and rolled on him. The Zulus were fast arriving but Lord William, with help from Sergeant Paddy O'Toole of the Frontier Light Horse, managed to mount the injured man behind him. He was, however, so dizzy that the sergeant, who had been keeping back the advancing Zulus, gave up his carbine and, riding alongside, helped to hold him on until they reached safety. Both Beresford and O'Toole were awarded the VC for their heroism in the face of the enemy, O'Toole being one of the first South African winners.

The regiment, as part of the 2nd Cavalry Division, was in the trenches during the entire First World War. As the Germans advanced in the first days of the fighting, the regiment was often called upon to make counter-attacks. In one such action Captain

Francis Octavius Grenfell, a notable polo player, was the first officer to win the VC. On 24 August 1914 he led the heroic charge of the 9th Lancers at Andregnies against massed German artillery and machine gun fire during the retreat from Mons. Later the same day Grenfell led another charge in aid of a trapped Field Artillery battery. Again in the face of unremitting enemy fire, he calmly led his men and rescued the battery. He was killed six months later in the trenches and in his will bequeathed his medal to the regiment *'to whom the honour of my gaining the VC was entirely due thanks to the splendid discipline and traditions which exist in this magnificent regiment'*. The regiment took part in other cavalry actions, the last one being on 7 September 1914 when a squadron of the 9th put the Prussian First Dragoon Guards to flight.

Sergeant Major David Spence, who won his VC for heroism in rescuing a comrade during the Indian Mutiny on 17 January 1858. As can be seen, he later became a Yeoman of the Guard.

The 9th Lancers were sent with the British Expeditionary Force to France in 1940 and had to make a fighting retreat. They were then posted to the Middle East playing a significant role at the Battle of Alamein where Corporal Nicholls was personally congratulated by General Montgomery for knocking out nine German tanks. The regiment fought with distinction throughout the Italian campaign till the war ended in the spring of 1945.

On 11 September 1960 they were merged with the 12th Lancers in a service at St. Michael's garrison Church in Tidworth, Hampshire, where the plaque commemorating the occasion reads: *'It is not the beginning but the continuing of the same until it be thoroughly finished which yieldeth the true glory.'*

Museum: Regimental Museum of the 9th/12th Lancers, Derby Museum and Art Gallery, The Strand, Derby DE1 1BS Tel 01332 716659

11th Hussars (Prince Albert's Own)

'The Cherry Pickers'; 'The Cherubims'

Dates	1715-1969 VCs 1
Motto	*Treu und Fest,* Faithful and Strong.
Anniversaries	23 October 23, El Alamein, 25 October, Balaclava Day.
Alumni	7th Earl of Cardigan, General who ordered the charge of the Light Brigade, the fictional Flashman, Anthony Beevor, historian, Prince Michael of Kent, cousin of The Queen, Nicholas Soames, grandson of Winston Churchill, politician.
Battle Honours	Warburg, Egypt, Balaclava, Salamanca, Waterloo, Bhurtpore, Balaclava, Inkerman, Sevastopol, Mons, Ypres, Somme, France and Flanders 1914-18, Tobruk, El Alamein, Volturno Crossing, North West Europe 1944-5.

The Cherrypickers, perhaps more than any other cavalry regiment, will always be remembered in folklore as part of the Charge of the Light Brigade. The 11th Hussars (Prince Albert's Own) hold more battle honours than any other cavalry regiment. Their commanding officer is addressed as Colonel rather than Sir and they have a tradition called Staff Parade performed every day at 9.50 p.m. to commemorate their famous colonel, the Earl of Cardigan, who died at exactly that time on 28 March, 1868.

Their nickname supposedly comes from an incident in the Peninsular War when the regiment was ambushed by French units when relaxing in a cherry orchard in Spain on 15 August 1811, near San Martin de Trebejo. But it seems just as likely to refer to the unique colour of their trousers.

The regiment was first raised in 1715 as Colonel Honeywood's Regiment of Dragoons in response to the Jacobite uprising and saw action at the Battle of Preston and in the second Jacobite rebellion at Clifton Moor in 1745. From 1755

An officer of the 11th Hussars, the Crimea, 1854. (Tim Reese)

they became known as the 11th Regiment of Light Dragoons. They fought in the Seven Years War at the Battle of Warburg in 1760, which was their first battle honour. They officially became the 11th Regiment of Light Dragoons in 1783.

With the outbreak of the French Revolutionary Wars the 11th were sent on campaign to Flanders and Holland where they took part in a number of engagements, including a cavalry battle at Le Cateau in 1794 – where they were to fight again in 1914 – and the siege of Dunkirk in the following years. A squadron of the 11th also went on General Abercrombie's expedition to Egypt in 1800-1 winning the right to bear the Sphinx emblem, which C Squadron of the King's Royal Hussars carries to this day on their guidon. During the Peninsular War they arrived in Spain in 1811 and fought at the victory at Salamanca in the following July. At Waterloo they were in the 4th Cavalry Brigade under General Vandeleur alongside the 12th and 16th Lancers.

The medals of Major-General Edward Louis Spears. As a musketry instructor lieutenant before the First World War he helped to ensure that the ranks of the 11th were filled with marksmen.

In February 1840 the dashing 11th Dragoons, led by their be-whiskered Colonel, the Earl of Cardigan, escorted the young Prince Albert of Saxe-Coburg and Gotha on his arrival in England from Dover to Canterbury. A few days later they formed part of the Royal escort at his wedding to the young Queen Victoria. Albert was so impressed by their turnout that they were renamed for him, the 11th Prince Albert's Own Hussars, and he remained their colonel-in-chief until his premature death in 1861. Lord Cardigan spent large sums of his private fortune on creating the new Hussar uniforms for his men. He was responsible for the crimson livery trousers they wear, which are based on the colour of the Royal house of Saxe-Coburg, as worn by Prince Albert on many occasions. The Colonel now called his men the 'Cherry Bums', later to become the 'Cherubims'.

On 25 October 1854 the regiment took part in the renowned Charge of the Light Brigade at Balaclava. The Light Brigade was commanded by their former Colonel, now Major General, the Earl of Cardigan, who personally led the charge at the Russian guns on that fateful day. The Light Brigade comprised the 11th Hussars, the 8th Hussars, the 4th Light Dragoons, the 13th Light Dragoons and the 17th Lancers. The 11th charged in the front line that day when only 79 men of their original 142 returned. The Light Brigade had started out with about 660 men. There were 245 casualties with 118 killed and less than 200 were still on their horses. Alfred, Lord Tennyson's poem on the charge is one of the most famous poetic works on military endeavour ever written.

Trooper Fowler hiding
in a cupboard, a tableau
in the Horsepower
Museum of the King's
Own Hussars.

Uniforms of the 11th
Hussars.

Half a league half a league,
Half a league onward,
All in the valley of Death
Rode the six hundred:
'Forward, the Light Brigade!
Charge for the guns' he said:
Into the valley of Death
Rode the six hundred …

… Cannon to right of them,
Cannon to left of them,
Cannon behind them
Volley'd and thunder'd;
Storm'd at with shot and shell,
While horse & hero fell,
They that had fought so well
Came thro' the jaws of Death,
Back from the mouth of Hell,
All that was left of them,
Left of six hundred.

When can their glory fade?
O the wild charge they made!
All the world wonder'd.
Honour the charge they made!

Lieutenant Alexander Dunn, a strapping young Canadian, aged only 21, was one of the finest swordsmen and horsemen in the British Army. He charged with the 11th Hussars in the Light Brigade. Having emptied his revolver at the surrounding Russians, he then set about them with his sword, saving both Sergeant Bentley and Private Levett. He became the first Canadian to win the Victoria Cross. He later died in an accident on a hunting expedition in Senafe, Abyssinia in 1868 while commanding the 33rd (West Riding) Regiment of Foot, (later to become the Duke of Wellington's Regiment) which was part of the 1868 British punitive Expedition against the Ethiopian Emperor Tewodros II. Dunn was buried near where he died and his grave was forgotten until 2001, when Canadian troops serving with the UN in the area discovered the grave and cleaned it up in the manner befitting the last resting place of a winner of the Victoria Cross.

During the First World War the regiment was on the Western Front from 1914 playing the role of most cavalry regiments at the time, fighting as infantry in the trenches and preparing for the mythical 'gap' when the Allies were in attack. During the Battle of Le Cateau in 1914 Trooper Patrick Fowler of the 11th Hussars found himself cut off from his squadron by the German advance in the French village of Bertry. He was taken in by a French woman, Madame Belmont-Gobert who with her daughter hid

11th (Prince Albert's Own) HUSSARS.
BATTLE HONOURS.
The Crest and Motto of the late Prince Consort.
The Sphinx, superscribed "Egypt."

"Warburg."   "Bhurtpore."
"Beaumont,"   "Alma,"
"Willems,"   "Balaklava,"
"Salamanca,"   "Inkerman,"
"Peninsula,"   "Sevastopol."
"Waterloo,"

HISTORY AND TRADITIONS.
The regiment was formed in 1715. It served in
Germany, 1760-3, and was present at the battles of
Warburg, Kirk-Denkern, Wilhelmstahl, Groebenstein, and
the siege of Cassel. It was fighting in Flanders, 1793-5, a
portion of the regiment being present during the same
period at the capture of Martinique and Guadaloupe. In
1799 it served with distinction in the campaign in North
Holland. It was present under Abercromby in Egypt, 1801,
and fought at Alexandria, and the advance on Cairo. It
served in the expedition to Hanover in 1805. It took part in
the Peninsular Campaign, and was present at El Bodon,
Salamanca and Burgos It fought at Quatre Bras and
Waterloo, and marched with the victorious army to Paris.
In 1825-6 it was present at the famous siege and capture of
Bhurtpore. During the Crimean War it was present at the
Alma and at Inkerman, and was one of the regiments which,
under the leadership of Lord Cardigan, its former Colonel,
rode "into the jaws of death" at Balaklava. It subsequently served before Sevastopol and at Eupatoria. In
1897-8 it served on the Punjaub Frontier in the campaign
under Sir William Lockhart.

Late Victorian Gale and Polden postcard of the 11th Hussars.

him for the next four years until the end of the war. German soldiers were even bil-leted in her house and used the room where he hid in a cupboard. On one occasion when the French lady had to move house, German soldiers helped by carrying the cupboard with Fowler inside to her new house. Towards the end of the war, when the British advanced, Fowler was able to escape. Fortunately, Major Drake from the 11th Hussars was nearby at the time and recognised him, otherwise he could have been shot as a deserter. Madame Belmont-Gobert was awarded the OBE after the war in recognition of her courage.

In 1928 the Cherrypickers became the first British cavalry regiment to become mechanised when they were converted to armoured cars. In the Second World War they won more battle honours than any other cavalry or armoured regiment. They became part of the 7th Armoured Division, the Desert Rats, and spent a large part of the war in the Western Desert, first successfully fighting the numerically superior Italians and then the German Afrika Korps until its expulsion from North Africa in May 1943. They fought at the Battle of Alamein. The regiment also landed in Normandy a few days after D-Day and fought across North West Europe all the way to Hamburg and later Berlin. It is a proud fact that the 11th Hussars spent more time in direct contact with the enemy than any other regiment in the British Army.

On 25 October 1969, Balaclava Day, the regiment amalgamated with the 10th Royal Hussars (Prince of Wales's Own) to become the Royal Hussars (the Prince of Wales's Own). In 1992 the Royal Hussars amalgamated with the 14th/20th King's Hussars to become the King's Royal Hussars. Unofficially, the regiment's traditions are perpetuated within C Squadron of that regiment.

MUSEUM: Horsepower, The King's Royal Hussars Museum, Peninsula Barracks, Winchester SO23 8TS Tel 01962 828539

FOR THE FALLEN

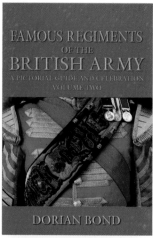

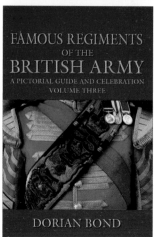

With proud thanksgiving, a Mother for her children,
England mourns for her dead across the sea.
Flesh of her flesh they were, spirit of her spirit,
Fallen in the cause of the free.

Solemn the drums thrill; Death august and royal
Sings sorrow up into immortal spheres,
There is music in the midst of desolation
And a glory that shines upon our tears.

They went with songs to the battle, they were young,
Straight of limb, true of eye, steady and aglow.
They were staunch to the end against odds uncounted;
They fell with their faces to the foe.

They shall not grow old, as we that are left grow old:
Age shall not weary them, nor the years condemn.
At the going down of the sun, and in the morning
We will remember them.

They mingle not with their laughing comrades again;
They sit no more at familiar tables of home;
They have no lot in our labour of the day-time;
They sleep beyond England's foam.

But where our desires are and our hopes profound,
Felt as a well-spring that is hidden from sight,
To the innermost heart of their own land they are known
As the stars are known to the Night;

As the stars that shall be bright when we are dust
Moving in marches upon the heavenly plain;
As the stars that are starry in the time of our darkness,
To the end, to the end, they remain.

Laurence Binyon, 1918

REGIMENTS FEATURED IN VOLUME II

INFANTRY REGIMENTS

1 King's Own Royal Regiment (4th)
2 Royal Northumberland Fusiliers (5th)
3 Royal Warwickshire Regiment (6th)
4 Royal Fusiliers (City of London Regiment) (7th)
5 Royal Norfolk Regiment (9th)
6 Royal Lincolnshire Regiment (10th)
7 Devonshire Regiment (11th)
8 Bedfordshire and Hertfordshire Regiment (16th)
9 Royal Scots Fusiliers (21st)
10 King's Own Scottish Borderers (25th)
11 Cameronians, Scottish Rifles (26th and 90th)
12 East Surrey Regiment (31st and 70th)
13 Duke of Wellington's Regiment (West Riding) (33rd and 76th)
14 Royal Hampshire Regiment (37th and 67th)
15 Sherwood Foresters (45th and 95th)
16 Seaforth Highlanders (72nd and 78th)
17 Connaught Rangers (88th and 94th)
18 Argyll and Sutherland Highlanders (91st and 93rd)

CAVALRY REGIMENTS

19 4th Queen's Own Hussars
20 5th Royal Irish Lancers
21 7th Queen's Own Hussars
22 8th King's Royal Irish Hussars
23 10th Royal Hussars (Prince of Wales's Own)
24 12th Royal Lancers (Prince of Wales's)
25 13th Hussars
26 14th King's Hussars
27 15th the King's Hussars
28 16th the Queen's Lancers
29 17th Duke of Cambridge's Own Lancers
30 18th Royal Hussars (Queen Mary's Own)
31 19th Royal Hussars
32 20th Hussars
33 21st Empress of India's Lancers

TERRITORIAL REGIMENTS

34 Honourable Artillery Company
35 Artists Rifles

ARTILLERY REGIMENT

36 Royal Horse Artillery

INDEX